Natural Law Republicanism

Natural Law Republicanism

Cicero's Liberal Legacy

MICHAEL C. HAWLEY

OXFORD
UNIVERSITY PRESS

OXFORD
UNIVERSITY PRESS

Oxford University Press is a department of the University of Oxford. It furthers
the University's objective of excellence in research, scholarship, and education
by publishing worldwide. Oxford is a registered trade mark of Oxford University
Press in the UK and certain other countries.

Published in the United States of America by Oxford University Press
198 Madison Avenue, New York, NY 10016, United States of America.

Library of Congress Cataloging-in-Publication Data
Names: Hawley, Michael C., author.
Title: Natural law republicanism : Cicero's liberal legacy / Michael C. Hawley.
Description: New York, United States of America : Oxford University Press, 2022. |
Includes bibliographical references and index.
Identifiers: LCCN 2021035249 (print) | LCCN 2021035250 (ebook) |
ISBN 9780197582336 (hardback) | ISBN 9780197582343 (epub)
Subjects: LCSH: Cicero, Marcus Tullius—Influence. |
Political science—Philosophy—History. | Liberalism. | Republicanism. | Natural law.
Classification: LCC JC81.C7 H39 2021 (print) | LCC JC81.C7 (ebook) |
DDC 321.8/6—dc23
LC record available at https://lccn.loc.gov/2021035249
LC ebook record available at https://lccn.loc.gov/2021035250

DOI: 10.1093/oso/9780197582336.001.0001

1 3 5 7 9 8 6 4 2

Printed by Integrated Books International, United States of America

For Irene Collins and Irene Hawley—my first teachers, and my best

Contents

Acknowledgments

This book began as my doctoral dissertation, and so I have been working on it in one way or another for more than four years. In acknowledging the many debts I have incurred over the course of that time, I am aware that I am committing an unjustified presumption in assuming that the reputations of those in question would be enhanced—or at least not sullied—by their association with this project. Still, I hope that I thank them better by naming them than by maintaining a discreet silence.

I first encountered Cicero as a high school freshman in Ned Ligon's Latin class. He helped me to see through Cicero's pardonable vanity to the brilliant theoretical mind behind it. But it was at Tufts that I first truly discovered political philosophy as the field that asked the questions that had always fascinated and driven me. Vickie Sullivan, Ioannis Evrigenis, and Rob Devigne were three of the finest teachers and guides I could have asked for. It is thanks to their cultivation and encouragement of me that I decided to pursue a career as a political theorist.

At Duke, I found a committee whose support was equally kind and generous. Ruth Grant first encouraged me to write my dissertation on this particular topic, and her feedback and support have been invaluable. Michael Gillespie has done more than anyone to prepare me to be a professional academic, and I have tried to reflect his lessons in my writing. Jed Atkins has cheerfully served as a sounding board for my ideas about Cicero, and his expertise in Cicero's thought is something I can never hope to match. Thomas Spragens insisted that I see the contemporary relevance of this largely historical project. All four have continued to provide me with thoughtful and generous feedback far beyond my expectations or deserts.

I have likewise benefited immensely from the broader political theory community at Duke. Jack Knight also provided insightful feedback on the Machiavelli chapter, and Alex Kirshner did likewise on several other disparate topics. Chris Kennedy, Brian Spisiak, Isak Tranvik, Elliot Mamet, Nolan Bennet, and Nora Hanagan all offered helpful comments, suggestions, and challenges. Samuel Bagg and Alexandra Oprea were especially thoughtful and insightful with their help.

A generous grant from the Koch Foundation made possible a postdoctoral fellowship at the University of Notre Dame. While there, I received invaluable mentorship and guidance from Michael Zuckert. Michael and Catherine Zuckert also welcomed me into the political theory workshop they hosted at their home, where I benefited from the insightful feedback of many excellent graduate students, especially Colleen Mitchell, Jonathan Gondelman, Kate Bermingham, Rob Wyllie, Sid Simpson, Robert Burton, and Matthew Hartman. While at Notre Dame, I also benefited from the assistance of the very generous Walter Nicgorski, whose knowledge of Cicero is truly encyclopedic.

During two years as a visiting assistant professor at Bowdoin College, I could not have asked for more supportive colleagues than Jean Yarbrough and Paul Franco. I am permanently indebted to both of them for their kindness and encouragement. At Bowdoin, I also encountered many wonderful and brilliant students. I want to thank especially Gabe, Nicole, Zack, Lorenzo, James, Isabella, Nikki, Victoria, Mollie, and Laura. Teaching and conversing with them helped improve this book more than I suspect they are aware.

I would also like to thank my editor, Stefan Vranka, for his thoughtful advice and kind support of this project and Kendra Millis for her work on the index. Two anonymous reviewers gave the work as a whole a thorough and generous examination. I believe the book is vastly improved thanks to their thoughtful comments, suggestions, and advice.

Finally, there are my family and friends, who have provided plenty of emotional support, relief, and diversion. Without them, I surely would not have made it to the end of this project. In particular, I am grateful for the friendship of John Currie, Theresa and John Owens, Mary and Rick Foley, Judy and Joe Bento, Josh and Catherine Lerner, Tom Cole, Katie Balch, Alicia Davis, Sam Zeitlin, and Nate Gilmore. Without occasional doses of sanity from them, I could hardly have persisted in writing this.

My father, George, has also been a friend, whom I can always rely on for support. To my brothers, Matt and Conor, I owe nearly all of my practical experience in such political matters as conflict, competition, negotiation, persuasion, and justice. Fortunately, they began giving these lessons long before I began the book, and they have charitably continued to do so throughout its composition. My maternal grandmother, Irene, first inspired my love of learning, and she continued to nurture it until her passing at the beginning of my graduate career. Finally, to my mother, Irene, my best friend and teacher, I owe an infinite debt that I can hardly hope to express here. The words fail. This book is dedicated to both the Irenes.

1

The Dream of a Republic

For all who have protected, aided, and increased
the republic, there is a special place set aside in
heaven, where they may enjoy an eternity of
blessedness. For nothing that happens on earth is
more pleasing to the foremost god who rules the
world than those councils and meetings of
human beings joined by justice which are called
commonwealths.

—*Rep.* 6.13

Introduction: A Grisly Scene

In December of 43 BCE, residents of Rome were treated to compelling evidence that the sword is indeed mightier than the pen when the head and hands of Marcus Tullius Cicero were nailed to the Rostra in the center of the city. Mark Antony had arranged this singular spectacle because the head in question had conceived—and the hands had written—a series of speeches, the *Philippics*, denouncing Antony's aspirations to tyranny and exhorting the Romans to revive the flagging liberty of the republic. Further requiting injury for insult, Antony's wife allegedly pulled out the offending tongue that had delivered the speeches and stabbed it repeatedly with a pin (Cass. Dio 47.8.4). Although Cicero's *Philippics* now rank among the finest oratorical examples of the Latin language, their persuasive and motivational power proved unequal to the military might of Antony and his new ally, Octavian Caesar. Within a year, the forces under Brutus and Cassius would be defeated at Philippi, and with them the Roman Republic was finally extinguished.

Cicero's main objective in the *Philippics* had been to respond to the rapid political developments surrounding the threat posed by Antony. But he had also used these speeches as an opportunity to present a vision for how the

Natural Law Republicanism. Michael C. Hawley, Oxford University Press. © Oxford University Press 2022.
DOI: 10.1093/oso/9780197582336.003.0001

Roman polity could be if it should survive the crisis. In them Cicero offers an account of what Roman republicanism and freedom mean. He claims that the Roman people are the source of all rightful political authority. Not only laws but magistrates, decrees, and even the army *belong* to the Roman people. Liberty (*libertas*) requires both that individual citizens be secure in their persons and property but also that the citizens as a body be recognized as the masters of their own political community. The recent rule of Caesar constituted slavery because these principles were denied, and laws were instead supported only by force. In all of this, Cicero does no more than affirm the basic republican principle we now refer to as popular sovereignty. The people may not always govern directly, but they are the original font of all legitimate state power.

Yet in these same speeches, Cicero also suggests another source of legitimacy. He defends the actions taken by Cassius and Brutus, who did not wait for legal authorization before they began to oppose Antony (or kill Caesar, for that matter). Cicero asks rhetorically: "By what right? By what law? By the very law which Jupiter himself approves: that everything done for the sake of the republic's safety be considered legitimate and just." Cicero goes on to say that *true* law is "nothing other than right reason, drawn from the will of the gods, commanding the morally right and prohibiting its opposite" (*Phil.* 12.28).[1] Cicero thus invokes in this public speech an obscure doctrine he usually confined to his more philosophical writings: natural law. He does not say here how this fixed, eternal, divine law can be reconciled with popular sovereignty and republican liberty. Are the people the ultimate source of political authority after all? Or is a just politics merely the process of conforming human institutions to the rationally deducible commands of nature and the supreme deity?

It would be easy dismiss the apparent tension in these claims by noting that they come in public speeches given in the heat of an intense political crisis. Under such circumstances, one could forgive a political actor for employing whatever rhetorical weapons came to hand, without caring much for logical coherence.[2] But in fact, Cicero's more considered and theoretical writings also feature the same central tension. His political philosophy rests on the pillars of popular sovereignty, republican liberty, and natural law. There, too,

---

[1] Unless otherwise noted, all translations from the Latin are my own.

[2] Valentina Arena sees something like this at work in Cicero's appeal to natural law here (Arena 2012, 266).

there remains some ambiguity about how these principles can be reconciled with each other.[3]

At any rate, the point soon seemed moot. It was not the theoretical puzzle of Cicero's republicanism that so provoked Antony and his wife. His personal attacks on them, coupled with his political standing as the leader of the senatorial faction, ensured his demise. With Cicero's death and the rise of the principate, there was no opportunity to see whether his principles could be combined in the real practice of politics.

Yet Cicero's intellectual legacy revived almost immediately after his proscription. According to Plutarch, near the end of his life, that same Octavian Caesar (now Augustus) who had consented to Cicero's execution went to visit one of his grandchildren. The boy had been reading one of Cicero's works, and fearing his grandfather's wrath, he attempted to hide the book. But the first Roman emperor—the man who had consented to Cicero's execution and abolished his republic—took the book, read some of it to his grandson, and then handed it back, saying, "a learned man, my child, a learned man and a lover of his country" (*Vit. Cic.*).

Whether apocryphal or not, the story is indicative of Cicero's philosophical afterlife. Cicero's thought remained admired long after the end of the republic to which he dedicated his career, and it appealed to a diverse list of readers. He seemed to offer something for everyone. Augustine, Ambrose, and other church fathers condemned many of the works of the pagans, but they exempted Cicero, whose ideas they freely borrowed.[4] Medieval scholastics, such as Thomas Aquinas, appealed frequently to Cicero as an authority. Cicero was immensely popular among the Renaissance humanists, particularly Petrarch, who considered Cicero his favorite Roman. Among the Reformers, Martin Luther implied that Cicero's prospects on Judgment Day were considerably better than those of many prominent Christians. After the Bible, the next book to be printed on Johannes Gutenberg's press was Cicero's *De officiis*, which Martha Nussbaum has called "perhaps the most influential book in the history of western political philosophy" (Nussbaum 2000, 178). Immanuel Kant and David Hume, two thinkers rarely in agreement, both acknowledge great debts to his work. In the words of Michael Grant, "the

---

[3] This is not to say that Cicero did not believe he could not reconcile them, only that he does not offer so explicitly an account of how this might be achieved. There are a number of suggestions in his philosophical works that illustrate his idea of how the two might fit together, as will be explored later.

[4] The most obvious example of this is Ambrose's *De officiis*, openly modeled on Cicero's work of the same name.

influence of Cicero upon the history of European literature and ideas greatly exceeds that of any other prose writer in any language."[5]

Cicero's immense influence suffered an abrupt decline in the nineteenth century, when influential German classicists and historians judged him to be derivative and uninteresting as part of a more general depreciation of Rome in favor of Greece. In their eyes, Plato, Aristotle, and the Stoics were real philosophers; the Romans were mere imitators. Cicero's intellectual exile continued through much of the twentieth century. The eminent scholar M. I. Finley captured a general spirit when he wrote with exasperation of the "nonsense" of taking Cicero seriously at all.[6] From being an acknowledged authority for some of the greatest political thinkers in history, Cicero had been reduced to an eclectic philosophical dabbler. He was considered so thoroughly unoriginal that his primary value to many scholars lay in the fact that they could mine his writings for clues about what other lost authors (especially the Stoics) had said.

Happily, the era of Cicero's neglect by scholars is ending. His reputation as a profound philosopher in his own right has enjoyed a nascent revival in recent years, thanks in large part to the efforts of such scholars as Walter Nicgorski, Jed Atkins, Joy Connolly, Daniel Kapust, and Benjamin Straumann. But scholarship is only now beginning to come to grips with his vast influence on the subsequent tradition of political thought. This book attempts to contribute to filling that large gap. Now, it would be a hopelessly sprawling endeavor to render an even cursory account of Cicero's total posthumous influence. But the relationship between popular sovereignty, natural law, and liberty provides a focal point that might allow one significant part of Cicero's legacy to be more fully explored—and explored in a way that shines light not only on other major thinkers but also on a problem that remains thorny today: are there any legitimate grounds for constraining the sovereign democratic people?

That, at any rate, is the task I have set myself in this work. In particular, I hope to shed light on the afterlife of Cicero's hope that the sovereignty of the people could somehow be reconciled with an immovable, eternal moral law and that the union of these two principles could undergird liberty for citizens. I argue that many of the seminal architects of early modern liberal philosophy and some of the most influential founders of the American liberal

---

[5] In Cicero 1960, 24.
[6] Finley 1983, 128n17. Fox (2016) helps to illustrate how the origins of this attitude lie at least in part in some faulty classical scholarship in the nineteenth century.

republic saw themselves as solving the puzzle Cicero had set and (in the latter case) realizing in an actual regime Cicero's dream of the natural law republic. Thus, the purpose of this book is to demonstrate the scope and significance of the influence of Cicero's ideas on those later thinkers.

There is a tradition (to use a somewhat amorphous term) of political thought centered on Cicero's original formulation. It is not a coincidence that Cicero's understanding of liberty is so strikingly similar to that defended by those much later writers: the freedom of the individual to be secure from interference, harm, or domination. Nor is it an accident that Cicero's peculiar interpretation of natural law so closely resembles the one they deploy to ground a theory of natural rights. Hugo Grotius, Samuel von Pufendorf, English republicans, John Locke, John Adams, and James Wilson constitute the core of an early modern Ciceronian tradition. They deeply engaged not only Cicero but also one another (that is, the antecedent thinkers in the same tradition), out of which interaction emerged a liberal republican theory and a real liberal republican regime.

By claiming this, I do not mean to assert that the themes originated by Cicero are the only significant sources of early modern liberal republicanism. One could not tell the whole story without also addressing Protestantism, the spread of commerce, the scientific revolution, and many other contributors. But I think it would be fair to see the core of early modern liberalism in the relationship of these Ciceronian concepts: a transcendent and universal moral law and an understanding of liberty as *both* the protection of the individual from arbitrary interference, harm, and domination *and* the collective right of the people to be the authors of their own politics. As a result, I do wish to make the strong claim that modern liberal republicanism, with its individual rights, popular sovereignty, and its appeal to a higher moral law, is profoundly Ciceronian in its origin.

On Longue Durée Histories of Liberty

In making this case, I am challenging several long-standing longue durée historical accounts about ancient and modern thought as well as the relationship between liberalism and republicanism. It is not that I intend to make similarly comprehensive claims about the whole sweep of Western thought. I make no pretensions of offering a rival comprehensive history. In fact, I consider the attempt to tell an authoritative story about "the ancients and the moderns" or liberalism and republicanism to be nearly impossible. One must either generalize to the point of uselessness or become a superficial dilettante on many subjects in which a deep engagement is required for mastery—likely one has to do both. Instead, I have opted to focus on a particular current in the great stream of political thought. But I do believe that this approach of focusing on a part allows one to engage questions about the whole in a way that is constructive exactly because of its narrower scope.

Of such grand theories of history of philosophy, Benjamin Constant's may be the most long-lasting and influential. He famously posits a fundamental difference between "The Liberty of the Ancients Compared with That of the Moderns." According to Constant, modern liberty consists of protections for the individual and private property against arbitrary harm or interference from rulers. Ancient liberty could be found in the ability to participate collectively in making rules for the community, against which the individual had no special rights or safeguards.[7] The same distinction can be found in "Two Concepts of Liberty" by Isaiah Berlin, who claims that there is "scarcely any discussion of individual liberty . . . in the ancient world." Berlin finds support for this contention in Nicolas de Condorcet's claim that individual rights were a concept unknown to the Greeks and Romans.[8]

Although he approaches the issue from a profoundly different perspective, Leo Strauss agrees that modern thought is characterized by a fundamental break with that of the ancients, inaugurated by Niccolò Machiavelli. According to Strauss, whereas classical political philosophy acknowledged the primacy of contemplation, modern political philosophy is characterized by an active commitment to the betterment of man's estate. Strauss explicitly denies that Cicero is any kind of exception to this division.[9]

To the extent that such stories of the division between the ancients and the moderns have been challenged at all, it has largely been through attempts to make room for Constant's version of ancient liberty in modernity.[10] It has become popular especially to look to the political thought and practice of Athens for resources to increase or improve democratic participation and

---

[7] Constant 1988.

[8] Berlin 2000, 201.

[9] Strauss 1953, 135.

[10] There are few but valuable exceptions to this trend, individuals who have pointed to the presence of an ideal of "modern liberty" among the Romans, including Benjamin Straumann, Michelle Clarke, Jed Atkins, and Chaim Wirszubski. I will discuss each of these further in this book.

deliberation.[11] Few have sought to find "modern" liberty among the ancients, and fewer still among the Romans in particular.

This view of a radical break has been taken still further, perhaps to its logical conclusion. Recognizing the pre-modern valence of natural law, some scholars have sought to sever the link between natural law and the natural rights that form the basis of the early modern liberal project. They have argued that Locke, Thomas Jefferson, and others did not themselves believe in the natural law doctrines they espoused, and that those arguments were only rhetorical cover used to smuggle in their truly revolutionary doctrines of rights.[12] Some of these scholars hope to make it possible for us to keep the natural rights parts of those theories while jettisoning the anachronistic natural law that undergirded them.

The argument of this book runs deeply counter to the alleged distinction between the liberties of the ancients and the moderns. Not only does Cicero espouse a "modern" doctrine of liberty, but it is his doctrine of liberty that inspires the truly modern ones. Moreover, I will attempt to show that Ciceronian natural law is, in fact, essential to the doctrine of natural rights advanced by Locke and the American founders. It is therefore not nearly so easy for us to disentangle them. If indeed we no longer accept the natural law foundation, we may have to grapple seriously with how to rescue natural rights (if indeed we want to rescue them at all).

Another grand historical story challenged by this book is the alleged quarrel of liberalism and republicanism. Some historians and political theorists have suggested that an alternative to liberal political values can be found in a tradition they term "republican" (Philip Pettit) or "neo-Roman" (Quentin Skinner). These neo-republicans contribute two important insights. First, they correctly call our attention to the fact that the modern period witnessed not only the emergence of a focus on individual rights in theory and practice but also a renewed insistence on republican self-government. We have come to view ourselves as citizens rather than subjects—not only as individuals entitled to security in our persons and possessions but also as rightful participants in political decision-making. Second, Pettit, Skinner, and others have correctly traced this commitment to republicanism[13] to the

---

[11] See, for instance, the work of Josiah Ober or Joel Schlosser, as well as many others.

[12] See Zuckert 1994; Pangle 1988.

[13] I include Skinner's "neo-Romanism" within the term *republican* at this point for the purpose of brevity. Later I show that Skinner's position—that the label of "republican" should be reserved only for those who reject outright all forms of monarchy—is rejected by nearly all the major figures of the republican tradition he identifies, including Cicero, Machiavelli, and Locke.

thought and practice of the ancient Romans. In fact, the Romans do appear far closer to us moderns than to the Greeks in outlook and circumstance. For the Romans as well as for us, the size and composition of the polity make the radical democracy of the Greek polis impossible. Indeed, many of the political terms we use—*citizen, republic, liberty*—come down to us from the Latin (in some cases directly from Cicero's own attempt to provide Latin with a political-philosophical vocabulary).

These neo-Roman insights offer a partial corrective to those accounts that posit a fundamental break between classical and modern political thought. But the neo-republicans undermine the value of this contribution by positing their own spurious dichotomy: liberalism versus republicanism. In conceiving of republicanism as a tradition and a coherent set of values *essentially* in opposition to liberalism, many neo-republicans have conjured up a new historical and conceptual divergence where there is none. Early modern liberals such as Locke were anything but hostile to genuinely *Roman* thought—particularly that of Cicero. Liberalism does not arise as a rejection of Roman republicanism.

However, it may indeed be that liberal republicanism *does* constitute a rejection of the kind of "neo-Roman" republicanism advanced in particular by Machiavelli, who tends to feature centrally in nearly all historical accounts of republicanism (and indeed also in the discourse around "the ancients and the moderns"). If one reads all republicanism through the prism of Machiavelli, one will find a politics that encourages conflict and contestation and is explicitly opposed to transcendent moral laws. But that is not Cicero's republicanism, and those very features of Machiavelli's theory that so distinguish him from Cicero are precisely the ones rejected by later liberal republicans. Understanding Cicero's role in inspiring early modern liberalism is key to grasping more fully the historical and conceptual relationship between liberalism and republicanism.

In this effort, John McCormick has offered some helpful preliminaries for preventing our view of republicanism from being so thoroughly colored by Machiavelli. McCormick identifies two republican traditions, one headed by Cicero and the other headed by Machiavelli. McCormick rightly insists that these two traditions are not only incompatible but fundamentally at odds.[14] McCormick's work focuses almost exclusively on the Machiavellian strain, which he clearly prefers (although, by his own admission, it is the Ciceronian

---

[14] McCormick 2011, 7–9.

tradition that triumphs historically). But I suggest, contra McCormick, that the distinction between the Ciceronian and Machiavellian versions is not that the former entrenches elite domination while the latter sides with ordinary people. There is indeed a friendliness to political elites in the Ciceronian tradition, but its defining feature is rather its acceptance of restraint—normative and institutional—on the otherwise sovereign people. The source of this restraint is natural law (which Machiavelli wholly rejects), and from it flows a number of other important features absent from or rejected by Machiavelli, including civic rights, constitutional checks and balances, and an ideal of negative liberty. As I argue in chapter 3, there is a strong case to be made that by imposing restraint on the people, Ciceronian republicanism is, in fact, far friendlier to the interests of the people (even as those interests are construed by Machiavelli) than Machiavelli's alternative is.

Thus, the argument of this book also challenges the "Cambridge School" historians and their neo-republican allies who elide the republicanisms of Cicero and Machiavelli. For this reason, I have included a chapter on Machiavelli, so that the contours of the Ciceronian tradition may appear in sharp relief. Indeed, although the focus of this book is on the non-Machiavellian current of republican thought, it may be that my most controversial judgment here concerns Machiavelli. I argue that the Florentine is *neither* the culmination of the classical republican tradition *nor* the forerunner of modern liberalism. The evidence presented here suggests that Machiavelli is something of a dead end, a *failed* challenge to the Ciceronian tradition, which ultimately wins out by giving rise to the phenomenally successful paradigm of liberal republicanism.

In making these challenges to such powerful historical accounts, I draw on some very valuable recent work by scholars. More than anyone else, Benjamin Straumann has begun to call attention to the importance of Cicero's legacy as a thinker. His work has brought Cicero into conversation with the too-often-overlooked Grotius, and he has even signaled that this connection implies a Ciceronian origin to Lockean liberalism.[15] Jed Atkins, Günter Gawlick, Matthew Fox, Phillip Mitsis, John Marshall, Martha Nussbaum, and Matthew Sharpe have all touched on Cicero's legacy for early modernity in stand-alone articles or as parts of larger projects.[16] The *Cambridge Companion to Cicero* contains a few chapters on Cicero's afterlife. Tim

[15] See especially Straumann 2016.
[16] Atkins 2014; Gawlick 1936; Fox 2013; Mitsis 2003; Marshall 1994; Nussbaum 2000; Sharpe 2015.

Stuart-Buttle has recently published a fascinating monograph on Cicero's influence on early modern debates over skepticism and religious belief. Finally, there are three edited volumes that deal specifically with Cicero's philosophical afterlife.[17] Aside from Straumann and Stuart-Buttle, however, these works tend to be episodic—they examine the role Cicero plays in a particular instance, or with a particular thinker (in the case of the edited volumes; the different chapters follow this pattern). I in no way aspire to tell the whole story of Cicero's influence—an impossible task for any book. But this book is an attempt to draw a coherent conversation on a particular connected set of topics out of the history of Cicero's influence, one in which a broad range of important thinkers participated. Each thinker engages not only Cicero himself but also other earlier contributors in the discussion. For that reason, I feel it is reasonable to refer to this conversation as a tradition of thought. But in calling it *a* Ciceronian tradition, I remain aware that it is not *the* Ciceronian tradition. There are many other such conversations sparked by Cicero, and I look forward to those being excavated as well.[18]

Organization of the Book

As I trace out the Ciceronian tradition I have identified, it was, of course, necessary to discriminate. Beyond the chapter on Cicero, I began this project with no real criteria to determine what belongs in the book and what is extraneous. As noted earlier, nearly every major thinker after Cicero in the Western tradition up through the late eighteenth century owes him a debt. Many of these have also explored issues of natural law, popular sovereignty, and liberty. Yet not all could be covered in a book. I have chosen to examine what I believe are the most significant theoretical moments in the development of the tradition. In the next paragraphs, I intend to offer less an outline of chapters than a logic of discovery.

I begin with Cicero himself and his attempt to build a republican theory grounded in his new interpretation of natural law. Cicero is not a systematic philosopher in the ordinary sense, and it is necessary to piece together his views from various works. I draw evidence from his most prominent theoretical political writings, particularly *De officiis, De re publica, De legibus, Orator,*

---

[17] Van Deusen 2013; Altman 2015; Kapust and Remer 2021.

[18] Two other such conversations that come to mind are Cicero's ideas about the relationship between rhetoric and statesmanship and Cicero's views on the limits of human knowledge.

and *De finibus*. But I also appeal to Cicero's speeches and correspondence when they offer clarification or insight, as many later authors were almost as likely to refer to these as to Cicero's more clearly philosophical works. The object here is not to offer a revolutionary new interpretation of Cicero's own political philosophy but rather to establish the fundamentals of his thought that will prove central to the development of this Ciceronian tradition.

After Cicero himself in chapter 2, I did not originally intend to write a chapter on Niccolò Machiavelli, whose thought and legacy scholars have endlessly fought over. The purpose of this book was to illustrate the non-Machiavellian tradition of Roman republicanism, after all. But I gradually realized that Machiavelli has so eclipsed Cicero in the scholarly discourse (and has so influenced the ways in which Roman thought has been viewed) that it is necessary to address the issue of Machiavelli directly. So chapter 3 illustrates Machiavelli's attempt to break republicanism out from the web of morally binding norms in which Cicero enmeshed it. In place of Cicero's cooperative commonwealth of natural law, rights, property, and peace, Machiavelli advocates for a violent, conflict-ridden republic organized for war and expansion. In this chapter, I seek to make the features of Cicero's republicanism sharper through contrast.

In chapter 4, I return to the Ciceronian tradition itself and examine the aftermath of Machiavelli's challenge to Ciceronian republicanism. If Machiavelli was right that security and justice for individuals were incompatible with republican political flourishing, it seemed one had to choose. Two nearly simultaneous intellectual movements arose, both looking to Cicero (and opposing the absolutism of Thomas Hobbes) but accepting different horns of the dilemma proposed by Machiavelli. Hugo Grotius and Samuel von Pufendorf sought to vindicate Ciceronian natural law and justice but accepted that republican self-government was a threat to these ideals. Across the Channel, English republicans looked to both Machiavelli and Cicero for inspiration to achieve republican self-government. But they rejected as limiting the natural law teaching about rights and limited government that Cicero had felt was essential to justice.

After this, I illustrate how Cicero's republicanism prevails over Machiavelli's challenge. The rift explored in chapter 4 proves not to last. I turn to John Locke, who re-establishes the connection between Ciceronian natural law and republican self-government. He shows the Machiavellian dilemma to be a false one. In chapter 5, I explore Locke's intimate engagement with Cicero's political philosophy. Locke brings back together the elements that had appeared irreconcilable after Machiavelli, restoring Cicero's fundamental linkage of justice and freedom. Individual freedom and security, as well as rights to liberty and property, are all essentially dependent upon the people's ability to control their government. Here we see how Lockean liberalism emerges out of the tradition of Ciceronian republicanism. I consider this the most important claim of the book; my larger argument stands or falls with the case I make in chapter 5.

In chapter 6, I examine the American founding. The period between the signing of the Declaration of Independence and the ratification of the Constitution looms large as the pivotal moment in many historical accounts of the alleged quarrel between liberalism and republicanism. More important, this period holds special significance for Americans today because it gave birth to institutions (and expressions of ideals) that still govern much of political life. I argue that the founding constitutes the culmination of the Ciceronian tradition in that it sought to realize in practice the theory of liberty and government first articulated by Cicero and adapted by Locke.

In the epilogue, I step back to consider how we might now think differently about our political ideals in light of the Ciceronian tradition. I argue that we lose a great deal by ignoring the tension at the heart of that tradition. Moreover, without the natural law that undergirds the Ciceronian linking of democratic self-government and universal moral norms, we may find it ever harder to unite those two in theory or practice.

In tracing out this historical conversation, I sought to avoid the trap of the hammer, to which everything looks like a nail. I understand that someone setting out to illuminate a portion of the legacy of a thinker may be inclined to see that legacy even where it is not. For that reason, I have tried to avoid placing the weight of my argument for Cicero's influence on instances where ideas or language seem merely evocative of his thought. Instead, I seek to focus as much as possible on cases where he is referred to by name or quoted directly. However, I also know that it is possible for writers to name-drop and quote-drop, using the authority of an earlier thinker to buttress an argument that would have been appalling or incomprehensible to him. It is just as misleading to credit Cicero with influence in such cases.[19] I have thus tried to hold myself to a doubly rigorous standard whereby Cicero's intellectual shadow is recognized only where there is clear engagement with his ideas and not merely his words.

---

[19] Cf. my review of Cary Nederman in Hawley 2021b.

The Ciceronian Tradition and Us

This book takes a historical approach to its subject matter, and its primary purpose is to sustain claims about the nature and history of an interrelated set of ideas. But I also believe there is more than mere historical interest to this exploration. Although it has recently come under attack from both the left and the right, the liberal republican paradigm still forms the dominant theoretical component of the present political dispensation. This is especially the case in the United States, where the Constitution explicitly embodies these ideals, but it holds true for most countries that have adopted liberal principles—however filtered and mixed—from figures such as Locke. We therefore will not adequately understand ourselves and the origins of our political situation if we do not grapple with the role Cicero's thought has played in shaping us and it. We still struggle today with reconciling our desires for individual freedom and collective authority and our belief that there is some moral standard independent of the public's judgment. We could learn much by seeing how the great minds of this Ciceronian tradition dealt with the same challenges.

Aristotle argued that a certain kind of political wisdom can only be acquired through experience. As a *novus homo* who rose to Rome's highest office without a military background, Cicero certainly earns himself a hearing in this respect. His forceful prose and masterful use of language undoubtedly contributed to his appeal as an authority for early modern thinkers. Still more fundamentally, Cicero's writings are supported by a more basic—and perhaps more important—kind of experience as well. In him, seventeenth- and eighteenth-century writers—including the American founders—could find a profound philosopher who had the experience of living as a free citizen in a free republic. Cicero's passionate and persuasive defense of the value of such a political order may be what most commended him to individuals who sought to realize liberty for states and citizens alike.

2

Cicero

Natural Law and Republican Liberty

> I shall employ every moment of the day and of the night in thinking,
> insofar as thought is required, of the liberty of the Roman people
> and of your dignity; nor I shall recoil from action and activity, where
> that is called for.
>
> *—Phil.* **3.33**

As Cicero's head and hands festered on the Rostra, it might have occurred to a sympathetic observer that Cicero need not have come to this end. Proscribed as a symbol of the doomed republican faction, Cicero instead could have benefited substantially from the political transformation taking place in Rome. According to Cicero's own account, years earlier, Julius Caesar had invited Cicero to join him and Pompey in what became the First Triumvirate (*Att.* 2.3). But Cicero turned Caesar and Pompey down on the grounds that such an arrangement would violate the fundamental principles of the Roman constitution. His refusal to join the First Triumvirate would largely exclude him from power as the republic teetered toward disintegration. His opposition to the Second provoked his execution.

With his death, Cicero became the second famous philosopher of antiquity to be executed by his own regime. Although he was certainly unwilling to die, the parallel might have pleased Cicero, who throughout his life took Socrates as his model.[1] Yet there is also a clear distinction between the two deaths, a difference that illustrates what the two men considered most important. Socrates died as a philosopher, condemned for his refusal to give up philosophy. Cicero died as a statesman, condemned for his refusal to give up the republic. Although he considered himself a loyal philosophical disciple

---

[1] See *Leg.* 1.15, among others. See further Nicgorski 2016.

Natural Law Republicanism. Michael C. Hawley, Oxford University Press. © Oxford University Press 2022.
DOI: 10.1093/oso/9780197582336.003.0002

of Socrates (along with Plato and Aristotle), Cicero insisted that the active political life must take priority over the contemplative life (*Off.* 1.158).[2] For him, the highest human activity is that devoted to founding, preserving, improving, or maintaining commonwealths (*Rep.* 6.13).

But a commonwealth is not just any political community. To be worthy of such devotion, a political community ought to be a *res publica*—a commonwealth or republic. Therein lay the problem. According to Cicero, these triumvirates were not merely dangerous political initiatives, but they threatened to destroy the *res publica* itself. Cicero's objection to the new arrangement was not based on mere legalism or formalism—the triumvirs were quite happy to legitimate their rule with new laws. Instead, Cicero saw the very idea of such concentration of power as violating not Rome's written laws but rather some more fundamental unwritten laws. The new political arrangement violated Rome's constitution, the norms and structures within which legitimate political action could take place.

Benjamin Straumann has ably shown how Cicero develops his idea of a constitution in part as a response to the political crisis of the late republic.[3] Cicero takes Rome's constitution to be a kind of higher-order sort of law, which determines what other laws are acceptable and how they should be enacted. But Cicero's own theory of Rome's constitution holds that it grew and changed over time, so an innovation (even on the scale of a triumvirate) could only be disqualifying if there were a standard *above* even Rome's constitution to which Cicero could appeal. It turns out that such a standard does exist for Cicero, and it ultimately undergirds his whole republican theory: the natural law.

For Cicero, a *res publica* is distinguished from other kinds of states by the fact that its people are bound together by a common acceptance of the principles of justice. Cicero adamantly denies that the principles of justice are historically or culturally relative; the natural law applies always and to everyone. The goodness of any political community can be evaluated by the correspondence of its laws and institutions to this universal standard of the natural law. So Cicero's profound rejection of the constitutional changes proposed by Caesar and others depended on his conviction that the Roman

---

[2] This is repeated, among other places, at *Rep.* 1.10. Cf. Lévy 2012. Strauss's claim that classical political philosophy prioritized contemplation over action (Strauss 1953, 135) founders in the case of Cicero.

[3] Straumann 2016. Rawson also describes Cicero's refusal to join Caesar and Pompey as rooted in constitutionalism (Rawson 1983, 106).

constitution as it had stood was the nearest approximation to the natural law yet achieved in human politics. Its destruction would mean the loss of justice and liberty together, replacing the people's rightful collective ownership of the polity and the Senate's rightful role as guardians of it with the arbitrary wills of the triumvirs.

Thomas Hobbes would much later famously establish a fundamental dichotomy between liberty and law, arguing that liberty exists only in the silence of the law (*Leviathan* xxi). For Cicero, however, liberty could only be achieved in a *res publica* and thus depends on the principles of natural law. In forging such a close link between liberty and natural law, Cicero set the agenda for the republican tradition that would follow. The concepts of liberty and natural law form the pillars of Cicero's vision of a good *res publica*. However, there is a tension between those pillars that—while often dynamic and productive—is not totally resolved in Cicero's thought. Later attempts to resolve this tension would eventually culminate in the development of liberal constitutionalism. The rest of this chapter explores how Cicero establishes this relationship between natural law and republican liberty.

Bringing Philosophy Further Down from the Heavens

Any attempt to describe the course of a discrete political tradition inevitably encounters the problem of where to locate the beginning of the story. All ideas have antecedents, and no philosopher thinks in a vacuum, so every inquiry into the origins of the tradition seems to point ever further back. Yet Cicero and the Roman republican tradition stand as a partial exception to this problem. *Res publica* is a distinctly Roman expression, having no exact equivalent in earlier Greek thought.[4] As the earliest political philosopher of Rome whose works have survived, Cicero seems by default to qualify as the first extant republican philosopher.

Yet Cicero often insists that he is a follower of Greek philosophy. His writings show the strong influence of his Greek philosophical training and his engagement with the different schools—especially the Stoics, the Peripatetics, and the Academics. In particular, Cicero adamantly and

---

[4] Schofield 1995. Indeed, it was Cicero who first introduced Plato's great work under the title of *Republic*. There is therefore some connection to the Greek concept of *politeia*.

repeatedly insists that he ought to be considered a follower of Plato, "that divine man," and he acknowledges that his *De re publica* and *De legibus* are overtly modeled on Plato's *Republic* and *Laws* (*Leg.* 1.15). It was Plato, after all, whose dialogues captured Socrates's project of bringing "philosophy down from the heavens and placing it in the cities" (*Tusc.* 5.10). For Cicero, all the other branches of philosophy worthy of the name are to some extent heirs of Plato and Socrates.

So must we concede on the basis of Cicero's own testimony that we can find nothing significant in his thought that we cannot get from the original source in Plato? This is the position implied by Leo Strauss, who writes that Cicero "who must be supposed to have known what he was talking about, was wholly unaware of a radical difference between Plato's teaching and his own."[5]

There is certainly something to Strauss's claim. According to Cicero, Plato does provide the model for the right kind of philosophical skepticism that avoids the opposing extremes of dogmatism and Pyrrhonism (*Off.* 2.7–8). Moreover, Cicero agrees that philosophy is valuable in the discovery and cultivation of the virtues necessary to lead a good life. Cicero is also happy to try to imitate Plato's dialogical style of philosophical writing.[6]

But Cicero remains fiercely independent with respect to the *content* of that philosophizing: "it is easy enough to translate [Plato's] ideas, and I might do that if I did not prefer to be myself" (*Leg.* 2.17).[7] Politics in particular seems to be a place in which Cicero sees a wide difference between himself and Greek philosophy. The sharpest articulation of his critique of Greek thought comes from the character Laelius in *De re publica*, who explains that Plato's city in speech "may be a noble state, but it is totally alien to human life and customs" (*Rep.* 2.21). In the same work, Cicero's character Scipio describes Plato's city as one "more to be wished for than expected, one that could not exist" (*Rep.* 2.52).[8] Part of the problem, according to Cicero, is that Plato's

[5] Strauss 1953, 135. As for Cicero's affinity for Aristotle, see Nicgorski 2013. Indeed, the idea that Cicero is merely an unoriginal mouthpiece for Greek thought comes in many variations, with some considering him a Stoic, others a Platonist, still others a Peripatetic. The sheer variety of such contradictory claims suggests that Cicero really is best understood as an original, if eclectic, thinker.

[6] Nicgorski persuasively demonstrates that Cicero follows Plato and Socrates in his understanding of the methods, themes, and aims of philosophy. According to Nicgorski, these features mean that "Cicero is a Socratic in a Roman toga." However, he also acknowledges important areas of divergence between Cicero and Socrates (Nicgorski 2016, 245–247).

[7] Zetzel makes a convincing argument that Cicero truly does hold that there are "strict limitations on the proper role" of Greek thought generally in Rome (Zetzel 2003, 121).

[8] This charge is essentially repeated in *De or.* 1.224. For more on Cicero's disagreement with Plato about realism and the best practical regime, as opposed to the best conceivable regime, see Atkins 2013, 56–64. Going further still, Timothy Caspar argues that Cicero's imitation of Plato in *De legibus* is primarily a matter of style, not substance (Caspar 2011, 160–161).

political philosophy is insufficiently grounded in the realities of the human condition. Cicero believes that his own extensive political experience gives him special insight into precisely this issue. The character Scipio expresses Cicero's own self-understanding when he declares:

> So I ask you to listen to me, not as one wholly ignorant of Greek ideas, nor as one preferring their ideas to ours—*particularly on this topic*, but as a Roman citizen . . . inspired from childhood with a zeal for learning, but having been educated much more by experience and native instruction than by books. (*Rep.* 1.35; emphasis added)[9]

It seems that at least on the level of *political* philosophy, Cicero understands himself as separating clearly from his Greek authorities.[10]

Although Cicero admires Plato's project of bringing philosophy down from the heavens, Cicero believes Plato has not brought it down far enough. He insists that political philosophy base itself on what sort of creatures human beings are, how they can and do live. Only by understanding humanity's full range of needs and capacities can we begin to imagine a just and stable politics.

Human Nature and the Ends of Politics

So what sort of creatures are human beings? Cicero begins at the most basic level: human nature is a mixture of the animal and the divine. We are both body and mind (*corpore animoque*) (*Fin.* 5.34).[11] The body we share with all other living creatures. We need shelter and sustenance. The mind allows us to participate in reason, which sets us apart from other animals and unites us with the divine (*Off.* 2.11). Humanity's mental faculties give rise to all of our

---

[9] Cicero expresses a similar sentiment in his own voice at the beginning of the dialogue: "I should be considered an authority, since some earlier men were skilled at discussion but from whom came no great deeds, and others performed admirable deeds, but were poor reasoners" (*Rep.* 1.13).

[10] Straumann likewise takes Cicero's thought to be importantly divergent from Plato and Aristotle, although he focuses primarily on the issue of constitutionalism (Straumann 2016, 191–237).

[11] Although this may seem self-evident, Cicero suggests that many rival political theories fail to grant one side or the other of our nature its due. The Epicureans envision humans as guided solely by pleasure, which is based purely in bodily sensation (*Fin.* 1.55). They fail to give humans' higher rational nature its just priority. Cicero is much more sympathetic to the Stoic point of view. But the Stoics flatly deny the existence of bodily goods (*Fin.* 4.26–28). They fail to recognize the obvious consequences of the fact that we are corporeal beings.

highest qualities and achievements. In particular, philosophy and politics are only possible because of our ability to reason, remember, speak, and comprehend cause and effect (*Fin.* 2.113; *Off.* 1.11). In separating us from the beasts and enabling our capacity for virtue, reason is the source of our "dignity" (*dignitas*). Cicero is one of the first philosophers to base his political argument in part on the inherent dignity of human beings.

This dignity has both hierarchical and egalitarian valences. On one hand, the lives of the statesman and the philosopher assume prominence as the highest forms of human life because they develop and contribute most toward our rationality and sociality, respectively.[12] Theirs are the most dignified of all human ways of life. On the other hand, Cicero ascribes to all human beings a common universal dignity based on their shared possession of reason. Cicero, in fact, insists that in our defining feature—our rational capacity—human beings are all far more alike than different (*Leg.* 1.29). An individual who recognizes this quality within himself sees that "his own natural capacity is a kind of holy likeness of the divine" and strives to act worthy (*dignum*) of this gift (*Leg.* 1.59). A. J. Carlyle goes so far as to identify this argument of Cicero's as the moment in which modernity appears in contrast to antiquity: "there is no change in political theory so startling in its completeness" as when "over and against Aristotle's view of the natural inequality of human nature [Cicero sets out] the theory of the natural equality of human nature."[13] Moreover, this equality of dignity implies a certain equality in freedom, which I will discuss further. Here it is important to see that Cicero's theory leaves no room for natural slavery, in stark contrast to Aristotle. Slaves may lack standing in society as a matter of fact (and Cicero never concerned himself with altering this fact), but Cicero nowhere grounds this arrangement in nature. Instead, he denies that anyone by nature has the right to command another (*Off.* 1.13).

Cicero thus does not find the origins of political society in natural relationships of superiority and domination, as Aristotle does in the *Politics*.[14] He sees political societies arising out of commonly shared human needs, answering both the corporeal and the rational desires of our nature. First, political life is necessary to secure essential bodily needs. The natural

---

[12] Nicgorski's *Cicero's Skepticism* (2016) is in many ways a meditation on Cicero's account of the relationship between these two forms of life and an attempt to account for Cicero's prioritization of the statesman over the philosopher. See also Hawley 2020a.

[13] Carlyle 1963, 8.

[14] As Zetzel emphasizes, Cicero likewise resists the temptation to obscure the origins of political society in myths, supernatural or otherwise (Zetzel 2017, 484–485).

world is at once bountiful and stingy to human beings. The rest of creation (plants, animals, and inanimate objects) exists for human use and consumption (*Leg.* 1.25). But in comparison to the animals, which the earth nourishes lavishly with food, we human beings "supply ourselves with food barely—or not even barely—with great labor" (*Fin.* 2.111). Although the earth produces much that makes human life possible and even pleasant, human beings could not enjoy those fruits without cooperation:

> Neither medical care, nor navigation, nor agriculture, nor the harvest and preservation of fruits and other crops could exist at all without human work . . . or indeed our houses, by which the power of the cold is defeated and the oppression of the heat is allayed, how could they have been produced for the human race, or afterward repaired—when they collapsed because of strong winds, or earthquakes, or simple age—if common life had not taught us to seek help from our fellow men in such instances? (*Off.* 2.12–13)[15]

Thus, human association is necessary in part because human beings are not naturally equipped to survive or thrive without cooperation. Since such cooperation requires "human administration," politics is likewise necessary for human survival (*Off.* 2.12).

But Cicero insists that human beings are also drawn to political life for higher, non-instrumental reasons. While human society eases the needs of our bodies, it is also absolutely required by the rational aspect of our nature. The latter makes us social, providing us with speech and a desire for fellowship for its own sake: "the same nature, through the power of reason, connects one person to another for a common speech and life . . . it drives him so that he prefers that social interaction and gatherings should exist and that he himself should attend them" (*Off.* 1.12). So strong is natural human sociality that even if all our bodily wants were perfectly satisfied, we would still crave society with others and would be miserable without it (*Off.* 1.157).[16]

Our rational and corporeal qualities combine to produce a third reason for associating: property.

---

[15] Cicero goes on to enumerate many other necessities (or near necessities) of human life that are dependent on cooperation, including the domestication of docile animals, protection against predators, the irrigation of fields, and the importation of goods not to be found locally.

[16] Cf. *Fin.* 3.65. This echoes Aristotle's view that humanity is naturally political and that even if our bodily needs were all met, we would still congregate for the sake of communal life (*Politics* 3.6.1278b17). But Cicero emphatically denies that we are naturally political in the full Aristotelian sense. We are only naturally social.

Commonwealths and states were set up in large part so that people could hold on to what is their own. For, while human beings were originally led by nature to congregate, nevertheless they first sought protection in cities with the hope of safeguarding their property. (*Off.* 2.73)[17]

Cicero does not believe that private property exists by nature; the natural world was created for humanity's use and belongs—at least originally—to all humanity in common (*Fin.* 3.57; *Off.* 1.21).[18] But individuals and groups have carved out pieces of this common stock for themselves by various means: occupation of vacant territory, conquest, agreement, lot, and so on (*Off.* 1.21).

This last point indicates that Cicero's reasons for the value of human association by no means imply that human beings have always lived in political groups or that they are naturally political. Cicero describes human beings as originally living in what we would now recognize as the state of nature. Cicero claims that "once, before there was any natural or civil law established, men wandered in a haphazard way over the land, holding just that property which they could either seize or keep by their own personal strength and vigor, by means of wounds and blood" (*Sest.* 42).[19] Cicero does not present a full theory of how humans escaped this state of nature, but he asserts that it must have been a product of human artifice.[20] Political association is not the original state of human beings, and we can live without it, but not if we wish to live well.

The Natural Law

Indeed, for Cicero, the creation and preservation of political communities is the highest possible human achievement because of the myriad goods that depend on our living together harmoniously. But not every political association is a good one. Our rationality allows us to see order in the universe, gives us a sense of right and wrong, and enables us to know our duties. A good state, a commonwealth, mirrors that order. A commonwealth, therefore, must be guided by the universal moral law, or natural law. According to

---

[17] See also *Rep.* 1.41.

[18] In contrast, see *Top.* 90, the deviation of which Barlow reasonably ascribes to the rhetorical nature of that treatise (Barlow 2012, 212).

[19] See also *Inv.* 1.2. For an extended discussion of the Roman ideas of the state of nature, see Straumann 2015.

[20] Cicero credits wise speakers with persuading people of the benefits of association.

Cicero, natural law can be deduced by our reason alone if it looks squarely at the rest of nature as well as ourselves.

The discussion of natural law offered by Cicero in *De legibus* is the most complete extant classical account of the natural law doctrine and perhaps the most influential in the history of political thought.[21] But just as *De legibus* is explicitly a sequel to *De re publica*,[22] so, too, does its natural law teaching depend on premises set forth in the previous work. That the final part of *De re publica* establishes the foundation for the first arguments of *De legibus* is indicative of the unified whole that the two dialogues form. In *De re publica*, Cicero offers a literal vision of the cosmic order that allows us to locate the place of human political life in relationship to the whole.[23] It is to this that we must turn first if we wish to understand the premises behind Cicero's doctrine of natural law.

De re publica concludes with the famous dream of Scipio.[24] In it, the character Scipio is guided in his sleep by his adoptive grandfather to the celestial realm, where he learns about the nature of the cosmos. Scipio is shown how the vastness of the universe is ordered by rational principles. The stars and planets revolve and orbit according to different intervals. But the grand effect of their diversity is complete harmony.

> That [harmony] comes about by the force and motion of the orbs themselves, which take place in distinct and unequal intervals—but yet with each part established by reason [*pro rata*]—and by moderating highs with lows, creates various harmonies with equal proportions. (*Rep.* 6.18)

Out of hierarchy, difference, and motion comes cosmic harmony. This harmony is established and ensured by a rational supreme god, who oversees all (*Rep.* 6.17). The god's reason permeates the whole.

At the beginning of *De legibus*, Cicero makes it clear that his forthcoming account of natural law depends on this understanding of a divinely and rationally ordered universe: "all nature is ruled by the command, power, reason, mind, or divine will (or whatever other word would more clearly signify what

[21] See Nicgorski 2016, 104.

[22] As expressed at *Leg.* 1.15, 1.20.

[23] It is important to note that while most of *De re publica* was lost until 1819 (and much is still missing), this section survived from antiquity and was copied very widely.

[24] At least, this is the last extant portion of the *De re publica*. There is some scholarly debate about whether some portion of text is missing after the conclusion of the dream (see Atkins 2013, 45n92). No one, however, contends that the substantive arguments of the dialogue continue after this.

I mean) of the immortal gods" (*Leg.* 1.21).[25] Because human beings alone among the rest of creation share in the reason (*ratio*) that characterizes gods, they possess a kinship with the gods and occupy a privileged place in the natural order. The divine reason that governs the cosmos and gives it order is itself a kind of law—in fact, the highest and truest form of law. Cicero thus offers his famous definition of natural law:

> Law [*lex*] is the highest reason [*ratio summa*], innate in nature, which commands what is to be done and prohibits the opposite. This same reason, when it is established and perfected in the mind of a human being, is law. . . . If this has been expressed properly—and indeed I think that it basically has been—it is necessary to seek the beginning of justice in law. For that [law] is the force of nature, it is the mind and reason of the wise person, the standard of justice and injustice. (*Leg.* 1.18–19)[26]

Natural law is thus identical with rational morality. Cicero is indeed far from being the first philosopher of natural law, although his is the fullest extant account. Many scholars have noted that this understanding of law appears inspired by the Stoic formulation, according to which the term "natural law" is redundant because the only law properly so named is the law of nature.[27]

Indeed, the account of natural law laid out in *De legibus* does bear a strong resemblance to the explicitly Stoic account offered by the character Cato in *De finibus*. But Cicero's thoughts do not perfectly conform to Stoic doctrine, as he himself makes clear. Cicero himself appears as a character in that dialogue and offers some pointed criticism of Stoic natural law theories, in particular their failure to recognize the significance of human beings' embodied state. Although our minds make us superior to the other animals, our bodies leave us with much in common with them. It is our bodies—their neediness and vulnerability—that make politics necessary.

---

[25] Cicero acknowledges that he might have to begin his argument establishing this position if his interlocutors do not grant it. Since Epicureans believed the universe to be chaotic and ungoverned by the divine (see *Fin.* 1.17–18; *Leg.* 1.21), we might expect the Epicurean Atticus to object. But he reservedly allows Cicero to continue, which we might construe as a recognition of the work the *somnium Scipionis* does for Cicero's argument here. It may also indicate, however, that the theological assumption underlying natural law has not been sufficiently proven. Atticus is never persuaded of this first claim, after all.

[26] This definition is reiterated at *Leg.* 1.33, 2.11, 2.13; and *Rep.* 3.33.

[27] See Asmis 2008; Watson 1971; Atkins 2013, 165. Atkins notes, however, that Cicero insists that this version of natural law is meant to appeal to followers of Plato and Aristotle as well (Atkins 2013, 166–168).

Cicero says that we can see the rudiments of the natural law in the fact that all living creatures have natural instincts of self-love and self-preservation. This self-love may include a desire for pleasure, and it certainly includes a desire for the basic necessities of life as well as for improvement of the creature's faculties. Because the universe is rational and purposeful, we should conclude that these natural impulses are intended by the creator—they are guides for how the creature ought to act. So, too, with human beings. Since human beings are both body and mind, their goal must be the preservation and development of both their bodily and mental faculties (*Fin.* 4.32–37). For the former, this entails food, rest, shelter, health, and freedom from pain. For the latter, this means the pursuit of virtue, which Cicero understands as excellence of the mind. The germ of mental and moral excellence can be seen in children's innate love of knowledge and instinctive sense of gratitude, which show the naturalness of the virtues of wisdom and justice, respectively (*Fin.* 4.18, 5.61). Just as the mind is superior to the body, so, too, is perfection of the virtues more important than health or other elements of bodily well-being. Natural law for human beings is all derived from these first premises: that human beings ought to love and preserve themselves and develop their capacities as far as their particular nature allows. Because they exist under this law equally with all other rational creatures, there is a "community of gods and men" (*Leg.* 1.23). Human beings must respect the fact that their fellows are co-citizens of the universal cosmopolis and also require these goods. The consequence of this last realization provides us with extensive duties that will be explored further.

The precepts of natural law, while drawn from our nature, are not mere suggestions or recommendations; they truly are *law*. Their source is the supreme deity, who is sovereign over all creation. In Scipio's dream, we see the ordered harmony of the universe maintained by the god's rational intelligence. The purposeful order of the universe means that we can infer that humans' natural impulses are also intended by the creator and are expressions of his will. As such, they ought to be obeyed as the commands of a rightful superior: "natural law summons to duty by its commands and averts from injustice by its prohibitions" (*Rep.* 3.33).

Cicero's espousal of natural law was not naive. He was well aware of the plausibility of the alternative view: that justice has no basis in nature. A half century before Cicero's birth, Rome had witnessed an astounding demonstration of rhetorical skill when the philosopher Carneades (an Academic of the same school as Cicero) gave two speeches in the city. The first was a powerful defense of justice that earned admiration from Cato the Elder and several of the characters featured in Cicero's *De re publica* (including Scipio, Laelius, and Philus). However, the next day, Carneades gave a second speech, more powerful still, debunking justice. Beyond demonstrating Carneades's potent skills as a dialectician (or a sophist), the strength of the second speech seemed to undermine the power of justice far more than the first had upheld it. The ensuing outrage from Cato, Laelius, and others pressured Carneades to leave the city.

We have no record of the original speeches, but in *De re publica*, Cicero takes the opportunity to reverse the outcome of Carneades's debate with himself, using the characters who were historically present.[28] Although the bulk of this work was lost until a discovery of a palimpsest in the early nineteenth century, Augustine and Lactantius preserve large sections of it, which would go on to provoke reactions from subsequent thinkers, such as Grotius and Locke. Cicero uses the debate as a way to vindicate natural law against the conventionalist attack.

Even with the material offered by Augustine and Lactantius, the debate is still incomplete. From Lactantius, we learn that Cicero allows the character Philus to make the case for injustice. His argument resembles those deployed by Thrasymachus, Adeimantus, and Glaucon in the first two books of Plato's *Republic*. Philus paints dueling portraits: one of a man who is just but is reputed to be supremely unjust, suffering torture and exile. The other man is secretly unjust but enjoys the rewards of his false reputation for justice. Philus asks rhetorically: "who would be so insane as to doubt which of these he would prefer to be?" (*Rep.* 3.27). Philus then goes on to argue that the same logic applies to nations—it is better to dominate unjustly than to be enslaved with justice. Successful imperial rule, in fact, depends on injustice. In short, Philus argues that injustice pays, while justice is costly. The nature of things does not redound to the benefit of the just.

The order of the speeches seems significant, as one expects Cicero to give the last word to his preferred position. Whereas in the original, Carneades defends justice first and refutes it second, Cicero's debate features first Philus's defense of injustice, followed by Laelius's vindication of justice. But what we have of Laelius's position is even less complete than Philus's. What we do have is Laelius's appeal to natural law, evidence for which he finds in the human realm and in the cosmos. He points to the god's rule over men, the mind over

---

[28] For more on this, see Zetzel 1996, 298.

the body, and reason over appetite as evidence of justly ordered hierarchy. He likens the commission of injustice to the reversion to being a beast, something no human would want (*Rep* 3.33–37).

Some commentators have argued that Laelius's rebuttal ultimately fails, perhaps that Cicero himself even intends it to. Jed Atkins suggests that Laelius never manages to refute the point that injustice is most useful for acquiring and maintaining empire.[29] On a deeper level, it is somewhat strange for an Academic skeptic—of the same school as Philus and Carneades himself—to side against them in favor of the more dogmatic (and Stoic) position of natural law. If human knowledge is as limited as Cicero otherwise claims, his embrace of natural law seems difficult to justify.[30] In the case of *De re publica*, the fragmentary nature of the text makes it impossible to come to a certain conclusion about what lesson Cicero intends the reader to draw. But it is noteworthy that Cicero expresses many of the arguments deployed by Laelius in his own name elsewhere. For instance, the description of natural law is echoed and expanded in the first book of *De legibus*. Similarly, the idea that behaving unjustly makes us like beasts appears again at *Off.* 1.34. These strongly suggest that Cicero himself does side with Laelius in this recreated Carneadean debate.

In *De officiis*, Cicero sets out to defend the proposition that the morally good (*honestum*) and the useful (*utile*) are never truly in conflict and that Philus's alleged disjunction between the two fails. Cicero maintains this position on the grounds that human beings are rational creatures whose highest interest *is* moral goodness. Therefore, obedience to this natural law is not only obligatory for us, but it is also ultimately to our benefit. Conversely, violation of the natural law entails its own punishment, as it estranges us from our nature: "whoever disobeys [the natural law] flees from himself and denies his human nature, and by this very fact will suffer the worst penalty, even if he avoids what is commonly considered punishment" (*Rep*. 3.33).[31] Thus, natural law does function like an ordinary law: it prohibits, commands, and supports its orders with threats of punishment and promises of reward.

This, then, is the outline of Cicero's doctrine of natural law. It binds each individual human being. But it has special consequences for politics. Just as the good human being must obey the natural law as it applies to him, so, too,

[29] Atkins 2013, 40–42. See also Zetzel 1996, 317.
[30] Here again, the failure in *De legibus* to persuade Atticus of the existence of the supreme deity also supports the skeptical view.
[31] See also Alonso 2012, 160.

must a good political community obey those particular precepts of the natural law applicable to whole political communities. However, Cicero never resolves the difficulty of how a skeptical epistemology could ever be brought to endorse a natural law that seems to depend on recognizing the existence of a supreme deity and even knowing the content of that deity's will. This problem would recur for Cicero's heirs, finally finding a solution (of sorts) in Locke.[32]

Justice and the *Res Publica*

For now, however, it is necessary to turn to the relationship between natural law and particular political communities. The vision of the cosmos in Scipio's dream is explicitly analogous to a *res publica*, with the supreme deity as the sovereign over the earth and the rest of the celestial bodies. A commonwealth must therefore somehow reflect the order of the universe microcosmically. Its laws must correspond to highest law; it must produce a harmony out of diverse parts. Cicero acknowledges the inferior dignity of written human laws in comparison to this highest law (*Leg.* 1.19). Whereas written human laws are particular and are limited by the flawed human wisdom that gives rise to them, the natural law is perfect—perfectly rational and perfectly just. Moreover, the natural law applies to all human beings equally in their capacity as rational creatures (*Leg.* 1.30). The fact of an objective, rational, natural law for everyone invalidates all forms of moral relativism. Cicero denounces as "the most stupid idea" the suggestion that people's institutions or laws can *determine* what is just. The common acceptance of robbery, deception, murder, or adultery would not, by the mere fact of popular approval, make those things just (*Leg.* 1.42–45). There is but one universal standard of right: "there will not be one law here, another in Athens, one law now, another in the future, but a single, eternal, unchanging law binding all peoples always" (*Rep.* 3.27–33).[33]

If the natural law thus is meant to apply across political communities, we are prompted to ask, what does natural law have to say about the commonwealth and its laws? How can human laws best approximate the natural law?

---

[32] See chapter 5.

[33] Cicero argues further for the universality of natural law based on human dignity at *De officiis* 3.27–28.

According to Cicero, human laws best reflect the natural law by enabling or promoting human beings' highest goods—self-preservation, the necessities of nature, and the pursuit of virtue. For all three of these things, we need political communities; more precisely, we need commonwealths.

Because the universe itself is a macrocosm of it, the very idea of the commonwealth holds an exalted position according to the natural order in *De re publica*. Despite the ultimate smallness and apparent insignificance of even the largest empire on earth (Rome), Cicero's Scipio is assured that great rewards wait in heaven for the leaders and preservers of commonwealths (*Rep.* 4.13, 4.29). Neal Wood insists that the best way to translate *res publica* is by "state," and he credits Cicero with being the first to conceive of the purpose of the state "in largely non-ethical terms."[34] But all evidence suggests that a *res publica* is not any state; Cicero makes it quite clear that the state (understood as the institutions of government or political rule) can and does persist under the conditions of tyranny but that the *res publica* cannot (*Rep.* 3.43–44; *Off.* 2.3).[35] To be a stable commonwealth, a group of people must practice justice.

In some fashion, such a consideration applies to all organizations, not merely commonwealths; even a band of pirates cannot operate without its members observing rules of justice at least with one another (*Off.* 2.40). Some element of agreement seems also necessary to make any organization work. But Cicero takes great pains to resist the conventionalist suggestion that agreement by itself makes something just and that any agreement about justice can form a commonwealth.[36] The laws of the commonwealth have to be evaluated by the just standard of natural law; they are not themselves the standard. Cicero denounces those who "consider just all things which have been established by a people's institutions or laws." He continues: "it is a sign of insanity to hold that these things are by opinion, not fixed by nature" (*Leg.* 1.42–45). This is why Caesar's proposed constitutional innovations are intolerable, even if they were approved by Rome's citizens.

Justice is the politically relevant portion of natural law. Whereas other elements of natural law apply to human beings taken in isolation, justice

---

[34] Wood 1988, 120.

[35] For more on Wood's inappropriate rendering of *res publica* as "state," see Barlow 2012, 218. Wood even appears to contradict himself on this issue (Wood 1988, 145).

[36] Hobbes provides perhaps the clearest contrast to Cicero's position here, when he argues that justice does not exist prior to agreement and contract (*Leviathan*, chap. 13). I will return to discuss the consequences of this contrast in chapters 4 and 5.

applies only to groups. So what is justice by nature? First, it takes account of the fact that natural law applies to everyone. Not only to be observed among the powerful, "justice must be maintained even toward the lowliest . . . even slaves" (*Off.* 1.41). Cicero then offers a succinct definition in *De officiis*: one must not harm others unless provoked by wrongdoing, and one must treat common property as common and private property as private (*Off.* 1.20–21). Injustice lies in the violation of these conditions *or* in allowing others to violate them when one is in a position to prevent it (*Off.* 1.23). This understanding of justice derives from human beings' common membership in the universal cosmopolis and our status as embodied beings.

Marcia Colish sees in Cicero's definition of justice a combination of "the traditional Platonic-Aristotelian *suum cuique* formula with values drawn from Roman law."[37] But Colish's view understates Cicero's divergence from Plato and Aristotle. The difference between Cicero and Plato and Aristotle (and, indeed, the Stoics) is especially noticeable in the last component of Cicero's definition of justice—the requirement to prevent wrongdoing committed by others. But even the apparently straightforward first rule of justice constitutes a change at least of emphasis and orientation from the Platonic-Aristotelian framework.

Plato and Aristotle would not likely disagree with Cicero's first rule of justice, the prohibition of unprovoked harm.[38] But neither arrives at that conclusion the same way Cicero does, and the underlying reasoning matters here. In Aristotle's *Politics*, the just is either conventional and therefore coterminous with the lawful, or it is about relations of equality—whether proportional equality or numerical equality.[39] Harming others is a violation of justice, therefore, either because it breaks the law or because it violates the rightful dynamic of proportional or numerical equality. In Plato's *Republic*, justice is eventually discovered to be "the minding of one's own business and not being a busybody" (433b). The just individual will therefore refrain from harming others because he will be focused solely on his own affairs (in particular, his soul), which are the only things of true importance (443a–e).

As noted, Cicero resists the identification of the just with the lawful. Also entirely absent from his definition of justice is Aristotle's concern for

---

[37] Colish 1990, 146.

[38] Socrates in Plato's *Apology* goes so far as to deny that one ought to harm someone else *even if* provoked by harm (25b–e).

[39] See Aristotle, *Ethics* 5.6.1129a30–1135a15; *Politics* 3.9.1280a11.

proportional and numerical equality.[40] Instead, Cicero places the avoidance of harm at the forefront. By nature—that is, according to right reason and supreme natural law—human beings are in fellowship with one another. Unprovoked harm is injustice because it violates this sacred fellowship. Cicero cites Plato's Ninth Letter approvingly: "we are not born for ourselves alone" (*Off.* 1.22). But even as he calls on Plato for support, he rebukes him for having only a partial understanding of justice. The normative obligation to human fellowship that Plato and the Stoics acknowledge not only prohibits us from committing injustice but also requires us to prevent others from suffering injustice when we have the power to stop it. By this standard, Plato's archetypal just man, the philosopher, is not sufficiently just: "they observe one type of justice, indeed, that they should harm no one else by inflicting injustice, but they fall into another; for hindered by their devotion to learning, they abandon those whom they ought to protect . . . such men abandon the fellowship of life" (*Off.* 1.28–29). The very thing that prevents Plato's philosophers from committing active injustice—a concern only for the health of their own souls—is what also prevents them from fulfilling the active duties of justice. It makes them indifferent.

Cicero places the central focus on the avoidance of unwarranted harm to the individual, who is therefore entitled to certain protections. On the other hand, it is insufficient for us to follow Plato's just man and mind our own business. Our fellowship with others demands that we actively aid them when they face injustice. This fact makes the republican value of community-oriented public-spiritedness a necessary component of being just; "our country claims one part of our birth" (*Off.* 1.22). It further makes a career in public service morally obligatory for those who are most capable of preventing injustice (*Off.* 1.28–29).

It turns out that the fundamental value of human fellowship also undergirds the second aspect of Cicero's understanding of justice: the protection of private property. Here Cicero departs even more from the traditions of Plato, Aristotle, and the Stoics. The traditional formulation of *suum cuique* that Colish finds in Cicero's definition becomes explicitly about respecting the distinction between public and private property. For Colish and Wood, this indicates the influence of Roman property law on Cicero's thinking.

---

[40] Cicero was certainly concerned with the issues of proportional (or aristocratic) equality and numerical (or democratic) equality, but he does not link them very closely to his definition of justice (*Rep.* 1.53).

Colish and Wood point out that the idea of private property receives no similar deference in the teachings of Plato, Aristotle, Polybius, or the Stoics.[41] In Plato's case, private property (not to mention private family life) is, in fact, forbidden to the guardian class of the Kallipolis. Aristotle objects to Plato's communism, but his objection is based primarily on the practical infeasibility of such a scheme and secondarily on the grounds that such an arrangement would restrict the performance of such virtues as liberality (*Politics* 2.3.1261b33, 2.5.1263b11).

Cicero's defense of private property on the grounds of human fellowship might at first seem odd. As noted, Cicero denies that any particular property is private by nature, and he recognizes that property is often acquired by conquest and other forms of injustice (*Off.* 1.21). Moreover, we tend now to think of property as a source of social division, rather than harmony. Why, then, would Cicero insist that respect for private property is an essential element of justice and thereby one of the moral aims of any good commonwealth?[42]

Cicero does maintain that the protection of private property against theft or widespread redistribution is an important moral imperative for the state (*Off.* 2.73).[43] But contrary to the charges that he is an unreflective apologist for the cause of the wealthy against the poor, the example of Cicero's life shows that while he certainly wished to protect his own property, he would not seek to enrich himself wrongfully at the expense of the poor. He scrupulously refrained from despoiling Rome's subjects when he served as governor—in stark contrast to Caesar, the self-styled populist.[44] In Cicero's account of the origins of real political organization, he suggests that the defense of property served the cause of the poor against the predation of the rich:

> For when the poor multitudes were being oppressed by those who had more wealth, they fled to some one man outstanding in virtue, who protected the weak against injustice, and with equity established, held the highest and the least under an equal justice. (*Off.* 2.41)

---

[41] Colish 1990, 146; Wood 1988, 130.

[42] It is noteworthy that Cicero's clearest definition of justice is offered in the first book of *De officiis*, where he claims to be at least loosely following the Stoic Panaetius. But Cicero elsewhere reveals that he understands the Stoics to consider private property morally irrelevant (*Fin.* 4.22). All of this helps to illustrate Cicero's independence from the Stoics who allegedly served as his authorities on this issue.

[43] He accepts the possibility of moderate redistribution, though, if it serves the common good. See Neumann 2015, 33–34.

[44] Hammer 2014, 27.

Private property is so important to Cicero because maintaining clear boundaries between mine and thine facilitates interactions of good faith between individuals, by removing the opportunity for one party to seize what belongs to the other.[45]

Republican Liberty

It is clear how two of the three major elements of Cicero's natural law translate into politics. Our embodied state makes it necessary to ensure that we have the basic requirements of life, that we are protected from physical harm, and that the material goods we rely upon cannot be taken from us without provocation. Our common fellowship under the highest god's supreme sovereignty gives us an obligation to respect others' claims to these goods as well. But what about our minds? Cicero admittedly follows Aristotle and Plato in considering the mental aspect of our nature vastly superior to the bodily. Plato and Aristotle had taken the logical conclusion from this and made education—especially education in virtue—central to their visions of a good political regime. Yet Cicero nowhere ascribes to the commonwealth a responsibility to train citizens in virtue.[46]

Indeed, given Cicero's view of the importance of structuring our political life according to the commands of the universal natural law, one might wonder why he does not follow his acknowledged authority, Plato, and endorse rule by philosopher kings, whose wisdom could keep the polity on the proper path. This would leave very little room for the activity of a sovereign people to make laws for themselves but would ensure the implementation of the natural law. Yet Cicero rejects this option outright. Part of his objection to such an arrangement is practical. One cannot count on kings to remain virtuous and just—like all men, they can be corrupted by power. Therefore, we cannot expect to enjoy forever a situation where one individual or successive individuals from the same family line are so superior in wisdom and virtue to the rest that they can govern effectively and justly. Kings easily transform into tyrants (*Rep.* 2.47). According to Cicero, this is what led the Romans and other early peoples to substitute laws for kings, which would address citizens equally and impartially (*Off.* 2.42). The rule of law had to be substituted for

---

[45] For a fuller account of Cicero's views about property in light of its potentially tainted history, see Hawley 2018.

[46] Straumann 2016, 191–240.

the arbitrary rule of an individual's will, and so it transpired that "a magistrate is a law that speaks, and a law is a silent magistrate" (*Leg.* 2.3).

But because Cicero believes the practical and the moral to be linked, it should be unsurprising that he levels a deeper objection to monarchy, one that applies even to a just king. Cicero has Scipio explain, "the people that is ruled by a king lacks a great deal, and above all it lacks liberty [*libertas*], which does not consist in having a just master, but in having none" (*Rep.* 2.43). Here Cicero raises the crucial issue of liberty, whose opposite is subjugation to a master. Cicero is the earliest extant political philosopher to defend this understanding of liberty as freedom from domination or interference. He is thus also by default the first to place this understanding of liberty at the center of his idea of the good political regime. How is it that Cicero's *apparently* teleological natural law doctrine could yield a politics in which citizens are largely free to pursue whatever form of life they prefer? How is it that natural law would tolerate such liberty?

To answer this, first it is important to understand exactly what Cicero means when he refers to *libertas*. For Cicero, liberty for the individual lies in the freedom to act that exists in the absence of arbitrary domination. He describes the common goal of kings and philosophers as "needing nothing and obeying no one, they might enjoy liberty, the mark of which is to live just as one pleases" (*Off.* 1.70).[47] For Cicero, liberty appears equally opposed to domination and interference.

This kind of liberty requires law in order to make it real. As Cicero says, "we are therefore slaves to the law so that we may be free" (*Clu.* 146). There is a connection here with Philip Pettit's understanding of republican liberty as the absence of arbitrary power over someone. In this light, subjection to a fair system of law does not make one unfree.[48] But, for Pettit, the mere equal subjection of everyone to a common system of law in which everyone enjoys "the capacity to stand eye to eye with your fellow citizens, in a shared awareness that none of you has a power of arbitrary interference over another" *is* freedom.[49] But Cicero makes it clear that those features are the *conditions* of liberty. Liberty itself still lies primarily in the absence of constraint that emerges from those conditions.

---

[47] See also *Stoic Paradoxes* 34.
[48] Pettit 1997, 5.
[49] Pettit 1997, 5. Pettit insists that when an individual whose freedom to act is constrained not by arbitrary power but by interference from a government in which he or she has power equal to others, this is not a violation of republican freedom. Pettit is forced into the logical contortion of declaring that such a person should be considered "non-free, but not unfree" (Pettit 1997, 26n1).

Cicero's defense of this sort of liberty is a striking philosophical first, and scholars have yet to fully come to grips with the significance of Cicero's innovation, which implicates not only his theory of freedom but also his doctrine of natural law. To see perhaps Cicero's most enduring contribution to the history of political thought, we need to compare his views here to those whom he so often claimed as his authorities: Plato and Aristotle.

Cicero's Greek philosophical predecessors had no love for the sort of negative freedom that would allow people to live as they chose, precisely because of how they construed natural law and human perfection. The City in Speech of Plato's *Republic*—to take the most prominent example—has no room at all for liberty understood as freedom from either interference or domination. Plato's Socrates elaborates on the principle that "in founding the city, we are not looking to the exceptional happiness of any one group among us but, as far as possible, that of the city as a whole" (420b). According to Plato, this requires forcing those with philosophical natures to rule, depriving them of private property and families. The paternalistic interpretation of the common good extends to the rest of the city as well, as citizens' whole lives— from birth through assignment to a class and profession, to mating, to the culture they can consume—are all determined for their own good.

However, Plato does not merely ignore this conception of liberty. The characterization of democracy in the *Republic* depicts such freedom as the "insatiable desire" of that regime (562c). This freedom is posed against obedience such that those who are inclined to obey are called "willing slaves" by democratic partisans (562c). The people under such a regime wish to "avoid having any master at all" (563d). Plato's description of democratic values is partially caricature and clearly unfriendly. But it appears to be a characterization based in the practices and rhetoric of Athenian democracy. In Thucydides's account of "Pericles's Funeral Oration," the democratic leader extols Athens in part because "the freedom which we enjoy in our government extends also to our ordinary life. There, far from exercising a jealous surveillance over each other, we do not feel called upon to be angry with our neighbor for doing what he likes . . . at Athens we live exactly as we please" (Thuc. 2.37–39).[50] Thus, we can see that Plato had access to some idea of freedom as the absence of mastery and living as one wants, yet he clearly rejects it in the

---

[50] This understanding of freedom closely resembles Cicero's definition in which one "lives as one pleases." There is a growing body of scholarship that argues that a freedom of this sort was indeed a feature of the Athenian democratic discourse. See Edge (2009); Cartledge and Edge (2009); Raaflaub (2004). Edge even posits some overlap between this democratic freedom and later Roman practices.

Republic in favor of a vision of a city unified in its goal of achieving a singular notion of the good life.[51]

Although Plato is sometimes elided into the neo-Roman republican tradition, Aristotle holds a far more prominent place in more influential accounts.[52] Yet, like Plato, Aristotle had access to a negative conception of liberty and rejected it. Aristotle does offer a famous dichotomy between slave and free person, but the distinction rests on the latter's full possession of reason, not his ability to live as he pleases (*Politics* 1.5). Indeed, Aristotle describes a free political state as one characterized by "ruling and being ruled in turn" (*Politics* 3.4), a situation that may admit of many constraints. Such constraint is incompatible with not being ruled at all, a desire Aristotle (like Plato) ascribes to the partisans of democracy: "another [mark of democratic freedom] is to live as one wants" (*Politics* 6.2). Aristotle goes so far as to describe as "tyrannical" the democratic habit of "tolerating everyone living as he wants." He complains that "living in a disorderly way is more pleasant to the many than living with moderation" (*Politics* 6.2).

For all their differences, Aristotle agrees with Plato that the goal of the just regime is the good life for its members. Not being enslaved is a necessary precondition for the good life, but that good life may entail considerable regulation of the lives of citizens. The good life requires a comprehensive system of education and even coercion in order to mold citizens into the virtuous kinds of people capable of living the good life. For this reason, even scholars who seek to show Aristotle as standing behind later developments of liberalism and republicanism acknowledge his disapproval of ideals of negative liberty. Thus, Fred Miller, who sees in Aristotle the origins of natural rights theories, admits that Aristotle's thought "does not accord freedom or liberty the central place it has in most modern theories, so that he is more inclined to endorse paternalistic and other authoritarian regulations."[53]

Aristotle's interest in cultivating virtue as the decisive component of the good life leaves little room for citizens "living as they want." As Thomas

[51] André Laks finds several different meanings of freedom in Plato's *Laws*, but the negative sense of liberty does not feature among them (Laks 2007). Plato's method of writing certainly raises the possibility that his intended teaching may be at odds with the surface meaning of his text. However, those scholars who read Plato in this way do not generally attribute to him an esoteric appreciation for this kind of negative liberty. Indeed, it is difficult to imagine why Plato would feel the need to conceal such a view, if he held it, since it would conform to the dominant political opinion of his city.

[52] E.g., Pocock 2009.

[53] Miller 1996. See also Long 1996. Malcolm Schofield is still more emphatic that Aristotle is uninterested in such a conception of liberty or political rights of any kind (Schofield 1996).

Lindsay puts it, for Aristotle, "freedom is not, as the democrats claim, an end in itself, but exists for the sake of happiness, which is an activity (*energeia*) of the soul in accordance with virtue."[54] Eric Nelson summarizes the agreement between Plato and Aristotle: "the freedom they value is the condition of living according to nature, and one of their cardinal assumptions is that most individuals cannot be said to be 'free' in this sense unless they depend upon their intellectual and moral superiors."[55] The common pursuit of the good life, the life according to nature, cannot then be reconciled with an ideal of freedom as non-interference, non-domination, or non-dependence. Greek philosophy's rejection of this ideal thus arises out of deep philosophical commitments, not historical contingency.

Cicero repeatedly aligns himself with the Platonic-Aristotelian tradition of construing natural law (e.g., *Fin.* 4.79–80). Yet he does not interpret natural law as foreclosing this negative version of liberty as they do; his natural law, in fact, seems to demand it. To understand why, we need to return to Cicero's explanation of the highest human end and the good human life, especially as found in *De officiis*.

We have already seen that Cicero understands us to be obligated to live according to the dictates of nature. With respect to physical goods and duties to others, nature speaks with the same voice to all. When it comes to our mental faculties, nature likewise commands us all to develop them to their fullest extent. But crucially, that development looks different for different people. For this reason, there is no uniform system that politics can or should impose that will promote mental development. The most illuminating illustration of this comes in book 1 of *De officiis*, where Cicero addresses the issue of choosing a course of life.

At first, Cicero's discussion there seems to follow closely the well-trodden Greek path. He asserts that the nature of humans greatly exceeds that of the beasts. This superiority lies in the human capacity for reason, while beasts are driven solely by instinct and the desire for base pleasure (*Off.* 1.105). Moreover, our rational nature also makes us social: "the same nature, by the power of reason, connects one person with another for the sake of fellowship of speech and life" (*Off.* 1.12). As Plato and Aristotle do, Cicero insists that reason ought to rule over the passions or appetites: "it is necessary that the appetites obey reason . . . to which they are subjected by the law of nature

---

[54] Lindsay 1992. Cf. *Nicomachean Ethics* 1102a5–7.
[55] Nelson 2004, 10.

[*lege naturae*]" (*Off.* 1.102). This understanding of nature elevates the philosopher and the statesman as the highest forms of life humanly possible. The philosopher most cultivates the human capacity for reason, while the statesman most serves human sociability by upholding and preserving the commonwealth (*Off.* 1.13, 1.153).[56] In all of this, Cicero says little that would separate him from Plato or Aristotle.

However, Cicero then complicates this picture considerably. It is worth quoting the relevant passage at length:

> For it ought to be understood that we are dressed by nature as it were, for two roles [*personis*], of which one is common, since we are all participants in reason and in that superiority by which we surpass the beasts, from which all that is honorable and proper derives and by which we discover a way of finding our duty. The other, however, is given specifically to individuals. For in the same way that there are vast differences in people's bodies . . . so too are there great variations in people's spirits. (*Off.* 1.107)

To the two roles here described, Cicero goes on to add two more: those thrust upon us by chance and those arising from our own free choice (*Off.* 1.115). Christopher Gill provides an influential interpretation of the so-called four *personae* when he asserts that Cicero's theory is meant to uphold Roman hierarchical class structures by convincing readers to mold themselves to fit whatever social position they find themselves in.[57] However, Cicero actually insists that the roles assigned by nature take precedence over those arising from social situation when we make choices (*Off.* 1.120).[58] As in the Greek case, nature remains normatively decisive.

But now, according to Cicero, each human being effectively has two natures: our universal human nature (*natura universa*) and our own particular nature (*natura nostra*) (*Off.* 1.111). The universal human nature functions in the same way that Aristotelian or Platonic nature would; it unites humans through reason and sociability. It gives us our universal moral obligations and enjoins us to cultivate the rational and social aspects of ourselves. But beyond this, according to Cicero, we ought to defer to our individual natures. Cicero provides a long list of qualities that might fall into this

---

[56] See also *Rep.* 6.3.

[57] Gill 1988, 171. See also Burchell 1998.

[58] For a fuller argument of the primacy of nature to circumstance in Cicero's theory, see Hawley 2020a, 20.

category: humor, seriousness, straightforwardness, irony, honesty, and craft-
iness are all qualities that it might behoove one person to cultivate but not
another. "Even in the case of the virtues, some men prefer to excel in some or
others" (*Off.* 1.115). Most important, Cicero insists that in the choice of life
path or career, "all consideration ought to be referred to the individual's own
nature" (*Off.* 1.119). As a result, some rightfully apply themselves to philosophy, while others pursue law or oratory, and so on (*Off.* 1.115).[59]

Cicero's overarching moral principle of *decorum* (propriety or seemliness)
places great weight on the particularities of individuals' natures: "for what
is most seemly for a man is that which is most his own" (*Off.* 1.113). Such
differences may go so deep that in the same circumstances, one person ought
to choose to die, while another ought to choose life. In short, Cicero's concept
of nature undergirds a vast diversity of human types and choices—which
cannot be conveniently grouped into a discrete number of classes, as in Plato's
Republic. Moreover, even though there may be objectively higher ways of life
according to the extent to which they reflect our rational and social natures
(the philosopher and the statesman), that fact is *rightly* irrelevant to any individual unsuited to them (*Off.* 1.110). As a result, it no longer makes sense
to conceive of politics as the arena in which we collectively seek *the* good life
together—since the good life will necessarily mean different things to each
one of us. Nor can the state function as a tutelary organization that educates,
guides, or constrains us to live the good life. Much less can it be expected to
adequately assign a life role to each of its members. Cicero is quite clear that
the development of each individual's nature and choice of life path is up to
the discernment of that individual alone and cannot be directed by someone
else—even by someone wiser (*Off.* 1.118).[60] Thus, Cicero's theoretically teleological natural law is in its practical application non-teleological—we do
not have some thick conception of the good life to seek together.

Thus, it should now be unsurprising that the primary purpose of the regime according to Plato and Aristotle (the achievement of the communal

---

[59] One might fairly point out that these particular life paths do not really capture the full diversity
of possible human choice and are actually only open to a Roman elite. As will be discussed more fully
in the next section, Cicero's thought on liberty often displays a tension between egalitarian and elitist
impulses. Of course, Cicero might also be able to defend his rather narrow list of examples as appropriate given the context that *De officiis* is formally addressed to his son, who is himself a Roman elite.

[60] It may seem that Cicero's position here is at odds with the very nature of *De officiis*, which is a
letter of advice from father to son. But the central feature of the first *persona* is that moral duties (the
subject of the work) *do* have universal validity, while the choice of life path remains up to the individual. Cicero can give advice with regard to the first, but his son must choose his own way for the
second.

good life through the pursuit of virtue) is entirely absent from Cicero's own descriptions of its purpose. Cicero variously describes the purpose of the state as the defense of property (*Off.* 2.73), the establishment of justice and common advantage (*Rep.* 1.39), and the satisfaction of sociability (*Off.* 1.12). Therefore, we can surmise that at the very least, Cicero's embracing of natural human diversity eliminates one aspect of Greek philosophy's vision of the ends of politics that is particularly antithetical to negative liberty.

More than this, we might even see in Cicero's account of individual nature a feature that *demands* something like negative liberty for its fulfillment. Cicero insists that our cultivation of our own particular natures ought to be the product of our own free choice (*Off.*, 1.115, 1.119–120). This natural obligation seems then to require that we are free to pursue that choice, at least within the limits of justice: "each should hold on to his own, so long as it is not vicious . . . for we must act such that we do nothing contrary to the demands of universal nature, but while holding on to that, let us follow our own nature" (*Off.* 1.110). We thus need something like liberty to ensure that we have the opportunity to fulfill this obligation. Resistance to brute command is a rightful and natural consequence of our rational natures (*Off.* 1.13). The baseline of common human dignity found in our shared rational nature also makes blind obedience to authority unworthy of us.

Thus, Cicero derives a principle of individual liberty from his conception of natural law and human nature. The teleological element of his natural law doctrine does not produce the paternalism of Plato's or Aristotle's politics but rather one of free choice. Because of our common human dignity and individual uniqueness, the *finis ultima*—the good life—looks different for each of us and requires that we enjoy the liberty to pursue it after our own fashion. The circumstances that make such a life possible still require politics, for all the reasons just discussed. But it will be a radically different kind of politics from that found in Plato and Aristotle. It will be a politics of *libertas*.

Natural Law and Popular Sovereignty

As a result of our natural individual liberty, a good political regime cannot be imposed from above but must be freely consented to by the people who make it up. Cicero explains that the people have a rightful ownership claim on their own political community. Using the genitive of possession, he insists that a *res publica* is the same thing as the *res populi* (the property *of* the people) (*Rep.*

1.39). As Malcolm Schofield explains, even the term *res publica* itself evokes a sense of ownership: "if the *populus* possesses its own *res*, it follows that it has rights over its management and use. And the ability to exercise those rights is what political liberty consists in."[61] Here we find the nascent articulation of the doctrine of popular sovereignty.[62] A free people *own* their commonwealth. All legitimate political communities must be commonwealths in this sense.[63]

Cicero does not invent this idea. He finds it, semi-inchoate, in the norms and practices of Rome. There is some evidence to suggest that the conflict over the Gracchan reforms reflected an attempt to locate the source of all legitimacy in this principle. Plutarch relates a speech of Tiberius Gracchus in which he argues that tribunes—legally untouchable—could be deposed if they violated the will of the people, since the people were the original source of all political authority (Plut. *Ti. Gracch.* 15.2–6).[64] The right of *provocatio*, which will be discussed further, seems to instantiate in the people an ultimate authority to judge offenses. But these claims of the people's sovereignty were thoroughly contested. The Gracchi were defeated, after all, and there were many ways in which the direct will of the people was often thwarted by the legal arrangements of the republic.

It is thus into a long-standing debate that Cicero enters in offering his theorization of popular sovereignty. From his definitional understanding of a *res publica*, he accepts the principle of popular ownership of the regime. For this reason, the whole *res publica*, not only individuals, can lose its liberty (and, with it, its very existence). Just as the individual citizen enjoys liberty when he is free to act unconstrained by arbitrary and unlawful power, so, too, does the political community. This liberty of the commonwealth is so morally important that its preservation demands even the ultimate sacrifice of one's life. Cicero's final speeches against Antony express his passionate commitment to recover and defend the liberty of the *res publica*: "Let us at last take our fathers' spirit and courage, resolving to regain the freedom that belongs to the Roman race and name, or else to prefer death to slavery" (*Phil.* 3.28). Cicero

---

[61] Schofield 1995, 76. Atkins concurs, explaining that the term *res publica* "plays upon the use of *res* in Roman law to designate property" (Atkins 2013, 131–132). Furthermore, "the fact that the people own the *res publica* implies the right to manage this property" (Atkins 2013, 138).

[62] Cicero never uses such a term, which appears in political discourse much later, but his theory certainly captures the basic features of the idea.

[63] As Schofield points out, Cicero's theory is a theory of legitimacy, which itself is not a particularly Greek concern (Schofield 1995, 66).

[64] Straumann 2016, 121–129.

proposes to lead in this effort by example: "I shall employ every moment of the day and of the night in thinking, insofar as thought is required, of the freedom of the Roman people" (*Phil.* 3.33).

The violation of the rule of law and the concentration of unchecked arbitrary power in the hands of any individual or group are the hallmarks of the loss of liberty. The aims of the individual and the political community to recover liberty then become united. According to Cicero, such was the case under Caesar's dictatorship, and his assassination returned Rome to liberty, albeit only briefly (*Phil.* 2.26–29, 2.80, 2.85–86). Denial of liberty (and, with it, of moral equality) is the real evil of arbitrary rule.

As we have seen, Cicero's definition of freedom does not resemble the Aristotelian ruling and being ruled in turn.[65] First, liberty is incompatible with being "ruled" at all, and Cicero does not use "ruling" words such as *regno, impero,* or *domino* when describing the just activities of government. If anything rules in a commonwealth, it is the laws, not humans at all. But even substituting "govern" or "administer" for "rule," Cicero's commonwealth still lacks the rotating element of Aristotle's formulation. As Schofield points out, Cicero's understanding of the *res publica* undergirds a whole political vocabulary with no "parallel in Greek generally or in Greek political philosophy in particular."[66]

The assumption of equal ownership over the body politic does not, in fact, require every citizen to be equally involved in the running of the commonwealth. As with any substantial piece of property, Cicero believes that it is often wiser to place the day-to-day running of the *res publica* in the hands of skilled managers. But, for the same reason as in the case of unchecked kingship, a purely aristocratic government (which Cicero understands as an aristocracy of merit rather than wealth or birth) cannot serve as a commonwealth. Such a state would benefit greatly from the deliberative wisdom of its governing body. True aristocracies also fairly reward the truly deserving according to their merit (*Rep.* 1.51–53). But in such a regime, the great mass of people still want for the liberty they lack under a monarch.

This idea that the people are the rightful owners of the regime might then seem to demand a democratic form of rule. Yet Cicero sets the tone for the Roman republican tradition's hostility to democracy along the Athenian model. Cicero's doctrine of natural law establishes the people's rightful

---

[65] See Connolly 2014, 1.
[66] Schofield 1995, 77.

ownership of their political community but also sets limits on what they can rightfully do. According to Cicero, democracy tends to be hostile toward both the wealthy and the virtuous. This is a violation of the fair partnership that should characterize a *res publica*—which for Cicero aims not at the greatest good for the greatest number but at a truly *common* good. Democracy fails to grant superior honor and responsibility to those who prove the best servants of the public good, offering political power to demagogues who flatter and fan the people's hatred of the wealthy (*Rep.* 1.53). It also fails to respect private property claims. In order to achieve its ends, Cicero believes, such a radically democratic populace will be inclined to raise up a tyrant to beat down elites of all sorts (*Rep.* 1.68).

Thus, Cicero suggests that each of the three simple forms of government is unstable and inclines toward revolution and tyranny. But they are unstable in large part precisely because, as partnerships of the whole citizen body, they distribute rights, honors, and responsibilities unfairly. Because they are unjust, they are also impractical—*utile* and *honestum* are inseparable.

Consent and the Mixed Regime

It seems as though Cicero has established two thoroughly incompatible standards of political legitimacy. He insists that there is one universal standard of political justice—one that is not relative to particular peoples or times. Yet his egalitarian (in one respect) understanding of human nature leads him also to insist that every good political regime is rightly owned by the particular people who make it up. How can this popular sovereignty be reconciled with a universal natural law? In fact, it turns out that Cicero's natural law doctrine functions as the grounding for his theory of popular sovereignty. Rights prove to be the concept that allows these two ideas to function together, if still in some tension.

A *res publica* depends on the consent of its members as a matter of justice and practicality. In *De re publica*, Cicero has Scipio give the famous definition of a commonwealth; in some sense, we might consider this the foundational moment of republicanism as a tradition of thought. Scipio offers the following definition:

> The commonwealth [*res publica*] is the concern of the people [*res populi*]. However, a people is not any collection of human beings gathered

in whatever way but a sizable group allied together by agreement about right [*consensu iuris*] and common interest [*utilitatis commune*]. (*Rep.* 1.39)[67]

Cicero's Scipio makes *agreement* about justice a definitional component of his commonwealth. He thereby introduces a requirement for something that at least resembles consent; the people must agree about what justice is. This condition flows in part from the fact that since a *res publica* is the common property of its constituent citizens, we could not expect it to function practically without some general consensus about how citizens ought to relate to one another. Cicero does not elaborate a detailed doctrine of consent (e.g., explicit vs. tacit). But it is clear that the requirement of consent is at least in part entailed by the requirement of justice. If people are free by nature, then all rightful association must be based on consent, not compulsion. Walter Nicgorski puts it simply: "for Cicero, to be fully human is to be free, and to be free is to be a consenting partner in the political community."[68] Cicero contrasts force (*vis*) with right (*ius*), illustrating that all political unity depends on one or the other. In this way also, he implies that right entails some element of consent.[69]

But it is not enough to consent to just any set of laws and institutions. Right entails consent, but consent does not entail right.[70] To qualify as a commonwealth, the people must agree to fundamental laws and institutions based on true justice and natural law. Justice exists independent of any consent, and for the consent to legitimate a regime, the people must consent to true justice. For this reason, Cicero's notion of popular sovereignty is not really a theory of "constituent power" as found in the Abbé Sieyès's famous distinction between a constituent power, which can legitimately form a constitution, and a constituted power, which is a body recognized by the constitution.[71] The people are rightfully the *owners* of the political regime, but they are not the absolutely free makers of it. In Cicero's theoretical account, they cannot

[67] This passage, too, was among those fragments of *De re publica* preserved from antiquity. It was made known to many subsequent thinkers through Augustine's citation of it in *The City of God. Iuris* in this context could also be construed as "law" or "justice." Schofield translates it as the latter (Schofield 1995). I have here rendered it as "right," because that seems to best approximate the various possible meanings at play, including justice.

[68] Nicgorski 2016, 175.

[69] Nicgorski 2016, 171.

[70] See Nicgorski 2016, 177.

[71] A number of scholars have recently explored this topic fruitfully, including Rubinelli 2020; Loughlin 2014; Loughlin and Walker 2007; Straumann 2019.

establish its institutions in whatever way suits them and have the resulting political entity qualify as a *res publica*.[72] The people's legitimacy *as a people* depends on their acceptance of the natural law's principles of right.[73]

This account of the people as normatively subordinate to the *ius* of natural law was contested in the late republic and through the principate. Dictators such as Sulla and Julius Caesar may have claimed authority from the people that would trump natural law, and Roman jurists would later attribute such authority to the emperor. Cicero as a politician undoubtedly makes use of this ambiguity when he relies on the allegedly supra-constitutional power of the people's mandate to move against the Catilinarian conspirators. But Cicero the philosopher takes greater pains to consistently construe the people's authority over the political community as downstream from their principles of natural law.[74] People have their qualified ownership claim to sovereignty because of the logic of the natural law. This principle, however, leaves the ultimate sovereignty of the people somewhat ambiguous. What precisely are the limits of this sovereign authority? What of the occasions when the two principles conflict? Cicero does not ever enumerate the limitations of this sovereignty, but his construal of how best to organize the powers of a *res publica* gives some indication.

For Cicero, a regime that corresponds to the natural law will avoid both the injustice and the instability characteristic of the three simple types of government. From this arises Cicero's doctrine of the mixed regime:

> If there is not an equitable balance in the state of rights and duties and responsibilities, so that there is enough power in the hands of the magistrates and enough authority in the judgment of the aristocrats and enough freedom in the people, then the condition of the commonwealth cannot be preserved unchanged. (*Rep.* 2.57)[75]

The drawbacks of each simple regime are to be ameliorated through combination, while at the same time preserving the unique goods represented by

[72] As Straumann puts it: "far from thinking that the people needed to act as a constituent power, Cicero put forward the very radical claim that there could not be a people in the relevant sense without there being first a core of constitutional norms to agree upon" (Straumann 2019, 275).

[73] Cf. Schofield 1995.

[74] Cf. Straumann 2019; Arato 2017.

[75] Although this succinct expression comes in *De re publica*, which was only rediscovered in the early nineteenth century, the general outline of Ciceronian mixed government can be found throughout those works of Cicero that were widely read in the early modern period, for instance, in *De legibus*.

each. For Cicero, Rome offers the closest approximation of this best practical regime, although it is a Rome of the past, deliberately and overtly idealized.

Cicero defends a mixture of the three types of government and a "blending" of rights and duties (*Leg.* 3.28). As both Atkins and Straumann have pointed out, separation of powers and a mixed regime are not the same thing: a mixed regime includes principles of at least two of the simple kinds of government (monarchy/order, aristocracy/merit, democracy/freedom), whereas separation of powers entails locating fundamental functions of rule (legislating, judging, etc.) in different bodies or offices.[76] Straumann, however, seems to take this to mean that clearly separating powers means that a regime cannot be mixed: "legally defined powers that compose the constitutional order are strictly separated, i.e., precisely *not* 'mixed.'"[77] But Cicero's vision of Rome includes both. It is true that many (though not quite all) functions of government reside in clearly delineated organs, but it is also the case that the *constitution* as a whole is a mixture of the monarchic, the aristocratic, and the democratic.[78]

Certainly, Cicero's defense of the mixed regime is influenced by earlier Greek models, particularly those of Aristotle and Polybius.[79] Yet many recent commentators have noted there is also something distinctively Roman to Cicero's account of a *res publica*.[80] Scipio signals this immediately before he offers his definition, when he claims to be speaking more from his experience as a Roman than from his study of Greek philosophy.

For Cicero, the nature of the balance in the mixed regime is important, and he depicts Rome's early history as the story of attempting to achieve the ideal combination of the different elements. At some point, however, a highly desirable (if still imperfect) arrangement was reached. Consuls and (in extremis) dictators represented the monarchical element in the constitution,

[76] Atkins 2013, 92; Straumann 2016, 152.

[77] Straumann here refers to Polybius's view of the Roman constitution, but he applies the same point to Cicero's view (Straumann 2016, 152, 174).

[78] Cicero does clearly separate out many important powers: the tribune's veto and the people's right to judge in cases of *provocatio* are examples. However, the Ciceronian concept of blending—where powers are not clearly distinct—can be seen in the rather amorphous but clearly extensive authority of the Senate in areas of lawmaking and execution.

[79] Although Polybius is often viewed as originating the idea that Rome's was a mixed constitution, Nippel has rightly pointed out that Polybius himself never uses the term (Nippel 1980, 19). However, as with Cicero, it is clear that Polybius portrays Rome as *both* a mixed regime and one characterized by a separation of powers. The literature on the relationship between the Polybian and Ciceronian views of the Roman constitution is quite large. In addition to Atkins 2013 and Straumann 2016, see, among others, Von Fritz 1954; Walbank 1990; Hahm 2009.

[80] In addition to which, Polybius himself was profoundly influenced by his observations of the Roman constitution, and thus it may be possible to think of him as a "Roman thinker" as well.

allowing for decisive response to crisis. The common people acquired the right to vote, the right to appeal harsh sentences to the whole community, and the office of the tribunes. The tribunes possessed veto power over all other magistrates and gave the people as a corporate body protection for their interests and at the same time a relatively benign outlet for their resentment of the nobles. Wood especially sees Cicero as contemptuous of the common people and unconcerned with their rights and even suggests that the idea of mixed regimes is in general a scheme for defending privilege and unjust inequality.[81] Nevertheless, Cicero explicitly endorses these concessions to the people, not only as necessary and expedient but also as their just dues (*Leg.* 3.23–24, 3.27). The people have (and ought to have) the ultimate power in the commonwealth. Yet Cicero does clearly prefer that the people defer to the wise and public-spirited nobles, who in many ways form the center of gravity of his ideal constitution. Especially in times of peace, Cicero envisions the nobles prudently guiding commonwealth.

That the best men *should* govern is a fundamental feature of Cicero's republicanism, which contains no whit of the election by lot found in Greek democratic practice. Cicero's commitment to popular sovereignty does not entail the belief that all citizens are equally qualified to do most jobs. But neither does Cicero follow Plato and Aristotle in envisioning a regime whose central purpose is the education of citizens in virtue. More important, Cicero does not promise that a properly established republic will always have the best men governing it. If the people choose wrongly, the most virtuous have no just claim to seize power. This is not because Cicero denigrates the political importance of either education or virtue. Precisely if the balance of power in the regime is to lie in the meritocratic/aristocratic Senate, it is of the highest importance that there be citizens of great prudence and moral virtue. In *De officiis*, he discusses in depth the necessary virtues through the literary frame of educating his son—and by implication other aristocratic young men—for future service as a magistrate.

But this education in virtue takes place in private. It is not the place of the state to shape its citizens—perhaps because it would be perverse to be shaped by an institution you yourself own. In addition, the idea of a general scheme of education could not possibly account for the wide diversity Cicero finds in human nature.[82] But statesmen can educate citizens through their own

[81] Wood 1988, 159.
[82] Hawley 2020a.

example. Thus, Cicero's Scipio says that the ideal statesman will strengthen the virtue of citizens through cultivating shame and applying praise (*Rep.* 5.6). Even average citizens must be sufficiently cultivated in virtue to consent to the regime and do their civic duty. They must know and love virtue enough to recognize it in the best citizens, for whom they should vote when the time comes.

Rights

This is not to say that there is no competition or conflict in Cicero's vision of politics. There is. But conflict is limited and channeled by the laws, such that the community is not harmed by it and may even profit by it. So the resulting order is not *essentially* characterized by feverish internal conflict and competition, as Machiavelli's version of Roman republicanism depicts.[83] Instead, the *res publica* should resemble the celestial order, in which various different bodies and motions combine to form an ordered harmony:

> For it works out that if the Senate is in charge of public deliberation, and if the remaining orders are willing to have the commonwealth guided by the deliberation of the leading order, then it is possible through the blending of rights [*temperatione iuris*], since the people have power and the Senate has authority, that that moderate and harmonious order of the state be maintained. (*Leg.* 3.28)

Here Cicero describes the good commonwealth as a regime of *rights*. The invention of rights had long been considered a late medieval or early modern invention, the theoretical development of which is taken as one of the great achievements of modern liberalism. From Constant and Condorcet to Berlin and Alasdair MacIntyre, the consensus ran that the concept of rights is entirely absent from the thought and even the vocabulary of the ancients—including the Romans.[84]

More recently, this view has come under attack by those pointing to the clear presence of rights in Roman law.[85] The meaning of *ius* in Latin is even

---

[83] In contrast also to Pettit's claim that the cultivation of political contestation is an essential characteristic of republicanism.

[84] See, for instance, Berlin 2000, 201; MacIntyre 2007, 67; Strauss 1953, 181–182.

[85] Critics include Atkins 2013; Clarke 2014; Donahue 2001; Wirszubski 1950.

more ambiguous than the word "right" is in English. Charles Donahue explains that *ius* can mean "a whole body of normative rules, a legal order, as well as 'right' in either sense of the English word." He finds hundreds of instances in Justinian's *Digest* in which *ius* clearly refers to "right" in our sense of a licit power or claim (to act or possess) that is held by an individual (*ius habere, ius esse alicui*).[86] According to Roman legal doctrine, these rights were held by law and convention, not by nature.[87] Nevertheless, they were wide-ranging, protecting many of those elements that Cicero considered key aspects of justice, including the possession and use of property and bodily security, as well as voting, a formal trial, and legal appeals.[88]

This Roman understanding of rights plays an important role in Cicero's political theory.[89] Precisely because rights are absent from Greek political thought and practice, Atkins suggests that the concept is one of the key resources that enabled Cicero to make "his original contribution to political philosophy."[90] Extrapolating Atkins's line of thought, we might say that Cicero takes on enormous significance as the earliest extant theorist of rights. Looking at him in this light, we find a very interesting foundational account of this concept that has since become ubiquitous. Cicero follows the example of Roman law in denying that rights are derived directly from natural law. Rights do not precede the political partnership. But he also rejects a view of rights as merely conventional or legal. They occupy a middle ground, as conditions of just relationships within a properly constituted commonwealth. Their ultimate grounding is thus somewhat ambiguous. They serve somehow as a link between the principles of natural law and liberty to be enjoyed in a political community. Rights are the manifestation of the people's liberty as a corporate body and as individual citizens. Political communities or their rulers do not have complete discretion to order the rights of their citizens as they see fit.[91] The proper set of rights is largely fixed by the requirements of justice in a political context. In this way, rights form a crucial

---

[86] Donahue 2001, 507–509.

[87] Wirszubski 1950, 69; Clarke 2014, 226; Atkins 2013, 139.

[88] See Atkins 2013, 124–128; Wirszubski 1950, 24–26.

[89] Cf. Colish 1990, 146; Wirszubski 1950, 86–87; Atkins 2013, 128. The following analysis is deeply indebted to Atkins 2013, 128–154.

[90] Atkins 2013, 121.

[91] As Atkins puts it, "Scipio's analysis of *res publica* clearly establishes non-coincidence between the rights that citizens possess as citizens and those conferred by the prevailing governing authority. It is his normative conception of political society that provides the space for the relevant zone of non-coincidence" (Atkins 2013, 139). See *Rep.* 3.35.

way of mediating between the demands of universal natural law and popular sovereignty, and they do so in a way that protects liberty.

The fundamental right, from which the other rights may be inferred to flow, can be found in the very definition of a commonwealth: the owner-ship claim—we can now say ownership *right*—that all citizens have over the regime. All magistrates ultimately owe their authority to the people. True, Cicero prefers that the people defer to the wisdom of the Senate, and he envisions voting laws that encourage such deference. But the people remain entitled to the ballot as a "safeguard" of their liberty (*vindicem libertatis*) (*Leg.* 3.38).[92] Deriving from their status as co-owners of the commonwealth, the people enjoy a matrix of other rights, which collectively both constitute and safeguard their liberty.

In some ways, we can see these rights as instantiations of popular sover-eignty, existing within a political community that otherwise filters popular sovereignty through the institutions of a mixed regime. They reflect partially the collective right of ownership over the society, but they also reflect the es-sential sovereign freedom of individuals. They are also, as Straumann notes, trumps over other political considerations.[93] But they are trumps not based directly in nature and are instead derived from people's status as members of the particular political community in question.

The right of *provocatio* is a compelling example of how Cicero envisions important rights both as protections for individuals and as expressions of the rightful power of the community as a whole. *Provocatio*—or appeal to the Assembly of the People—was part of the more general right to a fair trial. According to Cicero, it is "the characteristic of a free state . . . that no individual be deprived of life or goods without a trial" (*Dom.* 33). Anyone convicted could appeal the judgment to the people. For Cicero, this right is especially important to protect the individual against bodily harm (*Rep.* 2.62). But the right also reflected the just claim of the people as a whole to be

---

[92] Arena argues that the voting laws in *De legibus* reflect a "different conception" of the common-wealth from the one proposed in *De re publica*, "characterized by a 'quasi-alienation' of the people's sovereignty." She points to the fact that Cicero suggests in *De legibus* that the common people be compelled to reveal their votes to the *optimates*, thus giving them only *species libertatis* (an ap-pearance of liberty) (Arena 2016, 73–74). However, even there, Cicero maintains that the people are entitled by absolute right to their free suffrage. The evocation of *species libertatis* seems rather to refer to the fact that the people erroneously believe that voting *is* liberty, where Cicero himself sees it merely as a manifestation of the underlying political liberty that the commonwealth ensures to all.

[93] Straumann 2016, 171–172.

the final judge of matters within the community and was in this respect "the protectress of the state and the defender of liberty" (*De or.* 2.199).[94]

Michelle Clarke points to Cicero's prosecution of Verres as proof that Roman liberty and rights were about protecting individuals from bodily harm. But, in fact, we find here strong evidence that Cicero sees rights as about *both* protecting individuals *and* about the sovereign authority of Roman citizens. Cicero depicts with great pathos the scene in which a Roman citizen is publicly and brutally whipped and crucified without being allowed his appeal, while his plaintive cry, "I am a Roman citizen," is ignored. Cicero asks rhetorically: "does liberty, that precious thing, mean nothing? Nor the proud privileges of a citizen of Rome? . . . A Roman citizen could be bound and flogged in the marketplace by a man who owed his rods and axes to the favor of the Roman people?" (*Verr.* 2.2.3–5). In this passage, Cicero not only calls attention to the outrage inflicted on one citizen unjustly, but he also points out the perversity that the magistrate who carried out the illegal punishment owed his authority to the Roman people, whose right to be final judge he disregarded.

Cicero's prosecution of Verres calls attention to another central issue in Cicero's conception of the relationship of rights to liberty: the rule of law. Living through (and eventually dying in) the turbulent final years of the republic, Cicero was especially aware of the precariousness of liberty in an environment of lawlessness. The tendency of powerful individuals to impose their will on the community as a whole without regard to law destroys the rights of the people. Once again, Caesar stands as the negative example that demonstrates this danger. By appointing magistrates, passing and voiding laws, and ignoring legal procedures, Caesar essentially made himself monarch and destroyed the liberty of the Roman people as a collective and as individuals.[95]

Although it is not necessary for citizens in a commonwealth to be socially or economically equal to one another, the law must speak to them equally (*Off.* 1.88, 2.41). They are all equally members of the partnership. Thus, no commonwealth can possess laws that single out specific individuals for punishment or reward: "[Rome's founders] did not want laws to be carried out against private men—that is the meaning of *privilegia*—because there is

[94] For more about the right of *provocatio* and its relationship to the protection afforded citizens by the tribunes as expressed in the *Lex Valeria* and the *Lex Porcia*, see Wirszubski 1950, 24–26.
[95] See *Phil.* 2.64, 2.80–87; *Phil.* 3.12.

nothing more unjust than that, since it is the essence of law to be a decision or order applying to all" (*Leg.* 3.44).[96] The passage of laws that do not apply equally to all would indicate that the commonwealth has fallen under the control of a single tyrant or a tyrannical faction, which is advancing its own interests over the interests of the whole.

The worst form of unlawfulness is violence. Cicero contrasts modes of contention, by speech and by force, and determines that the former is worthy of human beings, the latter proper to beasts (*Off.* 1.34). In this respect, Cicero's republicanism is perhaps most clearly different from Machiavelli's, as we will see. Machiavelli, who read *De officiis*, transforms and reverses Cicero's argument about the superiority of laws to force or fraud and suggests that acts of violence are, in fact, necessary to the healthy functioning of republics. Not so for Cicero: unlawful violence toward citizens is anathema to the spirit of fellowship that characterizes a healthy commonwealth: "There is nothing more destructive for states, nothing more contrary to right and law, nothing less civil and humane, than the use of violence in public affairs in a duly constituted commonwealth" (*Leg.* 3.42).

The proper mode of contention is through speech, our rational, peaceful faculty. Cicero is perhaps best known as an orator and a theorist of oratory. It is not my intention here to add to the great volume of scholarship on Cicero's rhetorical thought.[97] The details of Cicero's theory of rhetoric are not important for our purposes. What is important is the stress Cicero lays on rhetoric as the proper vehicle for resolving conflict. In chapter 3, I will explore in some detail the significance of the divergence between Machiavelli and Cicero on the role of speech.

Cicero's mixed regime of rights, resting on some element of consent to true justice, is his solution to the apparent tension between popular sovereignty and universal natural law. Straumann points out that Cicero and other Roman republicans did *not* "put the main emphasis on the need for laws to create virtuous citizens and thus create the conditions for the good life."[98] This now clearly follows from Cicero's application of natural law to our diverse human natures. Straumann is also right when he argues that Cicero's constitutionalism is a response to the crisis of the late republic that seeks to

---

[96] This is strongly consonant with Jean-Jacques Rousseau's position on general laws in the *Social Contract* (2.4).

[97] For work on Cicero's rhetorical theory, see, among many others, Remer 2013; Rose 1995; Steel 2001; Garsten 2009; Hawley 2021a.

[98] Straumann 2016, 25.

reverse the decay of republican institutions by articulating a set of supra-political norms that could structure and limit political power. But the crisis of the late republic also illustrates the practical and moral necessity of popular consent to those norms. The late republic was characterized not only by armed conflict but also by increasing *dis*agreement about the fundamental political norms and the place of freedom in the political community. In the absence of general assent to those norms, a Ciceronian *res publica* does not, in fact, exist. Neither Cicero the philosopher nor Cicero the statesman ever manages to provide an institutional account of how such agreement can be preserved. He places his hopes upon the philosophical statesman.[99] Such statesmen—like Scipio and perhaps Cicero himself—perceive with relative clarity true justice and can respond to particular crises, providing the guidance and instruction necessary to produce the harmony out of diversity that is a well-functioning *res publica*.[100]

But Cicero needed to look no further than his own time to recognize that, in the words of James Madison, "enlightened statesmen will not always be at the helm" (*Fed.* 10). To rely on philosophical statesmen seems ultimately to revert to the problem of the just king—we cannot always expect to have them. Arena notes a shift in Cicero's thought—or at least his rhetoric—toward the end of his life, as the crisis of the republic grows more extreme and unmanageable. She describes a Cicero increasingly reliant upon appeals to natural law, using it to justify apparently extraconstitutional emergency powers in the desperate hope that order and harmony can be reimposed.[101] Recall again how Cicero in the *Philippics* seems to concede that the extraordinary military commands of Brutus and Cassius were not authorized by the Roman people or part of Rome's ordinary rule of law: "by what law, according to what right? By the right that Jupiter himself set down, that all things beneficial to the commonwealth be considered lawful and just . . . this is the law that Cassius obeyed" (*Phil.* 11.28). Similarly elsewhere, Cicero denies that the people's ownership of the regime gives them license to abrogate the liberty of particular citizens: "if the people had ordered me to be your slave, on the converse: for you to be mine, do you think such a command binding and valid? You see and admit such a command would be worth nothing" (*Caecin.* 96). It is, of course, dangerous to take Cicero's speeches—especially political or trial

---

[99] Nicgorski 2016; Powell 2012.
[100] For a full account of Cicero's ideal statesman, see Zarecki 2014.
[101] Arena 2012, 266. See also Straumann 2016, 116.

speeches—to reflect his considered theoretical opinion. But the emphasis on the natural law at the expense of the manifest will of the people suggests that Cicero's reconciliation of natural law with popular sovereignty retains serious tensions—if natural law requires politics based on the people's consent to just laws, what follows when that consent no longer exists? In such cases, Cicero seems to prefer to prioritize natural law over the people's claims, but that is not immediately reconcilable with the idea that the people's consent is a fundamental condition of just politics.

A Universal Republic?

If the decay of a republic exposes the fundamental republican tension in Cicero's thought, it is also true that his conception of a healthy republic exposes a wholly different tension. Although this book is largely concerned with the attempts to work out the first tension, it is important to discuss briefly the latter, since it, too, recurs throughout the tradition Cicero inaugurated and cannot be separated from the dynamics intrinsic to the first.

A commonwealth that does conform to the principles of justice stands in a complicated relationship with other political communities. The goodness of such a regime is such that even the sacrifice of one's own life is not too high a price to pay for its preservation. When the very existence of the commonwealth is threatened, it is permissible for even a private citizen to use whatever force is necessary to preserve the *res publica*. Perhaps self-servingly, Cicero sees his own execution of the Catilinarian conspirators in the same light (*Off.* 1.76; *Cat.* 4). Ultimately, Cicero does not view these acts as violations of the bonds of fellowship that characterize the commonwealth but rather as reflections of the highest imperative of those bonds: "the good of the people must be the highest law [*salus populi suprema lex esto*]" (*Leg.* 3.3). The good of the community must be allowed to trump any particular loyalty and our strong attachment to specific members of our own community. On this ground is tyrannicide justified (*Off.* 3.32). By raising themselves above the laws, violating the rights of the people, and eliminating their power to manage their communal affairs, Caesar and other tyrants threaten to destroy the *res publica* (*Phil.* 2.34, 2.116).

Yet Cicero's natural law doctrine clearly establishes certain obligations that we have toward every human being, obligations that constrain a commonwealth's pursuit of its own self-interest. He attempts to reconcile this commitment with his strong patriotism by adopting a modified version of Stoic cosmopolitanism, imagining every person as a citizen of at least two commonwealths: their immediate political community and the universal cosmopolis. Cicero's republicanism becomes the theoretical basis for the cosmopolitan theories of international law proposed by Grotius and Pufendorf. Cicero's position makes his version of republicanism interestingly compatible with the values of international peace and concord expressed in liberal cosmopolitanism and theories of international law.[102]

Cicero's insistence that the "commonwealth is dearer to me than life itself" (*Fam.* 10.12) falls tellingly short of Machiavelli's later boast that "I love my native city more than my soul."[103] Reason of state must ultimately submit to moral considerations. It turns out that there are some things so obscene, such as impiety toward parents, that one should not sully oneself by undertaking them even for the sake of the commonwealth.

As I suggested, Cicero's conception of that universal human fellowship in terms of the Stoic-inflected cosmopolis helps him harmonize his patriotic strain with the universal principles of natural law. Although many Stoic thinkers supposed that only the perfectly rational (sages and the gods) were citizens of the cosmopolis, Cicero takes a more egalitarian view, including all human beings (*Leg.* 1.23).[104] In this way, the universal human fellowship takes a more definite shape than just any vague community. It is a *civitas*, a state (*Leg.* 1.23). Like any good state, the universal *civitas* is governed by laws and justice: "there will not be one law here, another in Athens, one law now, another in the future, but a single, eternal, unchanging law binding all peoples always" (*Rep.* 3.27–33). The cosmopolis is governed by the supreme deity, who rules with perfect justice. From that cosmic perspective, even great human empires are but tiny constituents (*Rep.* 6.15–17).

It might then seem as though patriotic service to such (cosmically) tiny entities as commonwealths would be morally insignificant. But commonwealths gain their apparently outsize moral status by virtue of their imitation of or resemblance to the perfect cosmic order.[105] The concrete

---

[102] In contrast to the bellicosity of Machiavelli's republicanism and the provincialism of Rousseau's or Aristotle's.

[103] Cf. Machiavelli's *Letter to Vettori* 1513.

[104] Also *Off.* 1.51, 2.11; *Fin.* 3.64. For the alternative Stoic view of a cosmopolis of sages and gods, see Colish 1990, 39; Márquez 2012, 191. Cicero's rejection of the Stoic position here seems linked to his critique of Stoicism's blindness to our embodied state. The Stoic cosmopolis is a city in speech, inhabited by the minds of the sages. Cicero's cosmopolis includes all living rational beings, who are embodied.

[105] Atkins 2013, 67.

political community in which we live binds us more closely and carries with it greater responsibilities, because we are more intimately connected to one another within it. But we are all, in a sense, dual citizens. The laws of the commonwealth ought to reflect the laws of nature, which ought in turn to be the law governing the interaction of nations (*Off.* 3.69). Violence between nations, then, is to be considered a last resort, just as it is within the commonwealth. Peaceful and civic patriotic service takes priority over military achievements.[106]

And yet there is also a darker side to this reconciliation of patriotism and cosmopolitanism. Cicero is not unaware of the potential for tension between our natural patriotism and our responsibility to the whole of humanity. In Scipio's dream, even as Cicero's hero experiences the transcendent perspective in which he can survey the whole of the cosmos, his eyes are drawn repeatedly back to the little dot that is Rome's empire. Even Scipio is not free from the tendency to prefer his native land to the whole rest of the world. Cicero makes sure that Scipio is rebuked for his parochial overattachment (*Rep.* 6.17, 6.20).[107] But Cicero's own corpus suggests that he himself is not totally immune to the temptation to seek a reconciliation between patriotism and cosmopolitanism on grounds more favorable to his native commonwealth. We can see elements in Cicero's thought strikingly similar to the logic of European imperialists of the sort analyzed by Uday Mehta (1999) and Jennifer Pitts (2006). It is hardly a coincidence that Cicero functioned as "a kind of biblical text" for colonial officials and public policymakers during the height of Europe's colonial period.[108]

Cicero is obviously aware that Rome during his day—and even in the earlier period in which he imagines it to most closely resemble the ideal commonwealth of *De re publica*—ruled over a massive empire acquired by force. On its face, such an empire seems contrary to the principles of cosmopolitan fellowship. Cicero provides one justification: that, at least during the virtuous early period prior to the corruption of later times, Rome gained its empire through wars fought in defense of itself and its allies. But he also adds another kind of war to the *just* sources of Rome's extensive rule: war for the sake of empire (*bella de imperio*) (*Off.* 2.26). Cicero insists that this sort of war must be conducted even more humanely and restrainedly than wars of

---

[106] A principle that allows Cicero to claim his own achievements as at least equal to, if not greater than, those of military heroes Caesar and Pompey (*Off.* 1.75–77).

[107] However, he is ultimately instructed to return to Rome's service.

[108] Nussbaum 2000, 180.

self-defense, but that very insistence *confirms* that he views such wars to be potentially just (*Off.* 1.38). How can such wars be compatible with the natural law that mandates human fellowship and peace?

Cicero does not clearly answer. But perhaps Rome's wars for empire can appear justified if they are the means by which the peaceful and liberal commands of the natural law are brought into reality. Recall that the idealized version of the earlier Roman Republic found in *De re publica* was not simply an example of *a* commonwealth but was the *best* practical commonwealth (*Rep.* 2.66).[109] The laws of that Rome, while not exactly the same as the laws Cicero derives from natural law in *De legibus*, are nearly identical. The principle that there be "not one law here, another in Athens . . . but a single, eternal, unchanging law binding all peoples" is unlikely to come about in a world filled with countless different states. But if the state that best approximates the natural law in its own laws were to conquer the other states, they could be brought into conformity with the natural law.[110]

Cicero nowhere quite draws that explicit conclusion, but there is evidence from Augustine and Lactantius that he comes close in now-lost parts of *De re publica*. According to Augustine's summary of the Carneadean debate between justice and injustice, the case for injustice points out that a commonwealth "cannot grow without injustice . . . if an imperial state, a great commonwealth, does not subscribe to that injustice, then it cannot rule over provinces." Justice replies that subjugation is beneficial for those who cannot obey natural law on their own. "When the right to do injury is taken away from wicked people: the conquered will be better off . . . do we not see that the best people are given the right to rule by nature herself . . . why then does the god rule over man, the mind over the body?" (*De civ. D.* 19.21).

In *De legibus*, we find a passage that encapsulates the ambiguity between the explicit strain of proto-liberal cosmopolitanism and the undercurrent of republican imperialism. Near the beginning of the second book, Cicero and his interlocutors embark upon a digression. The passage is worth quoting at length:

> I believe that both Cato and all those who come from the towns have two fatherlands, one by nature and the other by citizenship. Cato was born at Tusculum but was given Roman citizenship . . . and had one fatherland by

---

[109] Cf. Atkins 2013, 64. As Nicgorski puts it, "Cicero's Roman particularism is founded on his very universalism" (Nicgorski 1993, 789).

[110] See Hawley 2020b for further discussion of this possibility.

place of birth, the other by law. . . . But of necessity that one takes precedence in our affections whose name "commonwealth" belongs to the entire citizen body, on behalf of which we have an obligation to die, to which
we should give ourselves entirely and in which we should place and almost
consecrate everything we have. . . . I will never deny that this [Arpinum] is
my fatherland, while recognizing that the other one is greater and that this
one is contained within it . . . has two citizenships but thinks of them as one
citizenship. (*Leg.* 2.5)

On the surface, this is simply a comment about the status of Roman citizens
who (like Cicero himself) hail from the towns (*municipia*) and not the city
of Rome. But Cicero's language invites the reader to connect the analysis to
Scipio's dream. Just as citizens of Arpinum and Tusculum owe greater allegiance to the more perfect commonwealth of Rome that encompasses their
small towns, so, too, would citizens of Rome or anywhere else be bound in
loyalty to the most perfect and universal commonwealth of the cosmopolis.[111] Such a reading reinforces the pacific and cooperative internation-
alism that characterizes the overt principles of Cicero's republicanism.

But Cicero's statement could prompt still further consideration. The towns
of Arpinum and Tusculum were once independent states themselves. Rome
subjugated them and eventually incorporated their inhabitants into Roman
citizenship. Cicero's ancestors may have died fighting to preserve Arpinum's
independence from Rome, but now he professes absolute loyalty to Rome and
considers himself an equal member of Rome's commonwealth. Cannot this
be the model by which Rome absorbs the rest of the world, achieving peace
and bringing human beings into conformity with natural law? Rome's actual
practice with regard to conquered peoples becomes the framework and justification for a true universal empire in accordance with the liberal demands
of natural law. As Xavier Márquez suggests, "Cicero's political community
is—in contrast to the modern national state but like Rome—potentially unlimited: it justifies an empire ruled by law that succeeded in integrating politically many of its conquered peoples, but an empire nonetheless."[112] Or, as
James Zetzel puts it, "Cicero's is the first extant philosophical justification of

---

[111] Caspar comes close to suggesting this reading: "Cicero seeks to inculcate an affection for the
natural law republic in those gentlemen who will be called upon to rule in it, or at least those who will
rule in the lesser versions that exist in their own republics" (Caspar 2011, 106).
[112] Márquez 2012, 204.

the Roman empire, and he was certainly the first person to equate Roman justice with the order of the universe."[113]

While Cicero's explicit statements about the general rules governing the foreign policy of a commonwealth support liberal-cosmopolitan norms of just and peaceful interaction, those statements coexist with this imperialist alternative. Cicero the Roman evinces a tendency to see his particular fatherland as exceptional. For him, Rome might just bear the potentially world-historical mission of bringing natural law to the unruly human race. Cicero tends to suppress this alternative, but it remains just below the surface of his theory of Roman exceptionalism.

Setting the Republican Agenda

Although Cicero's beloved republic did not recover after his death, Cicero's thought stood as the undisputedly dominant account of Roman republicanism for more than a millennium. Republicanism itself went out of favor, but to the extent that one wished to engage it, Cicero was the touchstone. From church fathers (who often took a dim view of much other pagan philosophy) to Renaissance humanists, Cicero served as the moral interpreter of the Roman Republic.

Augustine and Lactantius were especially important in this regard. While most of Cicero's corpus was preserved intact, nearly all of the crucial *De re publica* was lost until the early nineteenth century. Most of what later writers knew of this work thus came from passages preserved by these two early Christian thinkers. Both Augustine and Lactantius were deeply influenced by Cicero and incorporated much of his thought into their own. But they also viewed him as a representative of the errors of both pagan philosophy and pagan politics. Their engagement with him thus reflected their agenda of vindicating Christianity over and against the pretensions to self-sufficiency that they saw in non-Christian ideas of virtue, justice, and politics.

In the case of Augustine, he repeats the famous definition of a *res publica* from Cicero's *De re publica*. He summarizes the Carneadean debate and connects it to this definition, emphasizing Cicero's point that only communities bound by an agreement to true justice qualify as commonwealths. But

[113] Zetzel 1996, 298.

on this basis, Augustine argues that no state—and certainly not Rome—
ever was such a commonwealth: "where there is no true justice, then, there
can be no . . . 'property of a people'" (De civ. D. 19.21, 19.23). True justice
requires giving each his due, especially giving the true God proper wor-
ship. The Romans did not do this—and in addition robbed and plundered
the Mediterranean world. Thus, Augustine concludes, "a Roman res publica
never existed" (De civ. D. 19.21). For Augustine, the only regime that could
truly qualify as a commonwealth in Cicero's sense is the City of God. To include human regimes, one would have to broaden the definition to include
any community bound by common agreement in what it loves (De civ. D.
19.24).

Lactantius, by whom still more of De re publica was preserved, takes an
even dimmer view of Cicero's claims on behalf of the Roman polity. He claims
that Laelius's argument for the superiority of justice to injustice fails altogether, as all just defenses must fail if not grounded in Christianity (Div. inst.
17.8–34). Likewise, Lactantius makes explicit the tension between Cicero's
skepticism and his embrace of natural law (Div. inst. 6.6).[114]

But for all their opposition to Cicero's ideas, both Augustine and Lactantius
accept Cicero's ways of framing many of these central issues of politics and
justice. More important for later thinkers, they preserve key pieces of De
re publica. Along with Cicero's extant corpus, they helped Cicero's political
thought to remain powerful through late antiquity and the Middle Ages.

Although the latter period is often considered dominated by the ideas of
Aristotle, Cary Nederman has recently demonstrated that Cicero was at least
a comparable influence on the intellectual life of Europe during this time.[115]
Indeed, the logical unity of popular sovereignty and natural law asserted by
Cicero was accepted even as far as Aquinas (Summa 1.90.2).[116] Perhaps because actual republican political life did not flourish during this period, that
unity did not come under sustained direct challenge.

One must wait until Machiavelli's Prince and Discourses to find the most
powerful attempt to overthrow the Ciceronian understanding of a republic.
Machiavelli levels his attack by seeking to explode the two tensions in Cicero's

[114] As a polemicist, though, Lactantius does not cite Cicero in good faith, taking him out of context to be admitting that his skepticism cannot be reconciled with a belief in natural law. Cf. Kendeffy
2015, 66.
[115] Nederman 2020.
[116] However, Aquinas leans far more heavily on the Aristotelian teleological version of natural law
than on Cicero's less teleological alternative.

thought that were explored in this chapter. First, Machiavelli takes up more seriously than any other thinker the alternative of a universal—or at least indefinitely expansionist—republic, which lurks submerged beneath Cicero's endorsement of a pacific, cosmopolitan commonwealth. Machiavelli's preferred republic is avowedly warlike, oriented toward conquest. To make such imperial growth possible, Machiavelli also abandons the Ciceronian reconciliation between natural law and popular sovereignty. Liberating the people from the constraints of Ciceronian natural law, he hopes to enlist them as enthusiastic supporters of military expansion. In chapter 3, we turn to Machiavelli's challenge to the Ciceronian foundations of the Roman republican tradition.

3

Machiavelli's Commonwealth without Justice

The commonwealth is dearer to me than life itself.

—Cicero, *Fam.* 10.12

I love my native city more than my soul.

—Machiavelli, *Letter to Vettori* 1513

A Ciceronian World

Lending weight to G. W. F. Hegel's dictum that the owl of Minerva flies only at dusk, the Roman Republic collapsed a few short years after Cicero declared its constitution the model of the best practical regime. Indeed, Cicero lived just long enough to see his beloved republic extinguished before he himself was executed for his allegiance to it. The manner of his death ensured an immortal reputation as a martyr for republican liberty.

With the rise of the principate, one might expect that Cicero's reputation as a champion of the republic would have limited the influence of his works. But instead, it flourished, perhaps in part because the early Roman emperors—beginning with Augustus—sought to preserve at least the appearance of the old constitutional forms. Cicero's son was allowed to proclaim the death of Antony to the city of Rome. The story from Plutarch at the beginning of this book suggests that Augustus himself admired Cicero's patriotism.[1] The Stoicism of Seneca, Marcus Aurelius, and others bear the marks of Cicero's ideas. Cicero's rhetoric became the absolute standard for eloquence. In sum, Cicero's theoretical legacy thrived in spite of the sea change in political circumstances that followed his death.

---

[1] Cassius Dio reports that Augustus—then Octavian—argued for two days against Antony's decision to proscribe Cicero.

Natural Law Republicanism. Michael C. Hawley, Oxford University Press. © Oxford University Press 2022.
DOI: 10.1093/oso/9780197582336.003.0003

Although the advent of Christianity meant the loss or destruction of many pagan works, Cicero's found sufficient favor with many of the early church fathers that few of his texts were lost, and, as noted previously, Augustine and Lactantius preserved large portions of *De re publica*.[2] Ambrose went so far as to write a Christian adaptation of Cicero's moral thought, also titled *De officiis*. However, as the Roman Republic receded further into the past and political systems bearing little resemblance to it took its place, Cicero's rhetorical and moral thought (rather than his political theory) came to constitute his legacy.

This state of affairs lasted until the Renaissance, which witnessed the revival of republican government throughout Italy and the rise of civic humanism, self-consciously inspired by the pre-Christian classical world. Although J. G. A. Pocock has sought to portray this period as one animated by an admiration for Aristotle's thought, Quentin Skinner and Hans Baron have demonstrated compellingly that Cicero was by far the dominant classical figure, especially (but not only) for the Italian humanists.[3] In Mark Hulliung's words, "under the sponsorship of the civic humanists Cicero was restored to his position, lost during the Middle Ages, of citizen and advocate of the *vita activa*."[4] At the center of this movement was Petrarch, who proclaimed the superiority of Cicero over Aristotle and launched a massive search of monasteries' libraries for the lost works of the writer whom he called "the great genius of antiquity."[5] Following Petrarch's example, other luminaries of the age sought inspiration from Cicero's political ideas expressed in his theoretical writings, his speeches, and even his letters. Among these were Brunetto Latini, Giannozzo Manetti, and Leonardo Bruni, all of whom took seriously Cicero's political views on questions of virtue, the union of philosophy and rhetoric, political prudence, and the qualities of the statesman. The Ciceronian conception of *virtus* and his writings about the education of a gentleman (especially *De officiis*) spawned the creation of a number of humanist schools in Italy based explicitly on his thought. As Skinner puts it,

[2] In fact, some of the church fathers were troubled by the strength of their own affection for the pagan Cicero. Jerome tells of a fevered vision of his own judgment in which God asks "what art thou?" In response to Jerome's reply, "a Christian," God declares, "No. Thou art a Ciceronian." On the other hand, Augustine credits Cicero's lost *Hortensius* for his conversion to Christianity. Cf. Slaughter 1921.

[3] Pocock 2009, Baron 1938. Although the recovery of Cicero's philosophy was strongest in Italy, it is worth noting again that the second book off Gutenberg's press was *De officiis*. It was also one of the first off the first press in France (Skinner 1998, 196). See also, among many others, Marsh 2013; Schmitt 2013.

[4] Hulliung 1983, 9.

[5] See Skinner 2002, 84, 88.

"the key to interpreting the humanism of Petrarch and his successors lies in the fact that, as soon as they recovered this authentically classical perspective, they turned themselves into fervent advocates of the same Ciceronian ideals."[6]

It was into this world saturated with Cicero's thought that Niccolò Machiavelli appeared. But Machiavelli shows none of the deference to classical philosophy that so characterizes his humanist peers. Without mentioning them by name, he condemns Plato, Aristotle, Cicero, and others for failing to take their bearing from the "effectual truth" of how human beings do, in fact, act and live (*Prince* 15). Against the unrealistic moralizing of the ancient thinkers, Machiavelli confesses a grand aspiration to introduce "new modes and orders" that will revitalize the political life of Europe (*Discourses* 1.pr.).

But Machiavelli's condemnation of classical political philosophy does not extend to the classical *practice* of politics. He sees a great gap between the moralistic theories of ancient philosophers and the deeds their cities performed. He encourages his readers to imitate the actions of ancient polities and political men. For Machiavelli, the great success of one ancient state in particular demonstrates its superiority to all others and makes it most worthy of imitation: Rome, particularly Rome during its republican period. The dominance of Cicero's political thought—and especially his moral interpretation of Rome's role in the world—places him squarely athwart Machiavelli's path to achieve his great ambition. Machiavelli's project, then, can be understood at least in part as an attempt to fundamentally revalue the legacy of the Roman Republic and, with it, republicanism itself. With this revaluation, Machiavelli aims to overthrow the understanding of Roman republicanism—which was most powerfully expressed by Cicero and which had again become dominant among civic humanists of Machiavelli's age.[7]

Cicero's Rome—as the manifestation of the best practical commonwealth—was worthy of admiration because of its correspondence to natural law, its just institutions, its fair dealings with others, and its government by wise, public-spirited individuals who employed deliberation and discussion to resolve questions. Machiavelli looks to the same Rome and sees a republic worthy of emulation because of its willingness to engage

---

[6] Skinner 2002, 88.
[7] For more on the role of Cicero in the Italian Renaissance, see especially Baron 1938 and Skinner 2002.

in *injustice*, its warlike capacity for imperial expansion, and the often violent contestation between its classes. Whereas Cicero had defended a civil kind of contestation in speech, bounded by firm moral laws and protection for individuals, Machiavelli emphatically suggests that the logic of contestation accepts no such limitation. In short, the political vision Machiavelli puts forth constitutes a rejection of nearly all of the central components of the *res publica* found in Cicero.[8]

A Common Love of Rome

The contrast between Machiavelli and Cicero is perhaps all the sharper because of the numerous biographical and theoretical similarities one can find between them. Neither Italian came from an ancient noble lineage, yet both rose by their own talents to positions of authority in their cities. Their status as newcomers to political power ensured that they were never quite accepted among the ruling families in their respective regimes. Yet both demonstrated a passionate patriotism that was wholly unfeigned. They were compelled by shifting political circumstances into forced retirements, during which they produced their most influential works of political thought. Both also lived long enough to see their republics overthrown and replaced by autocratic government.

Machiavelli also immersed himself in classical learning, including the works of Cicero. Indeed, as noted earlier, the intellectual milieu of Machiavelli's time was saturated with Ciceronian ideas, and he himself clearly read Cicero's works. On the theoretical level, too, Machiavelli follows Cicero on a number of points. While both considered the merits of sole rulership, they strongly favored republican government. For both, republics are more to be identified by their dispersal of power into many hands rather than by any strict institutional arrangement. The freedom of a republic lies in its not being dominated completely either by a single individual or faction domestically or by an external power. The absolute rule of one man is incompatible with a republic, but Cicero accepts the possibility of monarchical, aristocratic, and democratic republics in which institutional arrangements

---

[8] This claim challenges the influential views of contemporary neo-republicans and Cambridge School historians, who see Machiavelli as the natural successor to Cicero, most notably Skinner 2002; Pettit 1997; and Viroli 2002.

prevent such domination. Machiavelli, for his part, speaks of "princes of republics" and republics founded by a single individual's will (*Discourses* 1.2, 1.3, 1.9, 1.12, 1.16, 1.20).[9]

Both agree with Aristotle that the best kind of political community has some mixture of the three simple regimes: monarchy, aristocracy, and democracy. For Cicero, this mixture ought to ensure that "magistrates have enough power, the council of leaders has enough authority, and the people has liberty" (*Rep.* 2.57).[10] Machiavelli's *Discourses on Livy* abounds with examples illustrating the superiority of a regime in which the vigor of a solitary executive is combined with some mixture of elite and democratic governance.

The two were critical of the tendency of some classical writers to imagine unrealistic and impractical political ideals without any connection to reality. In one of his most famous passages, Machiavelli writes:

> It has appeared to me more fitting to go directly to the effectual truth of the thing than to the imagination of it. And many have imagined republics and principalities that have never been seen or known to exist in truth. (*Prince* 15)

It is possible that Machiavelli meant to include Cicero—the author of the famous *Somnium Scipionis*—in that critique. But, as we saw in chapter 2, Cicero is quite sympathetic to the kind of complaint Machiavelli raises here. While Cicero considers himself a disciple of Plato, he rebukes him for depicting an ideal regime "totally inconsistent with human life and custom" (*Rep.* 2.21).[11] Thus, both Machiavelli and Cicero feel that a necessary feature of valuable political thought is a capacity to address the facts about how human beings actually do live and interact.

All of these commonalities contribute to the final point of agreement between the two men: the status of the Roman Republic as the best example of political organization that humanity has yet produced. For Machiavelli, as much as for Cicero, the Roman Republic is the best example

---

[9] This is one reason it makes little sense to read *The Prince* and *Discourses* as different projects. Moreover, in both works—and only in these two works—Machiavelli claims he is presenting his entire comprehensive political teaching. Cf. Strauss 1995, 17–19; Zuckert 2017, 22. This suggests that the two works form a coherent whole. When reading both of Machiavelli's works, one finds similar advice offered to republics and princes.

[10] See also *Leg.* 3.27–28.

[11] See also *De or.* 1.224.

of a political regime that history has yet furnished, and which it most behooves a founder of a state to imitate (*Discourses* 1.2, 1.6). Machiavelli agrees with Cicero that the Roman regime was brought to near perfection by a long historical process (*Discourses* 1.2). The mixed regime of consuls, Senate, assemblies, and tribunes was supported by Roman virtue, which in turn depended in large part on the politically salutary Roman religion (*Discourses* 1.11).

The ultimate disagreement between Cicero and Machiavelli is all the more intense because it takes place on the basis of these similarities. Both lay claim to the Roman Republic as the best regime that humanity has yet realized: a universal republic. But for Cicero, Rome's status is as a universally valid *example*, the blueprint of a regime in which the twin pillars of popular sovereignty and natural law make possible liberty and justice. Machiavelli, in contrast, sees Cicero as an example of the great chasm between classical political thought and action: Rome's greatness owed precisely to the fact that it did not act in accordance with Ciceronian natural law.[12] The real Rome was a machine built for empire. Machiavelli thus takes up the submerged alternative discussed in chapter 2: Rome as the universal republic because of its (almost) limitless ability to expand. Machiavelli accepts that universal standards of justice or natural law prohibit such expansion. So he abandons those standards and rejects one of Cicero's two pillars of republicanism. His far more overtly democratic republicanism seeks to liberate the people both from the oppression of elites and from the demands of any natural law, enlisting and unleashing them as the force that drives republican imperial expansion. In Machiavelli, we can see an attempt to wrest from Cicero the legacy of the Roman Republic.[13] The influence of Cicero on the preceding tradition, stretching from Augustine and Ambrose to Bruni, Francesco Guicciardini, and Petrarch, makes such an attempt a daunting one. In place of Cicero's decent commonwealth characterized by rights and based on justice and an adherence to a transcendent moral law, Machiavelli seeks to glorify a martial, imperial, turbulent republic in which conflict— not harmony—signifies political health and upon which justice has no essential bearing.

---

[12] Machiavelli holds a dim view of Cicero's political judgment, accusing him of a failure to see what was "easy to conjecture" and contributing to the downfall of the republic (*Discourses* 1.52).

[13] Hulliung writes of Machiavelli's "inversion" of Cicero, turning him "upside down" (Hulliung 1983, x).

A Common Good without Justice

We saw in chapter 2 how Cicero's definition of a *res publica*—a commonwealth—contains two features. First, a commonwealth must encompass a people united for common benefit. Second, that union must be based on an agreement about *ius*—right or justice.[14] Moreover, the justice agreed upon cannot be any conventional understanding of justice; it must conform to *true* justice, the justice ordained by the natural law. Only those political communities that meet this standard qualify as commonwealths. Undergirding this view is Cicero's understanding of a providential cosmos. Fortune may not always favor us, and we may sometimes have to adapt ourselves to unfavorable conditions, but the universe itself is not essentially chaotic or purposeless. The earth exists for human benefit, and human beings themselves exist in part to aid one another (*Off.* 1.22). Although vice-prone, human beings have a natural orientation toward moral virtue, and virtue of some worth is accessible even to ordinary people. Human beings have a natural sociality that drives them to pursue fellowship with others for its own sake—and not merely for instrumental benefits. There is therefore a natural common good in human association. Violations of this sociality, committed by one citizen against another or one state against another, are contrary to right reason and forbidden:

> For a man to take something from another for his own benefit to the other's disadvantage . . . destroys common human life and society . . . imagine if each limb had the idea to seize for itself the strength of its neighbor, necessarily this would weaken and destroy the whole body. (*Off.* 3.21–22)

For Cicero, as all human beings by nature are citizens of the universal cosmopolis of gods and men, the dictates of justice apply also to those outside our political community. This is the grounds for making justice a foundational component of a well-ordered commonwealth and for the action of the commonwealth to be constrained by justice in its internal and external dealings.

Those who fail to live according to this rule of human fellowship reveal themselves to be like beasts clothed in human likeness (*Off.* 1.105, 3.82). Human beings, as social and rational, ought to employ reason and discussion

---

[14] See *Rep.* 1.39.

to resolve their disagreements. Force is only acceptable in response to the bestial behavior of others: "there are two ways of contending, one by discussion, the other by force; since the first is proper to human beings, the latter to beasts, we should only resort to the second if it is not possible to make use of the first" (*Off.* 1.34). In particular, human injustice takes two different bestial forms: "deceit, like a fox, and force, like a lion; both are most improper to a human being, but deceit deserves the greater blame, for there is no injustice worthier of punishment than that of individuals who commit the greatest betrayals while appearing to be good men" (*Off.* 1.41).

Machiavelli's universe does not seem nearly so providentially ordered.[15] Neither Cicero's cosmos governed by natural law nor the divine order of Thomistic Christianity characterizes Machiavelli's view of the human condition.[16] Machiavelli's universe more closely resembles the chaotic flux described by Lucretius.[17] He writes: "all things of men are in motion and cannot stay steady, they must either rise or fall" (*Discourses* 1.6). Fortune is no friend to human beings but an enemy to be conquered. In the penultimate chapter of *The Prince*, Machiavelli addresses the issue of "in what modes [fortune] may be opposed" (*Prince* 25). Machiavelli employs two famous metaphors for fortune, whose rule over human affairs he seeks to overthrow. In the first, fortune appears as a violent river, "which, when they become enraged, flood the plains, ruin the trees and buildings . . . each person flees before them." The prudent individual anticipates this, building dikes and dams to contain the river's flood. In the second metaphor, Machiavelli's advice is still more proactive and violent: "fortune is a woman, and it is necessary, if one wants to hold her down to beat her and strike her down" (*Prince* 25).[18] In both examples, human beings cannot possibly aspire to live a life in accordance with the cosmic order. That order does not exist. Fortune is hostile—or, at best, indifferent—to us, so we must find some other way to achieve our goals.

---

[15] Some scholars have argued that Machiavelli leaves important room for God to determine the outcomes of human affairs. See Nederman 1999; De Grazia 1989. But even in these interpretations, this is not a rational God whose creation follows predicable laws, much less laws that are for the benefit of human beings.

[16] Duff 2011, 980.

[17] For more on Machiavelli's debt to Lucretius, see Rahe 2007.

[18] Strauss compares this aggressive orientation toward fortune with classical philosophy's resignation in the face of chance. He sees Machiavelli as thereby giving birth to the modern project of the conquest of nature (Strauss 1995, 299–300). As discussed in chapter 2, Cicero's life and political philosophy cannot be viewed as promoting resignation—they are oriented toward the active political life. But, for Cicero, neither nature nor our fellow human beings are inherently our enemies.

With no transcendent standard, justice becomes conventional, to be judged in light of its instrumental value and broken when advantageous.[19] For Machiavelli, the very origin of our sense of justice lies less in our natural concern for each other and more in our fear that we ourselves may come to harm (*Discourses* 1.2). To *appear* just is always beneficial, but to act because of a true concern for justice often leads a person to a bad end (*Prince* 19; *Discourses* 1.9, 3.34).

As a result, human beings also have no natural orientation toward virtue and no natural common good. Rather, Machiavelli assumes that an individual "who wants to make a profession of good in all regards must come to ruin among so many who are not good" (*Prince* 25). Faced with the caprice of fortune and the malignity of others, we find ourselves in a hostile world, so we naturally seek after power both to protect ourselves and to advance our other interests.

States, as collections of individuals, are not immune to this logic. When Machiavelli writes that "where one deliberates entirely on the safety of his fatherland, there ought not to enter any consideration of either just or unjust" (*Discourses* 3.42), it may seem as though this amounts to only a small break from Cicero, who certainly recognized that grave national peril changes the moral calculus of the statesman.[20] However, Machiavelli's doctrine of constant flux and his recommendation that states be often drawn back to their beginnings (*Discourses* 3.1) work together to transform the extreme case into the rule. All political decisions are about the safety of the fatherland.

Cicero considers the false liberality of those, like Caesar, who steal from some to give to others "the worst vice" (*Off.* 1.44). Yet Machiavelli mentions Caesar approvingly for the same behavior, emphasizing that one should be "liberal" with the property taken from those outside the state (*Prince* 16). He offers a general rule: "truly it is a very natural and ordinary thing to desire to acquire, and always, when men do it who can, they will be praised and not blamed" (*Prince* 3).[21]

Unsurprisingly, then, Machiavelli's definition of a republic contains no mention of justice at all. Republics differ from principalities in that they are ruled by many rather than one (*Prince* 1).[22] As for the common good,

---

[19] Thus, Machiavelli notes that a prince may be able to exploit in another prince a concern for justice caused by weakness (*Prince* 21).

[20] However, Cicero denies that any danger can completely trump moral considerations (*Off.* 1.159, 3.90).

[21] Compare to *Off.* 2.77.

[22] Machiavelli blurs this distinction throughout his works.

Machiavelli writes that it "is not observed if not in republics" (*Discourses* 2.2). This curiously periphrastic construction does not promise that the common good can be found at all. In fact, Machiavelli provides a vision of human life too riddled by conflict for there to be a good that all can share in. What republics can achieve is the good of the greatest number.[23]

As Harvey Mansfield points out, Machiavelli never mentions natural justice or natural law in *any* of his works.[24] In advising individuals, Machiavelli almost never mentions justice of any variety. When he does, justice is only considered in light of its instrumental value. Even Skinner concedes that when Machiavelli "erases the quality of justice" from Cicero's paradigmatic list of political virtues, he makes "an epoch-making break." But Skinner immediately insists that this "represents Machiavelli's sole quarrel with his classical authorities," describing the rest of his political thought as "impeccably Ciceronian."[25]

In truth, however, Machiavelli's erasure of justice is the linchpin for a wholesale attack on Ciceronian republicanism. Justice in accordance with natural law stands at the heart of Cicero's republican vision; it is impossible to excise it without great downstream consequences on the rest of the theory. This becomes apparent in the case of Cicero's two famous animal metaphors, which Machiavelli adopts but then puts to very un-Ciceronian use as guides to political practice. Machiavelli writes:

> There are two kinds of combat: one with laws, the other with force. The first is proper to man, the second to beasts; but because the first is often not enough, one must have recourse to the second. Therefore it is necessary for a prince to know well how to use the beast and the man. (*Prince* 18)

Machiavelli reverses the intention of Cicero's metaphor. Whereas Cicero warns against using force, Machiavelli insists that it is necessary, however bestial. It is also worth noting that the alternative to force for Machiavelli is not "discussion," as it is for Cicero, but "laws." Laws, after all, are state rules backed by force, a point Machiavelli himself makes when he writes in *The Prince* that good laws are simply the consequence of having good arms

---

[23] Zuckert 2017, 182–183.

[24] Cf. Mansfield 1998, xii.

[25] Skinner 1984, 215–216. According to Skinner, Machiavelli "remains content to fit his ideas into a traditional framework, a framework based on linking together the concepts of liberty, the common good, and civic greatness in a largely familiar way" (Skinner 1990, 137).

(*Prince* 12). Machiavelli leaves us with the choice between orderly and limited force on the one hand and unrestrained force on the other. Resolving conflict by means of rational discussion or persuasion no longer seems to be an option for Machiavelli. There is not even a real choice between violence and laws. One should therefore concentrate on nothing but war, "for that is the only art which is of concern to one who commands"; good laws are the consequence of having a strong military, so there is no reason to give advice about lawmaking (*Prince* 12, 14).

Although *The Prince* and *Discourses* contain chapters on almost any political topic that one might imagine—from "how much artillery should be esteemed by armies in the present times; and whether the opinion universally held of it is true" to "how a state is ruined because of women"—there is not one chapter devoted to rhetoric or persuasion.[26] Machiavelli teaches extensively how people can be forced, frightened, manipulated, or incentivized, but he does not seem to have considered it worthwhile to instruct political actors on how to *persuade*.[27] Rhetoric and speechmaking were a central component of Roman political practice, and Cicero argues that they are the primary ways in which rational creatures living peaceably together ought to engage in political competition. Moreover, with the Ciceronian revival in Italy, rhetorical studies had once again begun to flourish in Machiavelli's day. Yet Machiavelli pays them virtually no attention. In both *The Prince* and *Discourses*, Girolamo Savonarola most closely resembles a statesman whose power rests on his rhetoric, and Machiavelli points to him as a prime example of the general rule that unarmed prophets are always destroyed (*Prince* 6).

We might well wonder why Machiavelli feels discussion is a toothless form of political contestation. After all, Machiavelli includes speeches in his *Florentine Histories*, some of which seem to produce the speaker's desired effect on the listeners (*Art of War* 3.5). It may be that Machiavelli uses speeches there in part, as Thucydides sometimes does, to demonstrate the motives of the actors in question or to illustrate their reasoning. More revealing still is Machiavelli's suggestion in *The Art of War* that military leaders must be good orators (*Art of War* 4.138). Such captains do not debate with their troops about what course of action to take, but they frequently need to reassure,

---

[26] Nor, for that matter, is there even one chapter devoted to justice.

[27] This is not to say that Machiavelli does not himself practice a very subtle form of rhetoric and persuasion in his own writings. See Kahn 1994, 58; Remer 2009, 18. But Machiavelli himself might point out that the failure of his writings to gain him the employment he desires—much less the political power necessary to free Florence or Italy—is evidence that words without force cannot grant an agent direct political power.

inspire, or motivate them.[28] With the troops at one's back, however, one need not reason with others.[29] In the same section, we learn that "if words are not enough, you can then use authority or force" (*Art of War* 4.37). Citing Cicero, the most Machiavelli says on the subject of persuasion is that "though peoples, as Tully says, are ignorant, they are capable of truth and easily yield when the truth is told them by a man worthy of faith" (*Discourses* 1.4.1). But here is absent any actual persuasion, much less any rhetoric or deliberative give-and-take between people seeking the truth in good faith through discussion that so characterizes Cicero's view of republican practice. The centrality of the latter is reflected in both Cicero's own occupation and the number of works he devoted to the subject. For Machiavelli, the objective is to cultivate trust so as to be believed in the critical moment, not to persuade through the force of argument. Without a real common good, deliberation unsupported by arms cannot achieve much.

Leonine and Vulpine Virtue

We can glean from this that Machiavelli's republics are no more concerned with justice than are princes, and Machiavelli does not suggest they should be. As Strauss puts it, Machiavellian patriotism (and, we might add, Machiavellian republicanism) is a theory of "collective selfishness."[30] This selfishness is not bounded by independent considerations of justice. Justice and communal self-interest have no necessary connection. Machiavelli recommends that republics advance the good of the community over the interests of any individual citizen and all outsiders—regardless of questions of right. Cicero asserted that justice was the "queen of the virtues"; without it, the other virtues become political vices (*Off.* 3.28).[31] Having dethroned the queen, Machiavelli's theory of political virtue does much to confirm the second part of Cicero's claim.

Maurizio Viroli writes that "Machiavelli taught us with his writings and his life" that "civic virtue is not a martial, heroic, and austere virtue but a civilized, ordinary and tolerant one of citizens of commercial republics."[32] The

---

[28] See Hawley 2021a for a fuller discussion of this kind of rhetoric.

[29] It is telling that this statement is elicited by a question of how to prevent one's troops from fleeing. The true danger is not failure to persuade but the loss of force.

[30] Strauss 1995, 11.

[31] For instance, as we saw in chapter 2, Cicero believes that wisdom without justice leads philosophers to ignore harms taking place in their communities.

[32] Viroli 2002, 13.

evidence just presented here suggests already that Viroli is well off the mark. But it remains to be seen how far. In Cicero's metaphor of the fox and the lion, the lesson to be learned was that force and especially fraud were improper political tools for human beings capable of using reason to resolve differences and for whom virtue was an end in itself. In *The Prince*, Machiavelli takes up Cicero's example and draws precisely the opposite conclusion.[33] He accepts that the two methods are bestial and argues that the prince should practice both, using the methods of the fox to avoid traps (and set them) and the ways of the lion to frighten the wolves (*Prince* 18). Machiavelli emphasizes that the fraudulence of the fox is especially needful. In doing so, as we shall see, he turns Cicero's theory of political virtue on its head.

As a man who rose from obscure origins to the highest office in the Roman state, Cicero was anything but naive about the requirements of political life. He knew well the political benefits that come with appearing to possess all manner of virtues. But, as his normative theory of politics demands that individuals attempt to practice justice, the only way to gain such benefits and to achieve glory is "by being what we wish to seem" (*Off.* 2.43). The morally upright (*honestas*) and the useful (*utile*) are identical because human beings are rational creatures whose highest interest *is* moral goodness.[34] Machiavelli's theory of politics, unencumbered by considerations of justice for its own sake, does not share the limitations that Cicero accepts. In particular, Machiavelli teaches his reader that it is important to learn "how not to be good, and to use this and not use it according to necessity" (*Prince* 15).

Colish contends that Machiavelli only intends this as a reminder to the overly moral political elite that extreme circumstances sometimes necessitate conventionally unjust actions to secure the common good. She points

---

[33] Many scholars have recognized that Machiavelli takes this language from Cicero, but Barlow 1999 provides the most detailed treatment of the matter.

[34] Colish takes the opposite view. According to her, Cicero's unification of the *honestum* with the *utile* takes place by raising *utile* to be the criterion of *honestum*, making him a thoroughly "Machiavellian" politician for whom anything expedient is thereby also moral (Colish 1978, 86). However, Barlow and Fott have demonstrated that Colish's reading of Cicero rests on a highly selective set of quotations, often interpreted out of context (Barlow 1999, 632; Fott 2008, 158–159). Neither Barlow nor Fott goes far enough to demonstrate that Cicero's position is nearly the opposite of what Colish claims. While Fott finds "much similarity between Cicero and Machiavelli," he acknowledges that "Machiavelli appears to see a more frequent need for dishonorable action than does Cicero" (Fott 2008, 162). Barlow suggests that Machiavelli corrects and completes Cicero's defense of the political life, "which is not properly understood in terms of things above politics" (Barlow 1999, 628). Barlow's reading focuses on comparing *The Prince* only with *De officiis*. But when *De officiis* is read in light of Cicero's other works, it becomes clear that Ciceronian politics is best understood in terms of things above politics, even if the connection between them is not the central focus of that particular work.

to Machiavelli's apparent critique of Agathocles of Syracuse as evidence that Machiavelli does acknowledge moral limitations to action. There Machiavelli writes that "one cannot call it virtue to kill one's citizens, betray one's friends, to be without faith, without mercy, without religion; these modes can enable one to acquire empire, but not glory" (*Prince* 8).[35] But Machiavelli makes it clear that the contemporary problem of political fecklessness is not caused by political elites being so scrupulous that they need to be reminded that occasional acts of brutality or treachery are necessary. As if to make absolutely clear that he does not really condemn Agathocles, immediately after saying that one cannot call Agathocles's actions virtuous, Machiavelli repeatedly refers to the "virtue of Agathocles" (*Prince* 8). It seems that while "one" cannot call Agathocles virtuous, *Machiavelli* can.

Machiavelli makes it a methodological assumption "to presuppose that all men are bad, and that they always have to use the malignity of their spirit whenever they have a free opportunity for it" (*Discourses* 1.3.1). The princes and leaders Machiavelli is addressing are *already* quite bad; they are just not bad enough. Machiavelli titles chapter 27 of *Discourses* "Very Rarely Do Men Know How to Be *Altogether* Wicked or Altogether Good" (emphasis added). The examples he offers show that Machiavelli is uninterested in teaching men to be altogether good. In particular, he rebukes Giovampagolo Baglioni, the tyrant of Perugia, for failing to kill the pope and all his cardinals when he had the chance, an act Machiavelli terms "honorably wicked." "So Giovampagolo, who did not mind being incestuous and a public parricide, did not know how—or, to say better, did not dare [to kill the pope and the cardinals] . . . and he would have done a thing whose greatness would have surpassed all infamy" (*Discourses* 1.28).[36]

In a recent important book, Catherine Zuckert argues that Machiavelli does not truly advocate being "altogether wicked." She acknowledges that Machiavelli sees the utility of fraud in winning wars and gaining kingdoms, but she points to the case of Castruccio Castracani as evidence that "the use of fraud will not bring anyone glory."[37] This aligns with the views of Colish and Benner that Agathocles likewise deprived himself of glory with his monstrous crimes. Yet we learn in *Discourses* that no amount of vice poses an

---

[35] Colish 1978, 91. Colish also takes Cicero to be defending politically expedient actions as just, providing her with grounds for seeing Machiavelli as following Cicero's political ethics. Benner likewise sees Agathocles as Machiavelli's example of how virtue cannot be totally disassociated from ordinary morality (Benner 2013, 112–113).

[36] For more on this, see Scott and Sullivan 1994.

[37] Zuckert 2017, 353.

insurmountable obstacle to glory: "glory can be acquired in any action whatever, because in victory it is acquired ordinarily" (*Discourses* 3.42).[38]

Perhaps this is why, immediately after denying that it is possible to call Agathocles's actions virtuous, Machiavelli promptly refers to "the virtue of Agathocles" and describes his cruelties as "well used" (*Prince* 8). Machiavelli asserts that victory brings glory automatically in its wake. As a result, no vice, as long as it helps him achieve his ends, will thwart a man's aspiration for glory—and not only a man's aspiration. Machiavelli links Agathocles explicitly with the early Roman state, saying that Rome itself misled many of its neighbors into becoming "partners," which contributed to Roman wars only later to realize that they had helped pave the way to their own subjugation. Machiavelli generalizes his point to claim that fraud is probably always necessary to rise from a low state to "sublime ranks" (*Discourses* 2.13). Rome, after all, is the most glorious of all republics, its early fraud leaving no indelible taint. Moreover, Machiavelli hereby suggests that the relative failures of men such as Castruccio and Agathocles lay not in their vice or fraud but in their inability to hide their immoral deeds: "fraud . . . is less worthy of reproach the more it is covert, as was that of the Romans" (*Discourses* 2.13).[39]

Machiavelli's endorsement of fraud thereby inverts Cicero's relationship between being and seeming virtuous. He writes of the virtues of liberality, faith, humanity, honesty, and mercy: "by having them and always observing them, they are harmful; and by appearing to have them, they are useful" (*Prince* 18). Much of the middle chapters of *The Prince* are devoted to explaining how individuals can feign the possession of virtues, while reaping all the benefits of their corresponding vices. We saw in the previous section how Machiavelli rejects Ciceronian liberality in favor of a scheme whereby one plunders abroad to appear liberal at home. Keeping faith—which for Cicero is an obligation we have even to enemies—in Machiavelli's estimation is not something to be done even with friends and allies (*Prince* 18). He instructs a prince to "not depart from good, when possible, but know how to enter into evil, when forced by necessity" (*Prince* 18). It is, of course, impossible to acquire the useful reputation for virtue without occasionally performing good acts, but Machiavelli instructs his reader to abandon such a course whenever it is useful or necessary.

---

[38] Tarcov 1982, 707.

[39] Perhaps the failure of Agathocles and Castruccio is also that neither achieved any lasting victory great enough to overshadow his earlier crimes. Not their evilness but their *smallness* deprived them of glory.

Cicero bases his prohibition of fraud on his understanding of human beings as essentially rational and social. The rational part of our nature is what we share with the gods. Those traits allow us to communicate, to persuade others, and to resolve disputes by appeal to logic and evidence. The social aspect of our nature leads us to prefer to coexist peacefully and ensures that there is some common good to be found. This is why Cicero's political theory places such weight on rhetoric: debate, discussion, and persuasion are the proper methods for resolving political disagreements between social and rational creatures. For Machiavelli, it is not the part of us that is divine but the part that is bestial that we must rely on.

That Machiavelli focuses on overturning Cicero's critique of fraud should not be taken to mean that he underrates the value of force. Among such unscrupulous creatures as men, it is not enough to outsmart them; one must also simply be stronger. Cicero discusses at length the relative merits of governing by relying on fear or love. He concludes that love produces a far more lasting and reliable base of support, while fear inevitably engenders hatred (*Off.* 2.23–24). Machiavelli disagrees. Since human beings are by nature unfaithful, self-interested, and ungrateful, it is foolish to trust to their love for support. It is far more reliable to depend on fear (*Prince* 17), which in turn relies on force.[40] For Machiavelli, republics are not immune from this logic. It is in republics that Machiavelli recommends regular public executions, and he praises Scipio for forcing the citizens at sword point to swear not to give up the fight against Hannibal (*Discourses* 1.11.1).

Effacing Rights from Republicanism

Machiavelli's abandonment of the centrality of justice affects not only his advice about the virtues of the republican citizen and statesman but also— and perhaps more important—his institutional recommendations. In his thought about the proper structure of a republic, Machiavelli stresses the value of violating all three prescriptions of Ciceronian justice: the prohibition of harm, the requirement to prevent harm to others, and respect for property. Machiavelli makes no mention at all of rights—to life, security, or

---

[40] Although Machiavelli agrees with Cicero that hatred must be avoided, he denies that fear necessarily results in hatred. Hatred can be avoided by refraining from certain particularly galling uses of power: despoiling subjects and violating their women.

property—a concept central not only to Ciceronian republicanism but also to the lived practice of Roman political politics, as discussed in chapter 2. There is good reason to believe that the misconception that rights are not indigenous to republican theory can be traced Machiavelli's silence about rights and to scholars such as Viroli and Skinner, who have taken Machiavelli as the supreme exemplar of republicanism—and even of *Roman* republicanism specifically.[41]

Cicero's conception of rights as manifestations of just relationships links the liberty of the republic to the liberty of its citizens. One of the key advantages of living in a free, self-governing, and well-ordered republic was the enjoyment of the rights such a republic would secure for the individual. In turn, the rights of the people as a body ensured the proper balance and relationships that maintained the freedom of the republic and prevented it from collapsing into tyranny. *Libertas*—of the individual and of the political community—is thus one of the central purposes of the political community. Preserving it is an end toward which the statesman ought to work.

For his part, Machiavelli does emphasize the importance of the liberty of the political community. *The Prince* and *Discourses* abound with Machiavelli's illustrations of the superiority of "free" republics over principalities (worse off still are those political communities that are dominated from without). Yet Machiavelli goes on to leave little doubt that the freedom of the individual citizen is not only not central to his conception of political freedom but is often in conflict with it. Machiavellian citizens do not securely enjoy bodily safety, the protection of their property, leisure, or the right to fair trial that Cicero found so valuable about Roman practice. In his understanding of the common good achieved in republics, Machiavelli writes: "this common good is not observed if not in republics, since all that is for that purpose is executed, and although it may turn out to harm this or that private individual, *those for whom the aforesaid does good are so many that they can go ahead with it against the disposition of the few crushed by it*" (*Discourses* 2.2; emphasis added). This seems proof that Machiavelli's republican "common good" is not really common—as long as common means something shared by all. Any private citizen can be sacrificed for the benefit of the greater number.

[41] Eager to distinguish republicanism from liberalism, they have emphasized that the former offers a vision of liberty without rights, often denying that the ancients (including the Romans) even had access to a concept of rights. See Viroli 2002, 7; Skinner 2002, 211–212.

It may seem that, contrary to the foregoing, Machiavelli does intend to carve out protections for some of the same rights defended by Cicero, even if he does not use the term *rights*, or that he at least shares Cicero's concern for justice with respect to the lives and property of citizens. On the subject of property, Machiavelli cautions princes against violating the goods (or women) of the people. But he clarifies that this advice comes only because "men sooner forget the loss of their father than the loss of their patrimony" (*Prince* 17). In other words, it is better to kill a man than to steal his money—and this only because his heirs may seek revenge. Although he says that one of the benefits of republics is greater security in your person and property than you would enjoy under a prince, Machiavelli insists that republics ought to keep "the public rich and the citizens poor" (*Discourses* 1.37.1). Apparently, such security will not amount to much actual personal prosperity. For Machiavelli, wealth acquired by force at the expense of others is *preferable* to wealth acquired peacefully. As Machiavelli puts it, the successful rapacity of the Roman citizen army proves that "gold is not sufficient to find good soldiers, but good soldiers are quite sufficient to find gold" (*Discourses* 2.10.1). The plundering of others' property becomes advisable and praiseworthy, as long as it is the property of those outside your state (*Prince* 16).

As for bodily harms, Machiavelli proposes not only that they be done but that they should often be done all at once, so that people notice them less (*Prince* 8). At least, that is his recommendation for princes. When considering republics, Machiavelli is still more sanguinary, believing that only repeated spectacles of blood can keep people subservient to the laws: "one should not wish ten years at most to pass from one to another of such executions" (*Discourses* 3.1.3). The question of justice—that it might matter whether the condemned individuals *deserve* to die, or indeed whether they are even owed a fair trial—Machiavelli does not even mention. Thus, whereas Cicero's views about public trials focused on the vindication of individual rights and collective rights, Machiavelli praises public *accusations* for producing *fear*.[42]

Unleashing the People

On the surface, Machiavelli's rejection of the first pillar of Cicero's republicanism seems motivated by a desire to fully achieve the second. His rejection

---

[42] In truth, not all of Machiavelli's examples were executed, a fact Machiavelli chooses to omit as he emphasizes the fear of punishment that mere accusations can cause. This is part of Machiavelli's general tactic of making the Roman practices seem even more violent than they were.

of the centrality of justice and natural law is no more conspicuous than his embracing of a more popular kind of politics that empowers the common people. Machiavelli considers where the power in a republic (or any state) should rest, whether in the elites or in the people—and emphatically chooses the latter (*Discourses* 1.5).[43] That Machiavelli's politics has a more popular—even democratic—element has been noted by many scholars, but McCormick has gone furthest in calling attention to this facet of his thought. McCormick bases his view on Machiavelli's famous "two humors" theory, according to which every political community consists of the common people, who "desire neither to be commanded nor oppressed by the great," and elites ("the great"), who "desire to command and oppress the people" (*Prince* 9).[44] Machiavelli strongly endorses the Roman republican model over those of Venice and Sparta because the common people were far more able to assert themselves in the former (*Discourses* 1.5.3).

McCormick rightly calls our attention to the fact that the kind of republic Machiavelli favors gives more space for popular participation than other republican models.[45] But McCormick wrongly concludes from this that Machiavelli's democratic republicanism contains within it a commitment to justice, where "the people's decency or *onestà* entails a fundamental disinclination to injure others . . . the people are capable of superior moral judgments."[46] In other words, McCormick thinks that Machiavelli's embrace of the people is, in fact, an attempt to better realize the demands of justice.

McCormick makes much of Machiavelli's claim in *Discourses* 1.4 that Rome proves how "the desires of free people are rarely pernicious to freedom." McCormick argues that the people are passive and deferential unless provoked by a threat to their liberty.[47] Of the nobles, McCormick states, "their oppressive nature is just a fact, a natural fact," whereas "the people '*only* desire not to be dominated.'"[48]

Contrary to McCormick's claims, it turns out that the people's desire not to be dominated is *not* a "natural fact" according to Machiavelli. Rather, it is circumstance-dependent. Should the people ever be free of oppression and the suspicion of oppression, they, too, would seek to dominate.

---

[43] See also *Prince* 9.

[44] Cf. *Discourses* 1.5.2.

[45] However, it is not quite as democratic as McCormick claims, as Balot and Trochimchuk (2012) demonstrate.

[46] McCormick 2011, 25.

[47] McCormick 2011, 30.

[48] McCormick 2011, 146; emphasis in McCormick but not in Machiavelli's original. Cf. *Discourses* 1.5.

Machiavelli describes Rome's conflict over the agrarian laws as arising because the plebs—after acquiring the tribunate for protection—began to seek to aspire to domination: "it was not enough for the Roman plebs to secure itself against the nobles by the creation of the tribunes . . . for having obtained that, it began at once to engage in combat through ambition, and to wish to share in honors and belongings" (*Discourses* 1.37.1). McCormick suggests that Machiavelli blames the elites (*grandi*) for the troubles over the agrarian laws.[49] But the assignment of blame is beside the point. The example illustrates that Machiavelli does not believe that the common people are immune to the desire to rule.[50] Their interest in justice is entirely a function of their weakness (as Machiavelli suggests the concern for justice always is). As soon as their fear of being dominated is abated, they look to dominate others. Thus, freedom as non-domination appears as an *inherently* unstable ideal in Machiavelli's thought; once the people achieve their desired liberation fully, they will simply join the ranks of the aspiring dominators. Machiavelli distills this into a general maxim: "first one seeks not to be offended, and then one offends others" (*Discourses* 1.46.1). This follows naturally from the principle that the desire to acquire is universal (*Prince* 3).

The Predatory Republic

The entire basis of Machiavelli's preference for the Roman model lies in the fact that, according to him, Rome best achieved the goal of enlisting the people in the struggle to dominate others. A republic founded on the people is best "if a republic wishes to make an empire" (*Discourses* 1.5.3). The Roman people's desire for freedom was perfectly compatible with the oppression of others; in fact, the two were inextricably linked. Machiavelli writes of the Romans' impressive success in conquering other peoples whose ferocity was born out of their desire to preserve their liberty—a liberty Rome destroyed. Machiavelli's republicanism certainly does seek to preserve the liberty of the republic—its capacity for self-rule and its independence from other states. But he knows that the success of such a republic will result in the loss of

---

[49] McCormick 2011, 89.

[50] Vatter says: "people and nobles do not designate natural kinds" (Vatter 2013, 63). Zuckert notes how Machiavelli's prince can make and unmake the great—by appointing and dismissing particular individuals—as needed (Zuckert 2014, 90). See also Sullivan 1992, 315.

liberty—and sometimes total extermination—for its neighbors.[51] Whereas Cicero imagines Rome to have brought justice and liberty to conquered peoples by extending them citizenship, Machiavelli views (and approves of) Rome extinguishing the liberty of other peoples (*Discourses* 2.2).

As with his advice to individuals, Machiavelli suggests that republics may at times find the practice of justice useful. The rule of law can help channel class conflict into beneficial results and ameliorate the dangers that arise when the wronged seek revenge (*Discourses* 2.28.1, 3.1.2). But justice should never get in the way of the communal interest. Cicero maintains that there were certain actions so dishonorable or unjust that one ought not do them even for the sake of the commonwealth (*Off.* 1.159). Machiavelli rejects that idea and excludes considerations of justice from proper deliberation about the welfare of the state (*Discourses* 3.41.) He praises the Roman Republic for not hesitating to kill "an entire legion at once, and a city" (*Discourses* 3.49.1).

Machiavelli's entire endorsement of Rome as the best example of a republic is based on its excellent organization for imperial expansion. He considers different kinds of republics, including the aristocratic Venice and the austere Sparta. But he concludes that neither of those is well suited to expansion and conquest, which are necessary for intrinsic and extrinsic reasons. A republic concerned for its own safety can only ensure its security by accumulating enough power to defeat any threat. But, perhaps more important, as we saw, human beings are naturally acquisitive, so that conquest is a temptation that can never be avoided indefinitely—as the examples of Sparta and Venice demonstrate (*Discourses* 1.6). Machiavelli thus distills a general rule about free republics: "a city that lives free has two ends: one to acquire, the other to maintain itself free" (*Discourses* 1.29.3).[52]

For Machiavelli, the development of the Roman constitution was driven by the class conflict between the plebs and the nobles. This class conflict resulted in, among other things, the creation of the tribunate, which protected the

---

[51] This is still more evidence that Machiavelli is not some kind of moral consequentialist, seeking to do the greatest good for the greatest number. The Romans purchased their own liberty by killing and oppressing their many neighbors, and Machiavelli commends them for it. Hulliung writes that "Florentine Greatness" for Machiavelli means at bottom "the list of cities once free and now subject to the yoke of Florence" (Hulliung 1983, 14).

[52] McCormick denies this. He points to a passage from *Discourses* 1.6: "*if indeed* necessity brings [a republic] to expand" (McCormick 2011, 57; emphasis McCormick's). On this basis, McCormick claims that Machiavelli opens up the possibility of a non-expansionist republic. But McCormick's suggestion seems implausible. The preceding paragraph in the text contains Machiavelli's *proof* of the necessity of expansion. Machiavelli's "if indeed" simply connects that proven premise to its conclusion.

interests of the plebs. Machiavelli criticizes writers who (following Cicero) bemoaned Rome's internal strife. To Machiavelli, those who do this chastise Rome for the very source of its greatness.[53]

The Romans—unlike the Greek city states—also extended citizenship to their conquered enemies.[54] These innovations ensured that the Roman state never lacked for manpower and that the lower classes—by far the most numerous—could be trusted to serve in the army and bear weapons, because they felt assured that their interests were protected (*Discourses* 1.2–6). The verdict of *The Prince* is that republics are superior to principalities, because in them is "greater life, greater hatred, greater desire for revenge" (*Prince* 5). McCormick is not wrong that Machiavelli's theory contains substantial democratic elements, but those elements receive their justification from their utility in war-making, not from some appreciation of the justice of democratic arrangements.

The "Effectual Truth" of Machiavelli's Republicanism

Near the core of Machiavelli's challenge to Cicero lies a tacit accusation: the Roman Republic that Cicero so adores for its conformity to justice could only be founded and sustained by injustice, and Cicero and later admirers of Rome blind themselves to that fact. It is an update of Philus's position in *De re publica*'s Carneadean debate. Machiavelli makes much of Rome's mythical founding in fratricide and suggests that this illustrates the fundamental truth about founding new regimes: one *must* commit injustice. Still further, Machiavelli charges that it is not just the establishment but also the maintenance of a free republic that requires regular spectacles of violence to preserve it, to overawe the people, and to keep potential tyrants at bay. Finally, the greatness of Rome that earned it more admiration than other ancient

[53] In *Florentine Histories*, Machiavelli suggests that the class conflict in Florence failed to produce the same desirable result. But Machiavelli makes clear that this fact does not undermine his general rule about internal conflict. The problem lay in the fact that the Florentine populace triumphed too completely over the nobility, depriving the nobility of their martial virtues. This example further undermines McCormick's claim that Machiavelli invariably sides with the people in all instances of class conflict.

[54] Recall that in chapter 2, we saw that Cicero also defends the institution of the tribunes and the extension of Roman citizenship. But he values both of these because of their contributions to justice and liberty. As we see here, Machiavelli sees their advantage for war.

republics is attributable not to harmony but to the discord that enabled it to conquer the rest of the Mediterranean world.

Cicero is not, however, naive.[55] He knows, of course, that sometimes political necessity demands the suspension of ordinary moral considerations, hence his dictum: *salus populi suprema lex*. His own response to the Catilinarian crisis illustrates his commitment to that principle. But Machiavelli's own arguments reveal that human beings need little help in "being bad." In that case, a salutary teaching of political virtue perhaps needs less to celebrate those occasions in which force and fraud are necessary than to encourage political actors to seek alternatives.

Still, Machiavelli's alternative has considerable appeal. It is not difficult to see how his forceful presentation of the case could impress readers with its apparent realism (despite the fact that Machiavelli, too, is prone to manipulate history to support his arguments). For contemporaries, his cynical wit must certainly have been a refreshing counter to the hypocritical ecclesiastical politics of the Borgia papacy and the fecklessness of the Florentine state.

But the real importance of Machiavelli's challenge lies not in its allegedly greater historical accuracy. The goal of both Machiavelli and Cicero is to influence political thought and action. Here Machiavelli makes an implicit promise. He suggests to those enamored of the Ciceronian version of republicanism that they can do better: abandon the commitment to natural law, justice, rights, and harmony, and your republic will flourish. In *Discourses* 2.2, Machiavelli gives two accounts of why people prefer freedom to servitude: first, because "cities have not ever expanded either in dominion or in riches if they have not been in freedom"; and second, because people feel themselves secure in their properties and families and believe their children will have the opportunity to thrive.[56] In a Ciceronian commonwealth, these two impulses would be irreconcilable—we cannot all extend our dominion over others while at the same time all remaining secure in what we have. But in advocating the emulation of (his version of) the Romans, who excelled at preserving their freedom while eliminating that of others, Machiavelli claims that we can.

But a closer look at Machiavelli's depiction of his preferred version of republican politics undermines the plausibility of his promise and raises the

---

[55] For one, Cicero does not ignore the injustice of Rome's founding—he condemns Romulus's mythical murder of his brother as criminal (*Off.* 3.41). See further Hawley 2018.

[56] Viroli points to the second of these reasons as evidence for Machiavelli's similarity to Cicero yet fails to see how linking it with the first produces a radical difference (Viroli 2002, 59).

question of whether abandoning the constraints of justice for the sake of popular rule ultimately undermines popular rule itself. McCormick and other scholars who seek to excavate the democratic or popular Machiavelli are forced to consider Machiavelli's writings about princes and other elite political actors as "description." For instance, McCormick only seems to notice cases where Machiavelli "defines," "characterizes," or "refers to" the oppressive behavior of elites.[57] He tends to ignore instances where Machiavelli *advises* elites on how better to go about accumulating power or oppressing. There is no particular reason to believe that Machiavelli did not intend this advice with the same sincerity as his counsel to republics.[58] In fact, the nasty behavior Machiavelli recommends to elites is a direct consequence of his abandonment of a firm standard of justice. Not only the people but the elites, too, are unleashed—and Machiavelli's account of their psychology suggests that their ultimate goal is domination and oppression. An ambitious man who reads and learns from Machiavelli will have no qualms about how he achieves power—glory, after all, is the sure consequence of success.

And so it is hardly surprising that the people in Machiavelli's model republic are constantly subject to elite manipulation (e.g., through religious deception), coercion, and privation—all this even though Machiavelli identifies the "common utility" that people get out of "a free way of life" as the security to enjoy their lives, families, and possessions (*Discourses* 2.2). Machiavelli's citizens are in a constant struggle domestically and with external enemies. While he does indeed find in the common people a desire not to be oppressed or dominated, Machiavelli does not propose ever to satisfy that desire completely, since doing so would eliminate the political tension he finds so valuable in republics. Moreover, Machiavelli provides evidence that the freedom of his ideal republic ultimately destroyed itself. He admits that the Romans' conquests (the products of their constitution) had the ultimate consequence of destroying liberty everywhere—even in Rome itself (*Discourses* 2.2–3). In sum, Machiavelli's rejection of the limitations posed by Cicero's natural law to enhance popular sovereignty and freedom seem in the end to destabilize both popular sovereignty and liberty.

Although Cicero may have evinced more overtly elitist sympathies, the rights that distinguish his conception of republican freedom from Machiavelli's offer a way to provide the people with what Machiavelli himself

---

[57] McCormick 2011, 4.

[58] Machiavelli's letter to Vettori strongly suggests that his willingness even to *work* for a prince, expressed in the dedication of *The Prince*, is not feigned.

says that they want: peace, leisure, and protection for themselves and their property. Machiavelli may identify this desire in the people, but his political prescription deliberately thwarts the full satisfaction of it.[59] Cicero seeks to fulfill it. Put another way, it may be that Machiavelli's challenge only confirms Cicero's claim that natural law undergirds popular sovereignty and that the latter without the former is not theoretically viable.

Re-Evaluating Machiavelli's Legacy

Few historical thinkers have been as fought over as Machiavelli. In recent decades, two competing narratives have been especially prominent. According to one advanced by neo-republicans and members of the so-called Cambridge School of intellectual history, Machiavelli should be taken as an exemplar (perhaps the culmination) of the classical republican tradition tracing back to Aristotle and Cicero.[60] The other narrative makes Machiavelli the founding and originating thinker of modernity, setting political philosophy on the road to liberalism. From the evidence presented here, the claims made by the former about Machiavelli's close compatibility with classical Roman republicanism on the model of Cicero do not seem convincing.

But most of the critics of the neo-republican view, while they understand Machiavelli to constitute a break with classical political thought generally, make this argument in order to set up the claim that Machiavelli is the first great step toward modernity and liberalism.[61] Those who see Machiavelli as neither an exemplar of classical Roman republicanism nor a proto-modern are very few.[62] The following chapters will trace the effects of the rivalry between Machiavelli and Cicero on later thought. Yet the examination of Machiavelli in this chapter should already indicate that his critique of Cicero does not constitute a movement in the direction of modernity as we understand it. Early modernity's pacific, rights-based, natural law liberalism corresponds to Machiavelli's tumultuous, bellicose, and popular republic far

---

[59] See Sullivan 2004, 49, for a related discussion of how Machiavelli acknowledges the people's desire for security but refuses to satisfy it because of his emphasis on war-making.

[60] Pettit 1997; Pocock 2009; Skinner 1998; Viroli 2002.

[61] Rahe 2000; Tarcov 1982; Mansfield 1998; Sullivan 1992; Strauss 1995.

[62] Two partial yet notable exceptions are McCormick 2011 and Straumann 2016. McCormick asserts in passing that Machiavelli is an outlier in the republican tradition but does not develop a historical account in any depth to support that claim. Straumann provides more analysis, but he is focused on the singular question of constitutionalism.

less than it does to Cicero's commonwealth.[63] Those who see Machiavelli's break with classical thought as an important step in the direction of modernity need to consider how it is that the life of individuals in a Machiavellian martial republic would so little resemble what either contemporary liberals or democrats would hope for them.

Still, Machiavelli's vigorous new republicanism had a real effect, especially in the century and a half that followed. No significant subsequent thinker in the republican tradition would go so far as to sever the connection entirely between popular sovereignty and natural justice. But Machiavelli had succeeded in placing great strain on the connection between the two. What Cicero had taken as mutually supporting pillars now appeared to be in tension with each other. Machiavelli's challenge appeared to demand a choice: would freedom be achieved better by prioritizing popular sovereignty over justice or vice versa?

As we will see, Machiavelli's challenge to the republican tradition's Ciceronian foundations was successful only temporarily. In the long run, the liberal republicanism of Locke and the American founders demonstrates that Machiavelli offers false choice. They sought to repair the relationship between popular sovereignty and natural law. As a result, we might have to accept that Machiavelli is neither the heir to the classical tradition nor (on the practical level, at least) a forerunner of the moderns. It is not that he goes entirely unread or unused by the early liberal republicans. But what thinkers such as Locke, Adams, and Wilson find valuable in Machiavelli's thought is not original to him, while what *is* original to Machiavelli proves not to be valuable.

[63] This does not necessarily overthrow the claim that Machiavelli's philosophical innovations (e.g., the attempt to conquer *fortuna*) are foundational premises for certain forms of liberalism. But it does demonstrate that in Machiavelli's hands, these premises do not yield a *practical* image of politics that resemble later liberal or liberal republican theories.

4

Two Ciceronian Traditions in the Aftermath of Machiavelli

> It is an easy thing, for men to be deceived, by the specious name of Libertie . . . and when the same errour is confirmed by the authority of men in reputation for their writings in this subject, it is no wonder if it produce sedition, and change of Government. In these westerne parts of the world, we are made to receive our opinions concerning the Institution, and Rights of Common-wealths from *Aristotle*, *Cicero*, and other men, Greeks and Romans.
>
> —Hobbes, *Leviathan* 21

Scientific and Theoretical Challenges

Machiavelli had posited a chaotic and unpredictable universe, one that foreclosed any possibility of natural law. If the only way to protect oneself and achieve other ends is to acquire power, the acceptance of moral limitations places one at a potentially fatal disadvantage. Those who see reality clearly must come to accept violence and injustice as ineradicable aspects of political life. Conquering fortune and overcoming the ambitions of others requires hardheaded realism. One must choose: either the stagnant and corrupt principalities (and papacy) of contemporary Christendom clinging to the patina of a moral order or the violently contested politics of the classical republics. Put another way, one could cleave to the hollow moral universalism of natural law or seek to achieve a universal republic through warlike expansion. Machiavelli opts for the latter.

By the seventeenth century, Machiavelli's challenge had been confirmed in part (but only in part) by the new scientific methods and discoveries of men like Galileo Galilei, René Descartes, and Francis Bacon. True, they showed that the universe was not chaotic and unpredictable and ruled by *fortuna*. In fact, we might say the new natural science debunked the very idea of fortune,

Natural Law Republicanism. Michael C. Hawley, Oxford University Press. © Oxford University Press 2022.
DOI: 10.1093/oso/9780197582336.003.0004

understood as something inherently unpredictable; the motions of the heavenly bodies follow predictable laws. But the very articulation of those laws seemed to reveal that motion was not inherently purposeful; there were no natural or inherent ends that could be deduced from natural change.

These discoveries dealt a severe blow to the scholastic natural law tradition, which had depended on the teleological philosophy of Aristotle and Aquinas. On the continent, this development prompted a new attempt to provide a universally valid moral grounding for political legitimacy and justice that would be compatible with the new scientific discoveries. At almost exactly the same time, England found itself embroiled in civil war, the (short-term) outcome of which was the establishment of a republic but not a small city-state republic. Instead, England offered itself as an example of a republic that encompassed a whole modern nation. The struggle of the republicans to gain and hold power prompted an even more urgent—if more localized—struggle to articulate a theory of legitimate political power that would justify the English Commonwealth.

Throughout all the upheaval, Cicero's reputation and influence only grew. *De officiis* had been the first secular work to come off the Gutenberg press, and the spread of modern printing had produced a vast number of copies of all his extant works, in Latin and in translation. During this period, two parallel efforts of theoretical legitimation looked to Cicero's works for guidance and authority, seeing him as offering uniquely valuable resources for their projects. Taking Cicero's thought seriously, both movements followed him in trying to navigate the competing demands of universally applicable moral norms and the rightful claim of the people in any given state to be the ultimate source of political authority. Although neither movement would undertake to follow Machiavelli's overtly immoralist path, the persuasiveness of his challenge was reflected in the fact that popular sovereignty and natural law no longer appeared naturally complementary but rather in tension with each other. Thus, these two movements tended to take opposite horns of Machiavelli's alleged dilemma.[1] Hugo Grotius and Samuel Pufendorf doubled down on Ciceronian natural law. They accepted the idea of popular sovereignty in principle but articulated a contractarian doctrine that drastically reduced the practical impact of the people's sovereignty on politics.[2]

---

[1] Lee detects an underlying shared debt to Roman law (Lee 2016, 259).

[2] As Lee puts it, Grotius sought "to reconcile the ideal of popular sovereignty . . . with the constitutional necessity of civil government . . . a people may remain fully free and fully sovereign while under the government of a prince" (Lee 2016, 257).

Conversely, the English republicans placed enormous weight on the doctrine of popular sovereignty and were fierce advocates of Cicero's conception of freedom for the individual and the community alike. However, they made only halfhearted appeals to a standard of natural law, the chief salient feature of which (they claimed) established as natural the people's claim to be sovereign.

In these two movements, we also see Cicero deployed in reaction to the new ideas about sovereignty put forth by Jean Bodin and (more immediately) Thomas Hobbes. Hobbes and Bodin were themselves readers of Cicero, and both were indebted in certain ways to his thought. Daniel Lee shows that, contrary to his reputation as a thoroughgoing opponent of popular sovereignty, Bodin recognizes the existence and legitimacy of regimes based on the authority of the people and included republican Rome among them (*Six Books of a Commonwealth* 6.6).[3] Bodin even conceives of the Roman Republic of Cicero's time much as Cicero himself conceived it. This is to say that he holds that ultimate sovereignty lay with the Roman people, but they wisely chose to delegate its function to subordinate magistrates and the Senate.[4] Hobbes, for his part, draws explicitly from Cicero the idea that the sovereign could function as an artificial "person," who represented all its members as a unity (*Leviathan* 16).[5] Hobbes also accepts (grudgingly) the legitimacy of non-monarchical states. But though they took these and other concepts from Cicero, Hobbes and Bodin firmly oppose the Ciceronian project of locating legitimate government in the union of popular sovereignty and obedience to universal moral laws. Nor was either a friend of Ciceronian liberty.

However, the contributions of Bodin and Hobbes toward developing a deeper philosophical grounding for the concept of sovereignty meant that neither Grotius and Pufendorf nor the English republicans could ignore their arguments. Bodin and Hobbes offered an analytical understanding of sovereignty that stripped *popular* sovereignty of any particular normative weight and allowed both thinkers to thus sidestep the tension in Cicero's thought.

[3] Cf. Lee 2016, 221.
[4] Lee suggests that this vision of Rome runs counter to the mixed-constitution theories of Polybius and Cicero (Lee 2016, 221). But, as we saw in chapter 1, Cicero, in fact, sees no contradiction between the idea that the people are the ultimate political authority and the idea that they would be right to delegate most of this authority to the Senate and the magistrates through regular elections.
[5] In his letter to Archbishop Bramhall, Hobbes cites Cicero as his authority for this (Hobbes 1682). See also Simendic 2011.

The conflict of priority between the claims of the people's right to rule and the natural law does not appear fundamental to either thinker.

Bodin offers his famous and deeply influential definition of sovereignty: "the most high, absolute, and perpetuall power over the citisens and subiects in a Commonweale" (*Six Books* 1.8).[6] He describes it as *legibus soluta potestas*, power free from laws.[7] This analytical definition of sovereignty is indifferent to moral claims. It is not, as Lee points out, that Bodin was himself indifferent to the ways in which sovereignty was used or abused; he was extremely concerned with the proper use of sovereignty.[8] But for Bodin, wherever this supra-legal power in fact resided in a state determined the nature of sovereignty in that state. Thus, while Rome and other republics ancient and modern might have located that power in the people as a corporate body, other regimes placed sovereignty in the person of the monarch or in a council of nobles (*Six Books* 2.7). Popular sovereignty is but one form of sovereignty, and not even the most choiceworthy kind, according to Bodin. Bodin grants the people no original right to determine the disposal of sovereign power. He explicitly denies that the consent of the people—tacit or explicit—is a requirement for legitimate government (*Six Books* 1.8).[9] As a result, it is not an urgent question for Bodin how the people's claim to rule might be reconciled with universal moral laws.

Hobbes owes to Bodin much in his theory of sovereignty, which also takes the possessor of sovereign power to be above all human law.[10] Like Bodin, Hobbes acknowledges that sovereigns may be subject to laws of God or nature, but violating those laws yields no recourse to subjects:

> It is true, that a Soveraign Monarch, or the greater part of a Soveraign Assembly, may ordain the doing of many things in pursuit of their Passions, contrary to their own consciences, which is a breach of trust, and of the Law of Nature; but this is not enough to authorise any subject, either to make warre upon, or so much as to accuse of Injustice, or in any way to speak evill of their Soveraign. (*Leviathan* 24)

---

[6] I use the Knolles English translation throughout.

[7] This is to say, free from human laws. Bodin accepts that all people are still subject to the laws of nature and of God. But he denies that any human can enforce these against the sovereign (*Six Books* 1.8).

[8] For more on this, see chapter 6 of Lee 2016.

[9] This is not to say that Bodin sees no value in the people's consent. He thinks it greatly beneficial to the well-functioning of a state that the people consent in some fashion—especially to taxation. But this does not mean that the people's consent is morally necessary (*Six Books* 3.7).

[10] On Hobbes's debt to Bodin, see Dunning 1896; King 2013; Lloyd 1991.

However, unlike Bodin, Hobbes does ground the initial formation of a commonwealth in the consent of the people who make it up. He grants the underlying logic of the popular sovereignty doctrine: all legitimate political authority ultimately flows from the consent of the people subject to it (*Leviathan* 18).[11] However, once that consent is given, sovereignty is truly transferred. Unless the people opt for a democratic commonwealth (which Hobbes concedes is legitimate but insists is unwise), sovereignty then is located wherever the original contract places it. As the passage just quoted indicates, the failure of the sovereign to govern well—even the violation of natural or divine law—does not justify resistance. Indeed, unless the sovereign ceases to protect a citizen's mere life, that citizen must consider the sovereign's actions his own, "because they have authorised all his actions, and in bestowing Sovereign Power, made them their own" (*Leviathan* 24).

More important, Hobbes's conception of consent is extremely loose, in a such a way as to raise serious doubts about the meaningfulness of the people's choice. For Hobbes, consent can be obtained by threat and fear: "Covenants entred into by fear . . . are obligatory. For example, if I Covenant to pay a ransome, or service for my life, to an enemy; I am bound by it. For it is a Contract, wherein one receiveth the benefit of life; the other is to receive mony, or service for it" (*Leviathan* 14). As a result, it follows for Hobbes that a sovereign set up by the free choice of individuals in the state of nature (a "Commonwealth by *Institution*") is no more legitimate than sovereign power acquired in a war of conquest (a "Common-wealth by *Acquisition*") (*Leviathan* 18). The consent given by the people in both cases is normatively the same for Hobbes.

But the advantages in sidestepping the dilemma Machiavelli presented to the Ciceronian tradition came at the obvious cost of sacrifices of the goods that Cicero and his heirs considered essential. For both Grotius and Pufendorf and the English republicans, the Bodin-Hobbes vision of political authority sacrificed far too much of the necessary components to a good regime. It offered no this-worldly means to hold sovereigns accountable for violations of moral law. Nor did it locate the source of political legitimacy in the *uncoerced* consent of the people.

In this chapter, we can see the ways in which Cicero's ideas were drafted to support both the new natural law politics of Grotius and Pufendorf and the republican aspirations of the English commonwealthmen as the two

[11] Cf. Malcolm 2016.

groups responded not only to Machiavelli's proposed dilemma but also to the Bodin-Hobbes alternative. By exploring the profoundly different directions in which Cicero's thought was carried during this period, we can establish the grounds for understanding how Locke and the American founders reunited these Ciceronian traditions to give birth to liberal republicanism. Both movements appealed to the authority of Cicero and drew theoretical inspiration from him. For the English republicans, Cicero and Machiavelli were on much the same side: defenders of republican freedom against Hobbesian despotism. For the new natural law thinkers, Cicero was at times an overtly anti-Machiavellian resource, one whose ideas of natural law formed the basis of their own moral-political system-building. The latter share with Hobbes and Bodin a hope for a more orderly politics but would not join them in liberating sovereignty from practical moral restraint. In a sense, Machiavelli's critique prompted a sundering of Cicero's legacy into two: Cicero the republican statesman pitted against Cicero the natural law philosopher.

A Natural Law for Modernity: Grotius and Pufendorf

Even within the Christian tradition, theologians along with philosophers had appealed to a conception of natural law to ground their principles on something putatively accessible to human reason unaided by divine revelation. Aquinas and the scholastics had developed a complex natural law tradition, which drew somewhat from Cicero but was primarily based on Aristotelian metaphysics and teleology. This great project depended in large part on an understanding of the universe as teleological, the components of which are animated by intrinsic purposes. In the early modern period, the basis of this entire scheme was challenged by such individuals as Galileo, Bacon, and Descartes. As Charles Tully puts it, "the philosophers of the new natural sciences advanced a concept of nature as a non-purposive realm of atoms on which God imposes, by an act of will, motion and an extrinsic order of efficient causes or regularities."[12]

These new discoveries delivered a crushing blow to the foundation of the long-standing dominant natural law tradition. If there were no basis in fact for Aristotelian ends, a politics based on a teleological natural law

---

[12] Pufendorf 1991, xvii.

becomes difficult to defend. Moreover, the Reformation and the rise of the Westphalian state system meant that Europe would also be a place of wide (and widening) religious diversity. This created a new challenge for political philosophers: "a new morality able to gain the consent of all Europeans to the new political order and bring peace would have to be independent of the confessional differences which divided them, yet also permit belief in and practice of these rival religions."[13]

In response to this challenge, a group of philosophers sought to articulate a new natural law tradition, which would be grounded on premises not confessionally controversial (as far as possible) or undermined by the new discoveries of natural science. By far the foremost among these were Grotius and Pufendorf. First set forth by Grotius, the new version of natural law was shortly thereafter expounded and systematized by Pufendorf. In the intervening years, two events occurred that have occupied far more attention from contemporary political theorists and historians: the upheaval of the English Civil War and the publication of Hobbes's political philosophy. Yet the works of these two, especially Grotius's *On the Law of War and Peace* and Pufendorf's *Elements of Universal Jurisprudence, On the Law of Nature and of Nations*, and *On the Duty of Man and Citizen* (this last being a summary of *Elements*), enjoyed a dominant place in the intellectual life of Europe for more than a century. Their works would profoundly influence Locke and the American founders as they developed the theoretical basis of liberal republicanism.

A Common Ground

Grotius and Pufendorf suggest that, despite the new confessional and political divisions of Europe, a universal political doctrine—acceptable to all—could be found if it were based on something common and accessible to all human beings, regardless of situation. This doctrine would not require the now-untenable teleological presuppositions of the scholastic natural law tradition. Grotius and Pufendorf would settle on two such premises: the state of nature as a reconstructed natural position common to all human beings and the motivation of self-love which all human beings experience.[14] Influenced

---

[13] Pufendorf 1991, xviii.
[14] For more on this choice, see Pufendorf 1991, xix; Pufendorf 1994.

by his older contemporary Grotius, Hobbes would follow in accepting both of these premises as the grounds for his own new political science, which has led some scholars to include Hobbes as a member of this new natural law movement.[15] This impression is strengthened by the fact that all three share with Bodin a strong desire for peace and prefer monarchical government over republics or mixed regimes.

However, Hobbes's version of natural law is in an important sense *amoral*, identical with prudence.[16] For Hobbes, there is no morality applicable to humans as humans (i.e., in their natural state, stripped of all socially acquired obligations); all justice is positive and issues from consent and the commands of the sovereign. As a result, political arrangements and the rights and privileges of individuals are at the discretion of the ruler of the state; only a direct threat to the life of a subject breaks the subject's obligation to obey. Hobbes denies that there is some objective standard or perspective from which to judge the justice of political institutions and decisions.

Such a view is fundamentally at odds with the project of Grotius and Pufendorf. They sought a decent politics, subject to the universal demands of morality. For them, natural law is a *moral* concept meant to ground a political order and to give a standard by which to judge its justice. They thus construed not only natural law but also the state of nature and the status of rights, in a way thoroughly different from Hobbes. Indeed, Pufendorf sees himself in an important sense as a defender of his and Grotius's system *against* Hobbes.[17]

While Hobbes looked to natural science as the model for his science of politics, Grotius and Pufendorf looked to Cicero. Ciceronian philosophy was to form the backbone of this new natural law tradition, in much the same way that Aristotle and Aquinas provided the framework for the old scholastic one. The Ciceronian valences in Grotius's and Pufendorf's work are especially clear in distinguishing their views from Hobbes. In fact, Pufendorf writes in *The Law of Nature* that when arguing against Hobbes, "Tully hath left the most noble Testimony for our Purpose."[18]

---

[15] For instance, Tuck 1982.

[16] Hobbes defines a law of nature as "a Precept, or generall Rule, found out by Reason, by which a man is forbidden to do, that, which is destructive of his life, or taketh away the means of preserving the same; and to omit, that, by which he thinketh it may be best preserved" (*Leviathan* chapter 19). In chapter 25, Hobbes clarifies the amoral quality of these rules, arguing that justice comes into being only with a covenant and is determined by the will of the sovereign. Cf. *De Cive* 6.9. The sovereign, by definition, cannot be unjust. For Bodin, justice is not determined by the sovereign's will, but, as noted, he grants the people no intrinsic right to correct any violation of justice by the sovereign.

[17] As Craig Carr puts it, Hobbes is, in fact, Pufendorf's "self-declared primary antagonist" (Pufendorf 1994, 20).

[18] As quoted in Hochstrasser 2000, 63.

However, it is important to note that Grotius and Pufendorf do not simply deploy Cicero rhetorically or polemically to provide respectable classical cover for their project. The two foundational premises of their doctrine (the state of nature and the fact of human self-interest) are by themselves far from sufficient to simply derive the outlines of the moral political life characterized by peace, justice, and individual freedom that Grotius and Pufendorf desire. In fact, they may appear to be rather challenging or unpromising starting points. If individuals are inherently selfish and not naturally in society, how can they be reconciled to the duties and obligations that come with being in political communities? Cicero's political philosophy contains much of the underlying logic that Grotius and Pufendorf rely on to make their case.[19]

Pufendorf and Grotius both seek to offer a systematic account of natural law and its political implications. Matthew Fox argues that Cicero is not a figure with "an easily identifiable significance" during this period, because "Cicero's thought does not have any coherent philosophical system." As a result, "Enlightenment readers took inspiration from Cicero, but they did not as a rule think of him as the inaugurator of a theoretical vision that could be taken as more than a vague foundation for their own endeavors."[20] It is true that Cicero's theoretical writings do not amount to a single system. But as we have seen, they are largely coherent, and Grotius and Pufendorf do indeed find that Cicero's account of natural law and popular sovereignty was capable of bearing the theoretical weight they would put upon it.

In fact, Cicero provides unique resources for achieving the ends Grotius and Pufendorf outline, while avoiding the pitfalls of the earlier natural law doctrine. Like Aristotle, Cicero was a classical natural law philosopher. Unlike Aristotle's, Cicero's natural law was, at most, only loosely teleological. As discussed earlier, Cicero viewed the idea of positing a single best or natural way of life for all individuals to be a kind of Procrustean bed.[21] He derives our duties instead from our sociality, our common membership in a universal cosmopolis, and the demands of divine providence—not from a single best form of life that we all naturally aim at (and not as citizens of any particular state).

---

[19] Straumann argues persuasively that, despite his apparent equal reliance on Greek and Roman sources, Grotius's main ideas (and, through him, those of Pufendorf and others) arise out of Cicero and the Roman law (Straumann 2015, 6). See also Lee 2011.
[20] Fox 2013, 319. Fox's outlook is primarily on the later figures of the Enlightenment, whereas the current discussion focuses on much earlier figures. But, as we shall see, later Enlightenment thinkers also took Cicero seriously for their system-building.
[21] Cf. Hawley 2020a, 20.

Cicero's writings also contain versions of both of the premises from which Grotius and Pufendorf begin, making his philosophy compatible with their project from its very beginning. In his speech on behalf of Sestius, Cicero offers one of the earliest articulations of a state of nature, as it later came to be called. Cicero asks:

> Who of you does not know that the nature of things is such that, once— before natural or civil law had been discovered—human beings were scattered and wandered separately over the land, holding only so much property as they could seize or keep by their own hand and strength, with violence and wounds? (*Sest.* 42)[22]

Cicero goes on to posit that the establishment of law brought humanity out of this state of barbarism and laid the groundwork for civilization. Several aspects of this account prove striking. Not only does Cicero actually subscribe to the idea that human beings were once historically in a condition where they were stripped of all political institutions, but he also assumes that without those institutions, human beings would live isolated lives, characterized by violence. Moreover, Cicero calls special attention to the fact that such a situation would make property particularly precarious and costly to retain. Finally, Cicero posits the existence of a universally binding natural law—but one that is not simply inscribed on our hearts or expressed in teleological action toward a fixed end. Instead, the natural law would have to be "discovered." Grotius and Pufendorf develop this concept of a state of nature far beyond Cicero's depiction, but their innovations remain in keeping with the outlines of Cicero's original.

As for the other initial component of the new natural law project, several of Cicero's works grapple with the fact of our instinctive self-love. Most notably, *De officiis* revolves around an attempt to reconcile individual self-interest with duty. It presents this reconciliation as a means of achieving peace and social harmony, wherein members of political society understand their mutual obligations. Here, too, Grotius and Pufendorf follow Cicero's lead as they attempt to construct a theory of moral and political duties compatible with— and even derived from—our self-interest.

---

[22] This passage, among others that may be found in Lucretius, decisively refutes Skinner's claim that the concept of a state of nature was "wholly foreign" to Roman thinkers (Skinner 1998, 19).

Finally, Cicero appeared as an appealing source of guidance for reasons other than the actual content of his thought. As Grotius and Pufendorf sought to develop a theory that could resonate with Protestants and Catholics, it was advantageous that Cicero's appeal crossed sectarian battle lines. Already one of the most popular works surviving from antiquity, *De officiis* became especially ubiquitous with the spread of printing. Debts to Cicero were acknowledged by such Catholics as Erasmus and Thomas More, but also by Martin Luther, John Calvin, and Philip Melanchthon.

Grotius and Pufendorf make no secret of their reliance on Cicero; their major works contain hundreds of explicit references to him. In Grotius's case, Cicero is, in fact, both the first and the last authority invoked in his magnum opus (*De iure belli* 1.1.2, 3.20.7). Contemporary readers as well as modern scholars have noted that Cicero was at the heart of this new project. In particular, Straumann has illustrated the fundamental ways in which Cicero provides the basis for Grotius's system.[23] However, it appears that none has so far attempted to render an account of why Grotius and Pufendorf should have been so dependent on Cicero. After all, both Grotius and Pufendorf strongly prefer monarchical political regimes that bear little apparent similarity to Cicero's own republic. And yet behind this seeming opposition, it turns out that the political philosophy of Grotius and Pufendorf is an attempt to rework the Ciceronian dyad of natural law and popular sovereignty to derive the universally legitimate outlines of a commonwealth.

Natural Law and the State of Nature

Although Pufendorf wrote after Grotius and is considered by many (including himself) to be essentially a follower of Grotius, he made a far greater effort than his predecessor to present the new natural law project systematically. Pufendorf suggests that there are three sources of knowledge about moral uprightness (*honestum*):[24] reason (by which we know the natural law), civil law, and revelation (by which we learn divine law). The first applies to us as human beings, the second as citizens, the third as Christians (*De officio* 7). Sectarian division makes the last of these an unpromising source for

---

[23] Straumann 2015. See also Hochstrasser 2000, 57–58; Nussbaum 2000, 179.

[24] Note that Pufendorf and Grotius follow even Cicero's philosophical vocabulary. It is also noteworthy that the title of Pufendorf's most popular book, *De officio*, strongly recalls that of Cicero's own.

building a political philosophy acceptable to all.[25] Political divisions and the wide diversity of different laws and forms of government make the second similarly unsuitable. Pufendorf also adduces a deeper reason to look beyond civil law: just civil laws will ultimately be derived from natural law. We therefore must rely on knowledge universally accessible to unaided reason. In this, Pufendorf is following Cicero. For the same reasons, Grotius denounces conventionalism and relativism as obstacles to the establishment of a just peace.[26] Natural law is to be the basis of a universal political philosophy.

Citing Cicero, Grotius defines natural law as "dictate of right reason, shewing the moral turpitude, or moral necessity, of any act from its agreement or disagreement with a rational nature" (*De iure belli* 1.1.10).[27] Pufendorf accepts this definition verbatim but notes (rightly) that Grotius leaves rather vague what it would mean for something to be "in agreement . . . with a rational nature." He clarifies by suggesting that that phrase entails a recognition that "man has been made a social animal by the Creator" (*Elementa* 1.13.14). What Pufendorf means by this clarification, and the argument he produces to defend it, shall be explored. For now, it is simply enough to point out that this addendum, too, is in line with Cicero's view that it is precisely our rationality that makes us social.[28] Although he does not include it in his definition of natural law, Grotius agrees with this view of our natural sociality, paraphrasing Cicero (*Off.* 1.12), saying that even if human beings lacked for nothing, they would still be driven to associate with one another because of their desire for company (*De iure belli* prol.).

Given their view of human beings as naturally social, it may seem odd that Grotius and Pufendorf would find use in thinking about a state of nature.[29]

---

[25] Although both Grotius and Pufendorf deny that there is any contradiction between the dictates of reason and true revelation, only the former are available to all human beings qua human beings. Grotius even goes so far as to clarify that natural law is not subordinate *even to God*: "the Law of Nature is so unalterable, that it cannot be changed even by God himself. For although the power of God is infinite, yet there are some things, to which it does not extend." Grotius cites biblical text to demonstrate that "God himself suffers his actions to be judged by this rule" (*De iure belli* 1.1.10).

[26] Grotius selects the classical philosopher Carneades to be the mouthpiece for such moral skeptics, "so that we may not be obliged to deal with a crowd of opponents" (*De iure belli* prol. 5). In doing so, Grotius chooses for himself the same philosophical opponent as Cicero does in *De re publica*, instead of selecting any more contemporary figure. Zuckert sees Carneades as a stand-in for Machiavelli (Zuckert 1994, 127). See Straumann 2016, 55–63, for a persuasive argument that Grotius is seriously concerned with the classical conventionalist argument and his debt to Cicero in responding to it.

[27] Compare Cicero's definition in *Leg.* 1.18.

[28] *Off.* 1.12, 1.157. Note, however, that this posited natural sociality is not a claim about humans' natural *end state*, toward which human beings are moved by intrinsic processes; rather, it reflects a natural *need*, which may or may not be met, depending on human choice.

[29] Indeed, Zuckert points to Grotius's assumption of human sociality as evidence that he actually lacks a state of nature in his philosophy (Zuckert 1994, 137). But Grotius explicitly refers to one (*De iure belli* 2.5.9, 2.5.115). Grotius also does clearly imply a pre-political state (at least a hypothetical

Certainly, the assumed asociality of human beings in the philosophies of Hobbes or Rousseau seems more obviously compatible with the state of nature theorizing. In part, Pufendorf gets around this objection by denying (as Hobbes does) that humanity as a whole ever existed in such a state (*De iure naturae* 2.2.4). For Grotius, the state of nature is even still a reality in some places, such as on the high seas.[30] But, despite treating the state of nature as hypothetical, they argue we can use it to determine those rights, duties, and political arrangements that apply to all human beings without appealing to the support of divine revelation or conventional civil laws.

So what can we know about human beings in such a state? For that matter, how can we know it? On this latter question of method emerges one of the most significant differences between Grotius and Pufendorf. For Grotius, one powerful tool to distinguish what comes from nature and what comes from other sources (convention, revelation, etc.) is to look for what is common to human life universally, across cultures and times. For Pufendorf, our necessarily limited knowledge of the world makes such a method unreliable. He insists we must instead excavate the truth by imagining ourselves in the position of an individual without society and ask what such a person would know and do. For Pufendorf, this means that natural law is accessible to reason, but it does not mean that every individual must recognize it; knowledge of it is not simply inherent in us. A few first principles may be obvious to all, but everything deduced from those by rational methods is likewise included in natural law (*Elementa* 1.3.5).[31]

Despite this divergence of method, Grotius and Pufendorf agree about the first principle we discern in human beings: self-love. Both argue that the love of self is humanity's first and most natural source of motivation, expressed both negatively (our desire to avoid harm and death) and positively (our desire for things we find good and pleasurable). It is this quality that Pufendorf especially points to as a way of establishing that human sociability does not automatically allow us to assume human beings always live together in

---

one), in which rights were enjoyed that are no longer enjoyed with the formation of civil society (*De iure belli* 1.4.2). Such a position makes little sense without a state of nature doctrine. See Straumann for evidence that Grotius considered the state of nature not merely hypothetical but a real condition found, among other places, on the high seas (Straumann 2015, 147–156).

[30] This is only partly because of humanity's natural sociality. More concretely, since revelation does not conflict with reason, both claim that we *know* that humanity as a whole never lived in such a state through the testimony of the Bible.

[31] Locke would side with Pufendorf on this question. Cicero's preference for this position is also implied in the passage from *Pro Sestio* quoted earlier.

society (Pufendorf 1991, 132). Our wills, seeking out what we think is good, naturally lead us into conflict with others, where our love of self will always lead us to prefer our own good to that of others (Pufendorf 1991, 27). Once again, we see in this new natural law a recognition that human action is not oriented toward some natural end but rather arises from needs and desires, some of which may work counter to others.

Grotius and Pufendorf also argue that an awareness of God's existence is available to us in such a state—even without revelation. For Grotius, this is evident from the (alleged) universality of religious belief, found in all cultures and times. For Pufendorf, God is deducible from reasoning about causation to a first cause; and that God governs the universe he creates is revealed by the presence of order in it, that is, the regularity of cause and effect (Pufendorf 1991, 39).

From these two ideas, Grotius and Pufendorf argue that we can discern our first duties. Thus, the natural law for Grotius and Pufendorf functions like a human law—only it was not set down by human beings and applies universally, rather than to a specific people. This law consists of commands and prohibitions laid down by a sovereign (God) and backed by rewards and punishments for obedience or rebellion. This is a fundamentally different conception of natural law from that based on Aristotelian teleology. The law is not centrally defined by any natural ends. It takes into account natural human *needs*, but it does not posit them as some kind of end state toward which our motion naturally tends. For neither Grotius nor Pufendorf is it the role of the state to cultivate virtue in its citizens or guide them to the good life. In all of this, Grotius and Pufendorf follow the Ciceronian version of natural law, which likewise was analogous to human law and which generally avoided reference to natural ends, focusing instead on needs and duties.

For Pufendorf especially, the idea of God is essential for such a natural law to be coherent to us. Pufendorf argues that for something to be properly considered a law, it must not only be conformable to our reason as something in our self-interest, but it must also be commanded by a superior capable of rendering punishment for disobedience. Thus, only by recognizing God and God's will (or command) made manifest in our natural condition can we truly perceive natural law as *law*. Grotius is slightly more ambiguous about the place of God. He famously insists that the basics of his natural law doctrine "would still have some validity, even if we grant what cannot be granted without the greatest evil: that there is no God" (*De iure belli* prol. 11). This concession (the famous *etiamsi* of Grotius) has sparked considerable controversy and debate among readers about whether Grotius thus makes God superfluous to his doctrine of natural law.[32] However, Grotius seems merely to be asserting his strong anti-nominalist stance: that there are certain logical principles that even God cannot change without self-contradiction (*De iure belli* 1.1.5).[33] The law of nature is one such logical principle, in that it expresses conditions of life necessary to rational mortal creatures, in a way that could not be otherwise without contradiction.[34] Grotius still affirms that the natural law is, in fact, a divine law, with God's sanction ultimately supporting its commands. Moreover, in an argument that lays the ground-work for Locke's famous "workmanship argument," Grotius insists that God's legitimacy as universal lawgiver derives from his status as our omnipotent creator (*De iure belli* prol. 11).

As for how we can recognize God's command by reason and without the aid of divine revelation, Grotius and Pufendorf put forth the following ar-gument. From our awareness of our own self-love and our understanding of God as the cause of all things (two things already established by reason), we must conclude that we are obligated to preserve ourselves. After all, God, as a perfect creator, would not create in vain, so the universality and intensity of human self-love must reflect divine will. From our awareness that God, as creator of everything, is sovereign not only over each of us but over all other human beings as well, we see that we have obligations toward them, too. However, since our love of self is our strongest sensation, our duties to others must generally be assumed—at least provisionally—subordinate to our duty of self-preservation (*De iure belli* 1.2.1; *Elementa* 2.4.4). The atten-uated duties to others include not harming them or their property—except when there is no other hope of saving oneself. More than this, we must also help our fellows whenever this would not cost us unduly (although the limits

---

[32] St. Leger 1962. See also Haakonssen 1985, 248–249; Zuckert 1994, 121; Tuck 1982, 77–79.

[33] In his extensive commentary notes, Jean Barbeyrac proposes this reading: "this assertion is to be admitted only in the following sense: that the maxims of the law of nature are not merely arbitrary rules, but are founded on the nature of things, on the very constitution of man, from which certain relations result" (Grotius 2005, 89n1). It is unclear whether Barbeyrac means this to explain Grotius's position or to correct it. He also connects Grotius's position to Cicero's in *De legibus* that the divine is ultimately the source of obligation (Grotius 2005, 91n3).

[34] Many of the contemporary scholars who read Grotius's position as writing God out entirely of the justification of natural law translate Grotius's claim as saying that his natural law doctrine would hold just as much force without God as with. For instance, Tuck translates Grotius as saying that his natural law would "take place" even if God did not exist (Tuck 1982, 77). But the Latin reads, *locum aliquem haberent* ("it would have *some* place"; emphasis added). Grotius thus implies that *some* of the force of his claims does depend on the deity. God's existence is not irrelevant to Grotius's doctrine; its force would diminish without God to support it. Grotius merely claims that its force would not di-minish to nothing in God's absence.

of this duty remain unclear). To illustrate this principle, both rely on Cicero's list of examples of such aid: sharing one's fire, providing advice, and so on (Pufendorf 1991, 65; *De iure belli* 1.2.11). The first two laws of nature are thus (1) to preserve oneself but (2) to do it in such a way that does not conflict with the preservation of others (*Elementa* 2.4.4).[35]

Pufendorf argues that we must also accept all other human beings as "our natural equals" (*De iure naturae* 3.2.1). In part, this equality derives from a recognition of a simple fact: our common weakness. Pufendorf cites Hobbes's argument that each of us is powerful and intelligent enough to kill any other, given the right opportunity (*De iure naturae* 3.2.2). However, Pufendorf argues that Hobbes's argument for natural equality is insufficient. Equality has a deeper normative basis. We all also have a natural equality deriving from our equal *dignity* as rational creatures subject to the same ultimate sovereign, God, and thereby to the same natural law. Thus, we are entitled to say to each other: "I am not a dog or a beast, but as much a man as you" (*De iure naturae* 3.2.1). In this idea—that we have a certain moral equality in our shared rationality and subjection to natural law—Grotius and Pufendorf again follow Cicero, who posited a universal baseline of dignity based on human rationality.[36]

For the same reasons we possess natural equality, a state of nature is also a condition of natural liberty. Without a natural (earthly) superior, human beings are free to do whatever their will leads them to, as long as they are physically capable of doing it (*De iure elli* 1.2.5; Pufendorf 1991, 117). The fact that God plants in us not only reason but a free will suggests that this liberty, like equality, is not only a fact but has something morally valuable in it (*Elementa* 2.2.5). This liberty, as the freedom to do as we please and set our own life course insofar as we do not harm others, is Ciceronian.

From these two positions arises the clearest and most important practical distinction between the Ciceronian natural law tradition and that deriving from Aristotle: in the former, there are no natural masters and no natural slaves (*Elementa* 1.3.7).[37] Pufendorf states the position especially clearly. Against Hobbes, he accepts Aristotle's insistence that there are wide natural inequalities of mind and body among human beings: "thus much indeed is

---

[35] These principles will form the basis of Locke's natural law doctrine as well.

[36] *Off.* 1.106; *Leg.* 1.29, 1.59.

[37] Standing behind this practical distinction, however, is still the deeper theoretical divergence: whether the natural law expresses inherent and natural ends for beings (Aristotle) or whether it functions like an ordinary law for all rational creatures, based on commands and prohibitions backed by sanctions (Cicero).

most evident, that some men are endued with such a happiness of wit and parts as enables them not only to provide for themselves and their own affairs, but to direct and govern others. And that some again are so extremely stupid and heavy as to be unfit to govern themselves" (*De iure naturae* 3.2.8). Yet he denies the Aristotelian conclusion that this implies any right for some to rule others: "yet it would be the greatest absurdity imaginable to believe, that nature actually invests the wise with the sovereignty over the weak and imprudent, or with a right of forcing them to submit and obey against their wills" (*De iure naturae* 3.2.8).[38] Superior knowledge or virtue may make a person a better ruler, but it does not *entitle* that person to rule; it does not give that person a *right* of governing. As a result, it is "easy to discover the absurdity of that opinion, derived from the ancient Greeks, of some men's being slaves by nature." The only way to save the Aristotelian position is to rework it so that includes consent (*De iure naturae* 3.2.8).[39]

This is not to say that either Grotius or Pufendorf delegitimizes slavery completely; it is possible to choose to alienate your freedom to someone else. Grotius at one point seems to contradict Pufendorf's position against the naturalness of slavery. He cites Aristotle's distinction of natural slaves as an argument legitimizing absolutist government (*De iure belli* 1.3.8). However, as Grotius continues, he makes it clear that he is simply accepting that some people are less wise and well suited to govern themselves than others. This does not, however, *entitle* anyone to rule them. Grotius cites Cicero to explain that people must *choose* whether to give up their power and to whom (*De iure belli* 1.3.8). Thus, without admitting it, as Pufendorf later does, Grotius, too, reworks the Aristotelian position to include consent. The passage he cites from Cicero, however, does not actually justify such concessions but critiques them as examples of the people falling in with demagogues. Here we can see how Grotius manipulates Ciceronian natural law to justify an anti-republican conclusion.[40]

More profoundly, this abandonment of the idea of natural slavery also entails a rejection of Aristotle's notion of distributive justice, whereby one is entitled to different goods and even to political rule by merit or desert if one

---

[38] Lee and Straumann both illustrate the heavy reliance of Grotius on Roman law for his conceptual framework. Central to this framework is the Roman legal distinction between slaves and free persons (Straumann 2015; Lee 2016, 257–259). That Grotius nevertheless refuses to ground that distinction in nature suggests a willingness to break from Roman law when it violates the fundamental premises of Ciceronian natural law.

[39] See *Leg.* 1.30.

[40] Cf. *Off.* 2.4.

is outstandingly virtuous (*Nicomachean Ethics* 5.3; *Politics* 3.13).[41] Grotius and Pufendorf thereby reject a central feature of Aristotelian political philosophy: that the just regime will be ruled by those who deserve to rule. In doing so, they employ Ciceronian logic to move in the direction of later liberalism, which would likewise give up any expectation that a just political regime should ensure distributive justice of this sort. Grotius and Pufendorf happily enlist Aristotle throughout their works, but from this it should be clear that the core of their political theory—the source of legitimate political authority—is un-Aristotelian and thoroughly Ciceronian.

To return to the main line of the argument, what would life for human beings in the hypothetical state of nature look like? Grotius and Pufendorf give considerable thought to the condition of property in such a state. Integrating both Ciceronian and biblical accounts, both agree that the world was given to humanity in common (*De iure* 4.4.4). Therefore, all the natural world was once common property. In such a state, no one has a right, properly so called, to private property; Grotius and Pufendorf follow Cicero (unlike Hobbes) in conceiving of rights as existing only in political society.[42] However, we need to eat and drink in order to live. Thus, both Grotius and Pufendorf understand that a human being in such a state has a moral permission to "use things not claimed and to consume them up to the limit of his needs" (*De iure belli* 1.2.5).[43] Pufendorf posits that humanity would tacitly but universally consent to such an arrangement (*De iure naturae* 4.4.9). The alternative is starvation. Both Grotius and Pufendorf rely on an argument provided by Cicero to illustrate how such an arrangement both is and is not like a system of private property. Grotius writes: "this Cicero has explained in his third book, on the bounds of good and evil [*De finibus*], by comparing the world to a theatre, in which the seats are common property, yet every spectator claims that which he occupies, for the time being, as his own" (*De iure belli* 1.2.2).[44]

Imagining ourselves in the state of nature—dispersed and enjoying our equality, freedom, and usufruct property—Pufendorf acknowledges that we might at first find superficial attractions to such a state. But those attractions are far outweighed by the inconveniences. First, even though the law of nature

[41] Grotius makes this break with Aristotle explicit (*De iure belli* 1.1.8). Cf. *Politics* 3.13, where Aristotle claims that outstanding virtue would entitle one to rule.

[42] This will be discussed further.

[43] See also Buckle 1991, 29.

[44] Cf. *Fin.* 288. Straumann sees Grotius in particular as a link between Cicero and Locke on the issue of property rights (Straumann 2015, 179–180).

applies to us all, not everyone recognizes it or chooses to live according to it. Man is a fallen creature, and the commandment "Thou shalt not kill" would be superfluous, unless we were the sort of creatures who are inclined at times to kill one another (Pufendorf 1991, 10). Without political society, our lives and our limited property would be totally insecure against depredation by those who defy the natural law.[45]

This is not to say that Grotius and Pufendorf agree with Hobbes that humanity's natural state is one characterized primarily by war. Grotius calls on Aristotle and Cicero as authorities for the proposition that peace is the more fundamental condition of humankind (De iure belli 1.1.1). Pufendorf responds explicitly to Hobbes, suggesting that "the very equality of strength" that Hobbes sees as leading to the bellum omnium contra omnes, in fact, inclines us to peace: "for no sane man likes to be in a fight with an equal unless he is driven to it by necessity or encouraged by an opportunity for success . . . both lives are exposed to danger, surely neither gains as much from victory as is lost by the one who is killed" (De iure naturae 2.2.8).[46] Nevertheless, there would be enough such conflict and insecurity about the possibility of conflict to make life in the state of nature precarious. In addition, even those of us inclined to obey the natural law may contribute to the violence, poverty, and waste of the state of nature. Without a political superior, we are forced to be the judges and avengers of violations against ourselves. But we are inevitably poor adjudicators in our own case and thus liable to punish more than is just or in situations where punishment is not called for at all, prompting cycles of violence (Elementa 2.5.1–2).[47]

Finally, we must consider that the fact of our weakness is not only relative to one another but also absolute. Following Cicero, Grotius and Pufendorf acknowledge that the earth does not readily yield its bounty to the unaided industry of a single individual. In order to achieve anything like a comfortable existence for ourselves, we require the help of others. Moreover, we crave the company of others for its own sake. Thus, paraphrasing Cicero, Pufendorf writes, "man can render the greatest help to man after the Great and Good

[45] Pufendorf anticipates that someone might ask if natural law as he defines it requires a superior capable of punishing violators, how could there be common violation? Pufendorf notes that God as sovereign will punish the violators, but the distance of that punishment necessarily leaves some undeterred, as is still the case for a smaller number in society (Elementa 2.5.1). Locke will develop this idea further.

[46] Here Pufendorf lays the groundwork for an argument that would more famously be deployed by Montesquieu and Rousseau.

[47] Consider again Cicero's description of the barbarism of the state of nature in Pro Sestio.

God."[48] These two facts together constitute Pufendorf's proof of humanity's sociality: we need others to live, and we would choose to be with them for the sake of companionship even if we did not need them.

So Pufendorf summarizes the situation of human beings in the state of nature:

> Man, then, is an animal with an intense concern for his own preservation, needy by himself, incapable of protection without the help of his fellows, and very well fitted for the mutual provision of benefits. Equally, however, he is at the same time malicious, aggressive, easily provoked and as willing as he is able to inflict harm on others. (Pufendorf 1991, 35)

So far, this is very compatible with Machiavelli's pessimistic evaluation of humanity's situation. But whereas Machiavelli then recommends an amoral orientation where one does everything one can to acquire power and subdue others to one's own ends, Pufendorf and Grotius instead turn in a different direction, informed by Cicero's ideas of sociality:

> The conclusion is: in order to be safe, it is necessary for him to be sociable; that is to join forces with men like himself and so conduct himself towards them that they are not given even a plausible excuse for harming him, but rather become willing to preserve and promote his advantages.[49] The laws of this sociality [socialitas], laws which teach one how to conduct oneself to become a useful member of human society, are called natural laws. On this basis, it is evident that the fundamental natural law is: every man ought to do as much as he can to cultivate and preserve sociality. (Pufendorf 1991, 35–36)

Thus, just as Cicero does, Pufendorf finds our fundamental duty according to natural law to be the preservation of human sociability. Moreover, just as Cicero renders it, this duty is not really selfless but rather born out of our deepest self-interest.[50]

---

[48] Cf. *Off.* 2.11. Locke will repeat Pufendorf's term, "Great and Good God" (*deus optimus maximus*), causing some readers to read this as implicit paganism. These readers do not recognize Pufendorf's mediation of Cicero here. See chapter 5.

[49] We might see in this expression an early version of Adam Smith's insight that the most efficient way to get others to become useful to us is to make ourselves useful to them. Cf. Hawley 2019.

[50] Pufendorf distinguishes strongly his view from that of Aristotle. According to Pufendorf, we are not natural "political animals" but are instead constantly tempted to violate the conditions of political life (*De iure naturae* 7.1.4).

The Politics of Natural Law

To achieve such a political society, it is not enough for independent individuals to form loose associations for mutual protection.[51] The natural conflicts of our wills with each other and the human tendency to prefer free-riding over contribution to common defense would make such an arrangement impossible. What is needed is a "perpetual union of the wills of all" and "some power [*potestas*], which shall be directly before their eyes, capable of inflicting suffering on those who oppose the common interest." Here the theories of sovereignty of Bodin and Hobbes seem to inform the logic. The only way to achieve all of this is for each to submit his will to the will of one man or assembly, such that what it wills can be taken as the will of all. Because of natural human freedom and equality, such an arrangement can only legitimately take place through free agreement, a contract: "no sovereignty can actually be established, unless some human deed or covenant precede. Nor does a natural fitness for governing presently make a man governor over another, who is as naturally adapted to subjection, nor . . . is it therefore lawful for me to force it upon him against his inclination" (*De iure naturae* 3.2.8).[52] The Grotian-Pufendorfian conception of the contract represents a formalizing of Cicero's position that the legitimacy of government depends on agreement. As Michael Zuckert says, "Grotius was not the first political philosopher to incorporate covenant or agreement in his doctrine, but, I would venture to say, he elevated it to a role it had never previously held in the tradition of natural law."[53] But, while Cicero's republic institutionalizes recurring mechanisms for the people's consent to be given or withheld (the ballot, assemblies, and the tribunate), Grotius and Pufendorf limit the expression of consent to a far narrower moment in time.

The state that emerges from this agreement is conceived of as a moral person (*persona*) composed of the citizens that make it up (Pufendorf 1991, 136–137).[54] For this concept of representation, that the sovereign is an artificial person that represents the people, Pufendorf's apparent proximate source is Hobbes. But here even Hobbes—the great critic of classical republicanism—admits to be following Cicero in this at least: "a *Person*, is the same that an actor is . . . and to *Personate*, is to *Act*, or *Represent* himselfe,

---

[51] Of the sort imagined by Robert Nozick (1974).
[52] Note again the rejection of Aristotle's position.
[53] Zuckert 1994, 124.
[54] See also Skinner 2002, 61–62.

or another, and he that acteth another is said to beare his Person, or act in his name; in which sence *Cicero* useth it where he saies, *Unus sustineo tres Personae, Mei, Adversarii, & Judicis*" (*Leviathan* 16).[55]

The political regime that arises here seems to have nearly the same absolutist quality of a Hobbesian leviathan. The subjects are supposed to have alienated their wills to a sovereign (they are not themselves sovereign anymore) whose decisions are final and to be taken as their own. But there are crucial differences. Hobbes sees natural human equality and freedom as mere facts; they function in many ways as an obstacle to the ultimate goal of peace. As a result, for Hobbes, civil society can be understood as substituting constraint and inequality for natural freedom and equality. But, for Pufendorf, freedom and equality are normatively important human characteristics. They therefore constitute firm limits to what such a regime can legitimately do. Coercion, as a violation of natural law, is an illegitimate way to get a person to consent to the contract, and anyone who dissents from it retains his natural freedom and remains outside the newly created state (Pufendorf 1991, 136). More important, because the decision to form a political union takes place among equals, Pufendorf insists that there are, in fact, two agreements, not Hobbes's singular pact. The first unites all into one body ready for a state. The people must self-form as a discrete political unit. After choosing a form of government, however, the people must then make a new contract, between the rulers and the ruled. By this agreement the rulers bind themselves "to provide for the common security and safety, the rest bind themselves to obedience" (Pufendorf 1991, 137).

This idea of a second contract makes for a crucial distinction from Hobbes. Hobbes vehemently denies that there is any agreement between the sovereign and the people and, with it, any duties that the people could compel the sovereign to perform. In his view, the social pact takes place only among the people: to obey the sovereign. The people alienate all of their rights (except for immediate self-defense) to the sovereign. Justice is then whatever the sovereign determines it to be.[56]

Grotius and Pufendorf, however, remain within the Ciceronian framework, seeking to unite natural law and popular sovereignty.[57] Taking free consent to the contract seriously, they establish the principle of popular

---

[55] See *De or.* 2.102. See Hawley 2020a for more on Cicero's theory of *personae*.

[56] See Hobbes, *Leviathan* 7–20.

[57] Here they break not only with Hobbes but also with Bodin, who explicitly rejects the Ciceronian view that some kind of agreement about right is necessary to establish sovereignty. See Lee 2016, 172.

sovereignty on meaningful—and not merely formal—ground. All legitimate political power rightly derives from the free consent of the people. But the grounds for that principle derive from natural law; it is natural law that demands the contract, and it is natural law that sets the conditions for its acceptance (equality and the absence of coercion).

It is important to see how this argument, derived from Cicero's premises, leads Grotius and Pufendorf to oppose four different and very influential sorts of arguments about the legitimate source of political power. The difference with Hobbes is clear: obedience cannot be coerced, nor is the determination of moral questions such as the nature of justice within the purview of a political authority. But, by establishing centrality of natural freedom and equality, Grotius and Pufendorf oppose at the same time both the divine right of kings and the Aristotelian argument of distributive justice; neither noble birth nor superior wisdom and virtue entitle one to rule. Finally, Bodin's general indifference to the source of legitimate sovereignty is also ruled out. For Grotius and Pufendorf, political authority depends on real consent.

Indeed, the very right of the state to enforce its laws and to punish violators derives from the people who make it up. Grotius explains that the state has no rights that it does not acquire from individuals, which means that the right of punishment must naturally have belonged to individuals originally: "just as every right of the magistrate comes to him from the state, so has the same right come to the state from private individuals. . . . Since no one is able to transfer a thing he never possessed, it is evident that the right of chastisement was held by private persons before it was held by the state."[58]

However, for Grotius and Pufendorf, popular sovereignty has its full effective reality only for a moment. Whereas Cicero's commonwealth reflects the principle of popular sovereignty in its ordinary operations: through elections, the tribunate, popular assemblies, and so on, Grotius's and Pufendorf's people assent to the second contract and then nearly vanish as a political force. As Grotius explains, the people may choose to give up all of their power to some person or body for a variety of reasons (*De iure belli* 1.3.8). Grotius does concede that they *may* choose to give up only some of their power and rights, while retaining the rest. Grotius therefore establishes the possibility of a still more limited government. But he does not dwell long

---

[58] As translated by Tuck 1982, 62.

on this alternative.[59] Even in cases where the people completely surrender their rights, the specter of the people as originally sovereign remains in one important way, as will be discussed. But overall, Grotius and Pufendorf both clearly prioritize the demands of natural law over the claims of popular sovereignty—or, indeed, sovereignty of any kind. On their construal, a sovereign's will is not subject to any *human* superior but is not exempt from the demands of the natural law (*De iure belli* 1.3.7).[60] So even an absolute sovereign king or assembly may not legitimately break a promise, since natural law demands the keeping of promises (*De iure belli* 1.3.16).[61]

On the grounds that human beings have equal moral dignity and are under natural law even in the state of nature, Pufendorf and Grotius are able to avoid Hobbes's relativism and positivism. Instead, they follow Cicero in accepting a universally applicable framework for justice. Since the basic rules of justice apply to human beings as human beings, there is a standard external to the state by which to judge and critique it. Rights, as a moral quality whereby we can justly command a person or possess a thing, are not alienated by forming this compact (as they are in Hobbes's construal). On the contrary, it is only by forming political society that rights come into meaningful existence.[62] Pufendorf likens the original social pact to a bridge, connecting our limited duties in the state of nature to the more complex web of rights and duties that govern us in society (Pufendorf 1991, 68). The latter derive from our consent, and some may be specific to our particular political community. However, these new rights and duties are still natural in an important sense. Stephen Buckle explains that "they are natural in just the sense that the law of nature is natural: that is, they are either necessary to peaceful social existence, or possess a rational utility to that end."[63] For this reason, consent is not all that is required for a good and just political order. The institutions and actions consented to must serve the ultimate purpose of

---

[59] This is another difference from Hobbes, who insists that the act of alienation be total (with the exception of the right of immediate self-defense). English Grotians take this alternative and develop it further.

[60] In this, their construal resembles Bodin's.

[61] In direct contradiction to Machiavelli, and in line with Cicero's universalism, Grotius insists that promise-keeping is an obligation we have even to enemies (*De iure belli* 3.20–23). Cf. *Prince* 18, *Off.* 3.90–107.

[62] For this definition of rights, see *Elementa* 1.8.1. Pufendorf insists that there are no rights, properly understood, in the state of nature, because the persons or objects over which one could have a right are under no obligation to present themselves for the use of whoever claims the right (Buckle 1991, 80). Grotius does not share Pufendorf's technical exclusion of rights from the state of nature, but he agrees that rights are only ensured in society (*De iure belli* 1.1.4).

[63] Buckle 1991, 81.

advancing human good through cooperative society. This echoes one aspect of Cicero's idea of a *res publica*, which is formed in part out of an agreement about justice—the justice agreed upon must be true justice. But it becomes apparent that Grotius and Pufendorf view the people's active maintenance of their sovereignty as most likely to be an obstacle to the application of this justice.

Citizens in entering society therefore do suffer a loss of their natural liberty. Duties to obey just commands from the sovereign, to pay taxes, and to interact civilly with their fellows now bear upon them. Perhaps most significantly, citizens must be willing to risk their lives in defense of the community. Grotius and Pufendorf have a much easier time explaining this duty than does Hobbes. For Hobbes, our entire purpose in joining the social contract is to secure our lives, which makes it difficult to explain why a person would then risk his life on behalf of it. But, for Grotius and Pufendorf, our desire for our self-preservation is only one of the causes that lead us to joining society. We also have a natural desire for community, *and* our service to that community is commanded to us by God through natural law, who can render far greater punishments for our defection than earthly suffering.

The citizens' duties are joined by new rights they enjoy and also the corresponding duties of their new sovereigns. In society, what formerly existed as a loose moral permission to *use* things to satisfy our needs becomes a real right to keep and hold property (*De iure belli* 2.2.2). Citizens have rights to equal treatment and protection under the law. The concept of *ius* here builds upon the usage from Roman law and Cicero's thought that conceives of subjective rights—rights a person holds. Armed with these rights, citizens may not be punished for private thoughts or actions that harm no one (Pufendorf 1991, 160–161).[64] Nor can they be taxed unduly. The government has the right to tax only for the purposes of defense and to ensure the prosperity of the people (Pufendorf 1991, 153).[65] As for sovereigns, they have an extensive set of duties: to uphold justice fairly and impartially, to cultivate virtue in themselves and forsake idle pleasures, to appoint honest and competent individuals as ministers, and so on (Pufendorf 1991, 151–154). All of these duties flow from the sovereign's ultimate duty of advancing the common interest,

---

[64] Straumann points out that in construing justice as Cicero does (i.e., as concerned with providing rules for behavior that prevent harm), Grotius explicitly again rejects Aristotelian distributive justice (Straumann 2015, 119–129).

[65] In an argument with important ramifications for the next century, Pufendorf insists that without prior agreement, colonists cannot be taxed for the debts of the mother country (Pufendorf 1994, 266).

Pufendorf argues, citing Cicero's famous principle, "the safety of the people is the highest law" (Pufendorf 1991, 151).[66]

A sovereign's failure to adhere to these duties would entail significant consequences. Perhaps most unlike Hobbes, Grotius and Pufendorf articulate a (very limited) right of rebellion. The sovereign holds power not as a personal possession (as Bodin had argued was the case for many monarchies) but as a kind of usufruct.[67] Although Grotius and Pufendorf insist that citizens must bear a certain amount of ill treatment or poor government, they agree that a sovereign who makes himself the enemy of the people justifies their rising against him.[68] In this, they follow Cicero's famous justification for tyrannicide, which he derives from natural law.[69] But the great weight of their arguments focuses on limiting the scope of this permission to rebel. Grotius establishes quickly that we have no obligation to obey the commands of a sovereign that violate the natural law (*De iure belli* 1.4.1). This seems to be a significant limitation on political authority—and in fact, it does illustrate again the clear priority Grotius places on natural law over sovereignty of any sort. But Grotius denies that this right of non-obedience is the same as a right of resistance. It functions more as the right of a conscientious objector—to refuse to obey but not to actively resist unjust commands. He denies absolutely the right of private persons, as individuals, to make such resistance, for doing so would ultimately work to violate or defeat the very purpose of the natural law—human society (which could not survive if every citizen could, on the prompting of conscience, rise against the political authority) (*De iure belli* 1.4.2). Ultimately, it is only in the direst necessity, when an absolute sovereign designs to destroy the nation, that Grotius find a right to violently resist. In cases where the monarch does not hold all the sovereign power, however, Grotius acknowledges a wider set of situations that might justify resistance (*De iure belli* 1.4.11).[70]

Tuck identifies this right (along with property) as one of the two anti-absolutist elements of this political theory.[71] In fact, the complex web of rights and duties that Pufendorf and Grotius depict as the essence of a just political order means that the entire system is non-absolutist. However, it is true that the right of rebellion does form the ultimate moral guarantee of

---

[66] Compare to *Leg.* 3.8.
[67] Lee 2011, 386.
[68] *Elementa* 2.5.22.
[69] *Off.* 3.19, 3.23, 3.32.
[70] These exceptions would prove relevant to some English Whigs.
[71] See Tuck 1982, 79.

all the others. There is no other feature of the regime required by natural law that would give the people a moral regular means of ensuring good government and by which their consent could be renewed.

Finally, because the natural rights and duties apply to all human beings once they have entered society, there are laws of mutual obligation between states as well. Indeed, the central thrust of Grotius's work in particular was the articulation of international laws and norms. Both Grotius and Pufendorf thus also disagree with Hobbes that the international realm ought to be characterized primarily as a state of war (*De iure naturae* 2.2.9; *De iure belli* 1.1.1). In suggesting that sovereigns, too, have obligations toward one another, Grotius aims at a kind of nascent cosmopolitanism, whereby the countries of the world coexist peacefully in mutual cooperation. Sovereigns' mutual responsibilities stretch from the rights of envoys to the proper conduct of wars. The attempt to stitch together an international order that would bind a contentious state system together under the principles of justice is the particular contribution of Grotius to the development of modern cosmopolitanism. But, as Martha Nussbaum points out, Grotius's dependence on Cicero to achieve this end makes Cicero the true originator of this effort.[72]

In all of these arguments, it seems, Grotius and Pufendorf were heavily indebted to Cicero's thought. From the framework for natural law to the fundamental duty of sociability, rights emerging only in society, anti-relativism/positivism, and, finally, cosmopolitanism, they draw upon Cicero's framework to present a new normative theory of politics that might gain acceptance in the new Europe. In this way, Grotius and Pufendorf abandon Aristotelian natural law and the Aristotelian model for politics. They still make great use of Aristotle's insights, but the basis of their new political doctrine would be wholly incompatible with Aristotle—thus illustrating by contrasts the great gulf between Aristotelian and Ciceronian politics. Grotius and Pufendorf follow Cicero in denying that humans are naturally political and, more important, that there are natural masters and natural slaves. As a result, they also abandon the idea that political justice requires that the worse obey the better. Instead, they follow Cicero in establishing a requirement of consent for all political authority, implying a natural moral equality among human beings, grounded in a hypothetical state of nature. The natural law they appeal to offers commands and prohibitions but does not direct us to our telos

---

[72] Nussbaum 2000.

or perfection. Rather, it provides structure and order to our relationships with others, preventing harm and enabling mutually beneficial cooperation.

In one important particular, however, they diverge from Cicero: the issue of republican government. Neither Pufendorf nor Grotius excludes democracy and aristocracy as legitimate forms of government. Pufendorf, however, rules out mixed government as inherently unstable and prone to collapse into one of the three simple forms (*De iure naturae* 7.5.10). It is not certain whether either read Machiavelli's account of turbulent, violent republics, but Pufendorf at least witnessed from afar the chaos brought about through English republican aspirations in the English Civil War.[73] He condemns "a certain class of writers"—contemporary and classical republicans—who insist that all legitimate government is popular government. Without ruling out the legitimacy of other regimes, both Grotius and Pufendorf conclude that monarchy is the most effective form of government for achieving the ends of peaceful coexistence and cooperation that natural law demands. They thereby drastically reduce the practical application of the doctrine of popular sovereignty.

Grotius's and Pufendorf's desire to establish peace leads them then to abandon one of the fundamental conclusions of Cicero's natural law teaching. They reject the idea that the moral equality of human beings need necessarily translate into anything like institutions that offer all some voice in the running of the public business (*De iure naturae* 3.2.2). Faced with the apparent tension between realizing in practice the demands of natural law or the people's claim to popular sovereignty, they minimize the latter (without eliminating it), to achieve a stable politics according to the natural law.

An English Commonwealth

The rise (and fall) of English republicanism took place at roughly the same time as the emergence of the new natural law tradition, flourishing between the publication of Grotius's *On the Law of War and Peace* and Pufendorf's *On the Law of Nature and of Nations*. Unlike the natural law theorists, who formed a discrete project in which Pufendorf identifies himself clearly as the follower and expositor of Grotius's system, the English republicans

---

[73] And there is evidence that at least close associates of the two read Machiavelli. See Tully 1980, 7.

cannot be characterized as a single coherent project of political thought. The movement's intellectual leaders spanned political orientations from limited monarchists to outright advocates of regicide and from defenders of aristocratically dominated mixed regimes to proponents of radical democratic reform. Few appear primarily as political philosophers, making truly profound or novel contributions to the history of political philosophy, but rather they are active political actors. As such, many of them adopted different and even inconsistent positions as the political situation changed. Perhaps the most extreme example of this was Marchamont Nedham, who began his career as a partisan of Parliament, became a royalist, wrote propaganda on behalf of the Commonwealth after the execution of Charles I, and finally returned to defending monarchy after the Restoration.[74]

Most of the other individuals making up the loose constellation of figures considered English republicans—such as James Harrington, John Milton, Algernon Sidney, and Henry Neville—maintained greater consistency than Nedham, but their writings generally reveal them to be primarily concerned with the particular political developments going on around them. As such, it is impossible to discuss their works together as forming a single political philosophy, nor is it the purpose of this section to do full justice to the diversity of their thought and its antecedents.[75] Rather, I aim to show that most of these figures saw themselves as inheritors or revivers of a republican outlook—an outlook for which Cicero appears as perhaps the most universally accepted authority. There is a general tendency among the thinkers (and even among the more purely political actors) of the English republican movement to treat Cicero as a common resource for the practice of republican politics. In particular, they appeal to Cicero as the source of the doctrine of popular sovereignty, the argument that all legitimate political power flows from the people. In this, the English republicans take the opposite horn of the dilemma from Grotius and Pufendorf. Whereas Grotius and Pufendorf minimized the role of popular sovereignty in order to secure a politics faithful to the demands of natural law, the English republicans downplayed (although often without entirely abandoning it) the concept of natural law to foreground the concept of popular sovereignty as the foundation of legitimate politics and the cornerstone of liberty.

---

[74] Worden 1995, 315–316, provides an account of Nedham's colorful career.
[75] There are several large scholarly works that attempt to do precisely this, such as Sullivan 2004; Rahe 2006; Skinner 2002; Skinner 1998; Pocock 2009.

In this choice of the English republicans, the influence of Machiavelli appears far more clearly than it does with Grotius and Pufendorf. As illustrated in chapter 3, Machiavelli vigorously challenged the notion that healthy republican government could be compatible with the limitations of universal moral norms. He preferred to unleash the tumultuous power of the people in the service of a militant republic unconstrained by anything like a doctrine of natural law. Many scholars of this period have gone to great lengths to demonstrate that Machiavelli's particular version of republicanism dominated the English movement.[76] Machiavelli did prove to be an important inspiration for some of the leading republicans, especially Harrington and his friend Neville. The former cited Machiavelli dozens of times in his major political works, and the latter even faked a letter purported to be written by Machiavelli in order to show this republican hero as sympathetic to the Protestant sensibilities of the English revolutionaries.[77]

But there is some difficulty in demonstrating that Machiavelli is the central inspiring figure of the overall project of the English republicans. Even Harrington and Neville deviate quite substantially from some of Machiavelli's core doctrines. Other figures ignore or explicitly reject Machiavelli. Milton's deeply Christian—if unorthodox—republicanism has almost nothing in common with Machiavelli's impious and irreverent philosophy.[78] For his part, Nedham displays a good working knowledge of Machiavelli and credits his analysis on occasion, but his general attitude toward Machiavelli is hostile, siding explicitly with Cicero over Machiavelli on the central normative questions of politics.[79]

Indeed, much of the argument for crediting Machiavelli as the central inspiration for English republicanism lies in the simple fact that the movement in question *was* republican and so was impressed with classical Rome—its stories, heroes, and institutions. Since those are also Machiavelli's own interests, it may seem as though the English writers must have derived their

---

[76] Especially noteworthy here are Pocock (2009) and Skinner (1998). To a certain extent, Sullivan also falls into this camp, although she takes far greater pains to illustrate the ways in which the English republicans rejected some of Machiavelli's core arguments.

[77] Harrington 1977, 871; Neville 1691.

[78] As Rahe puts it, "at no time did John Milton allow the thinking of Niccolò Machiavelli to shape in any fundamental way the manner in which he wrote about, defended, and surreptitiously tried to guide the nascent English republic" (Rahe 2008, 104).

[79] Pocock, the most insistent advocate for the Machiavellian roots of English republicanism, is forced to present an arduous story of the circuitous route by which "patterns of Machiavellian thought" (note: not necessarily *Machiavelli's* thought but rather something mediated by a number of minor authors) became "domiciled" in an England that Pocock himself admits was dominated by a political and conceptual framework incompatible with it (Pocock 2009, 333–348).

insights from the Florentine. But interested readers in the first half of the seventeenth century in England possessed a far clearer and more direct link to genuinely classical political thought (especially of the republican variety) in the form of widely published works of the Greeks and Romans both in the original languages and in translation. The English republican movement saw a flourishing of interest in and appeals to these ancient defenders of liberty. Among the Greeks, Aristotle was often invoked. More important still were the Romans. Historians such as Livy, Tacitus, and Sallust enjoyed wide popularity. But the works of Cicero, the only great Roman *theorist* of republican liberty, were even more widely read. Although anyone who attended university during this period would have read his works (along with the others mentioned) in Latin, the late sixteenth century saw the publication of an English translation of *De officiis* that went through at least five editions and became a bestseller. Dozens of editions of Cicero's *Philippics* were also published during this period.[80]

The influence of Machiavelli's distinctive version of republicanism on the English republicans as a group seems strongest in (some of) the latter's desire to realize a far greater political role of the common people than was commonly allotted to them. But, unlike Machiavelli, the English republicans tend not to advance this goal simply by appealing to the greater strength—especially for war-making—of a popular commonwealth. Instead, they insist (in a manner wholly foreign to Machiavelli) that the key political question is the legitimate source of authority, and they follow Cicero by answering that question by appealing to the concept of popular sovereignty. In so doing, they also revive an interest in the question of what liberty means for a citizen in a republic that encompasses a whole nation, instead of an ancient Greek or Renaissance Italian city state. Here, too, we find a number of English republicans engaging with Cicero as they attempt to link the common liberty of popular sovereignty with the private liberty enjoyed by individual citizens. Despite their disagreements and ideological divergence, these thinkers largely share an ideal of liberty according to which citizens can only ensure their ability to live freely, secure in their bodies and property, by retaining a meaningful say in the affairs of government. In other words, individual liberty is analogous to and dependent on political liberty.[81]

---

[80] Skinner 2002, 313.

[81] Skinner refers to these individuals as "neo-Romans" instead of "republicans," precisely because some of them are open to *some* elements of monarchical government (Skinner 1998, 11). Nonetheless, following Cicero's definition of a *res publica* (which can likewise tolerate monarchical elements), I retain the more common usage of referring to these individuals as "republicans."

Cicero as Republican Symbol

The period between the outbreak of the English Civil War and the Restoration was politically chaotic. Whereas most of Europe had experienced the Wars of Religion through the rough but theoretically simple dichotomy of Protestant against Catholic, England presented to the world the spectacle of vicious conflict *between* Protestants. At times, it appeared to many of the parties that the question of the true, authentic Protestant regime was at stake in the conflict. Thus, some writers, such as Milton, preferred to couch their arguments primarily in a biblical and theological register. But the demands of political polemic meant that narrowly sectarian arguments might fail to move an audience of heterogeneous religious beliefs. Thus, for reasons similar to those of Grotius and Pufendorf, English republicans found that pre-Christian classical authors occasionally could function as commonly acceptable authorities—less decisive authorities than the word of God but also less religiously controversial. Many of the English republicans were willing to cite any authority in support of their arguments, without regard to the potential tensions between their sources' views. Aristotle, Cicero, Livy, Tacitus, the Bible, Roman law, Machiavelli, and the tradition of English historical precedents all make appearances in their writings. But as a symbol—a martyr, even—of republican liberty, Cicero seems to have held undisputed preeminence.

Cicero's reputation was such that he could be called upon not only as a scholarly authority in texts meant for an educated and leisured audience but even in parliamentary debates and public political statements. In Parliament, Sir Thomas Hedley denounced kingly prerogatives that place property of subjects "in the absolute power of another," noting that Cicero and Tacitus demonstrate the danger this poses.[82] In response to King Charles's refusal to assent to their demands for control over the militia, Parliament adopted Cicero's maxim of *salus populi suprema lex* and on that ground assumed control on their own authority. Cicero's principle thus provided the explicit justification for the first law ever put into effect by Parliament without royal assent, a significant waypoint on the road to the Civil War. When Charles subsequently tried to arrest five members of Parliament, they used language drawn from Cicero's *Third Philippic* to denounce anyone who attempted to carry out further such arrests as "a publick enemy of the Common-wealth."[83]

[82] As found in Skinner 2002, 320.
[83] For more on these two incidents, see Skinner 2002, 326.

When Robert, Lord Brooke, exhorted his officers to take up arms against the king, he appealed to "that great commonwealthman of the Romans, Cicero."[84] In all of these cases, Cicero's status as a symbol of republican liberty was sufficiently established that appeals to him could be made not only in theoretical tracts for scholarly readers but also in political rhetoric meant for public consumption and even in acts of law.

As for the thinkers and theoretical writings that are the primary focus of this chapter, Cicero had similarly high standing. Perhaps the most arresting statement came from Neville, whose enthusiasm for Cicero was so great that he incurred charges of impiety from Oliver Cromwell's government after allegedly declaring in the House of Commons that he preferred Cicero to the Bible.[85] Returning to his famous *A Defense of the People of England* several years after its initial publication, Milton saw fit to append two retrospective paragraphs to the end of the work. He uses this short addition to express his desire that the work will entitle him to the same status with respect to the liberty of his country as that enjoyed by Cicero at the end of his consulship (Milton 1991, 253). Nedham gets to the point more concisely when he describes Cicero as "the Oracle of Humane Wisdom" (Nedham 2011, 39). From all this, it becomes clear that scholars have underestimated Cicero's importance in shaping the development of English republicanism.[86] The leading English republicans were engaged in serious political contestation and certainly did not manage to articulate a common ideological doctrine of similar consistency to that of Grotius and Pufendorf. They often adopted, discarded, or modified their arguments and justifications for action as circumstances required. In doing so, they drew from a variety of modern and ancient sources for authority or inspiration. But the name of Cicero stands out as one of the most important republican shibboleths. No less an authority than Hobbes suggests that reading not Machiavelli but classical authors was a central cause of the English Civil War. He lists two names for particular opprobrium:

It is an easy thing, for men to be deceived, by the specious name of Libertie . . . and when the same errour is confirmed by the authority of men

---

[84] Strider 2013, 68.

[85] See Sullivan 2004, 187.

[86] A partial exception to this is Skinner. However, Skinner's failure to adequately distinguish Cicero's political vision from that of Machiavelli ensures that the specifically Ciceronian contribution to English republicanism is lost in a relatively undifferentiated swirl of "neo-Roman" thought.

in reputation for their writings in this subject, it is no wonder if it produce sedition, and change of Government. In these westerne parts of the world, we are made to receive our opinions concerning the Institution, and Rights of Common-wealths from *Aristotle, Cicero,* and other men, Greeks and Romans. (Hobbes 1996; emphasis in original)

Skinner agrees with Hobbes on this point, saying, "there is a great deal to be said for Hobbes's explanation," pointing out that Hobbes "mounts a furious attack on Aristotle, and even more on Cicero and his followers, for equating monarchy with tyranny."[87]

"The Original and Fountain of All Just Power"

Despite the easy changeability of his allegiances, Nedham's *The Excellencie of a Free-State* proved wildly popular, not only among contemporaries but later in America as well. Adams, for instance, engages Nedham thoroughly in his own great republican opus.[88] Nedham sets himself the task in this work to defend the benefits of the English commonwealth: "that Princes as well as the People be governed by Law; that Justice might be impartially distributed . . . that England might become a quiet Habitation for the Lion and the Lamb to lie down and feed together; and that none might make the people afraid" (Nedham 2011, 7). Nedham explains that "the end of all Government" is to ensure "the good and ease of the People, in a secure enjoyment of their Rights" (Nedham 2011, 25). These goals—peace, justice, rights, ease, and the absence of fear—seem decidedly anti-Machiavellian.[89] Indeed, Nedham contrasts his view of the proper moral ends of government with advocates of "this strange *pocus* called Reason of State." He associates it with modern Italian thinking, which "admits Ambition to be a reason, Perferment, Power, Profit, Revenge, and Opportunity, to be reason" (Nedham 2011, 105–107). He then offers an extended excerpt to illustrate such thinking "in *Machiavels*

---

[87] Skinner 2002, 308.

[88] Jefferson also had a copy of it in his library (Colbourn 1965, 220).

[89] Sullivan recognizes that Nedham breaks with Machiavelli on the issue of political immoralism. As she puts it, "Nedham's divergence from Machiavelli . . . seems to derive from the same interest— namely, his interest in the security and liberty of the people, which Machiavelli does not share" (Sullivan 2004, 134). Sullivan is right that Nedham does draw a number of useful practical lessons from Machiavelli, but she is also right that none of those overthrows the fundamental discontinuity in their ultimate aims.

own language . . . in that unworthy book of his, entituled, *The Prince*" (Nedham 2011, 120–124).[90]

The passage Nedham cites comes from chapter 18 of *The Prince*. It contains Machiavelli's argument for why princes ought not to keep faith. Nedham is not alone among the English republicans who are greatly concerned that people entrusted with political authority be held to their word. Harrington, for instance, insists that those entrusted with political authority be outstanding in faithfulness and constancy (Harrington 1977, 534).[91] Walter Moyle cites Cicero's analysis of the example of Regulus, who died rather than violate his promise—even to an enemy—as evidence for the importance of oath-keeping (Neville and Moyle 1969, 217). In part, this concern is part of a broad polemical point that justifies calling even kings to account for broken promises. But English republicans' concern for promise-keeping turns out to have deeper theoretical significance; it pertains to a dominant view among the English republicans about the nature of political authority itself.

According to nearly all the major English republican writers, the true source of legitimate political authority lies in the people. Unlike Grotius and Pufendorf, the English writers do not merely acknowledge the doctrine of popular sovereignty as part of a founding moment or held as a last reserve against tyranny; they tend to make it a centerpiece of their political thought. Political power is delegated by the people to certain individuals and institutions, Because of this, those particular individuals and institutions hold their power in trust from the people—and their faithfulness to that trust is therefore of the highest importance. Institutions must ensure that fidelity to the people is maintained.

Nedham's account of this dynamic is illustrative, and it is perhaps telling that the first and last authority cited in the *Excellencie* is Cicero. Nedham's logic of popular sovereignty follows Cicero closely and explicitly. To establish the fundamental principle of popular sovereignty, he needs first to demonstrate that human beings are naturally free and that the political authority must then derive from consent. The sole authority he produces for this argument is Cicero, "that Oracle of Humane wisdom," and his claims in *Off.* 1.4 and 1.19 that human beings naturally prefer to decide things themselves

---

[90] Even when Nedham credits Machiavelli with a valuable insight, he is less than complimentary. When citing Machiavelli's preference for republics over principalities, he writes that "It was a Noble saying, (though Machiavels)" (Nedham 2011).

[91] Harrington also describes the archon of Oceana, Olphaus Megaletor, as "inviolable in faith" (Harrington 1977, 598).

and are resistant to obedience. According to Neville, one can make three deductions from Cicero's account of human nature:

> First, that by the light of nature people are taught to be their own Carvers and Contrivers, in the framing of that Government under which they mean to live. Secondly, that none are to preside in Government or sit at the Helm, but such as shall be judged fit, and chosen by the People. Thirdly, that the People are the onely proper Judges of the convenience or inconvenience of a Government when it is erected, and of the behavior of Governors. (Nedham 2011, 39)

Nedham summarizes these three deductions from Cicero in one maxim: "that the Original and Fountain of all just Power and Government is in the People" (Nedham 2011, 39). He goes on to claim that this maxim is the foundational principle for all other principles of politics (Nedham 2011, 69). So, in sum, Nedham credits Cicero with establishing the fundamental premise of just politics: popular sovereignty.

Also like Cicero, Nedham does not believe the people themselves are fit to actually make all of the laws and other decisions of state. There is great need for leaders of intelligence and discretion, and even mixed government, with an executive somewhat insulated from public opinion. But at the basis of all such authority must be the people's consent. Moreover, unlike Grotius and Pufendorf, who accept the necessity of consent at the beginning of a regime but then take that consent to be binding indefinitely, Nedham insists that the people's sovereignty be the animating spring of government continually. The people's ultimate authority must be reflected in regular elections to the popular assemblies (Nedham 2011, 48–56). The people may choose one magistrate or form of distribution of governmental powers at one time but may later withdraw their consent and reorder things anew.

Although his political philosophy is far more overtly Christian, Milton's argument on the issue of popular sovereignty is remarkably close to Nedham's. Like Nedham, Milton grounds the principle of popular sovereignty on man's natural freedom. Refuting the claims of royal divine right, he paraphrases Cicero's account (without naming him) of the state of nature and the origin of civil society: "for that very reason men first came together, not so that one might abuse them all, but so that when one injured another, there should be law and a judge between men . . . when formerly men were scattered and dispersed, some eloquent and wise man led them into civil life" (Milton 1991,

TWO CICERONIAN TRADITIONS   125

195). After establishing the naturalness of human freedom, he, like Nedham, draws the conclusion that political power derives from the people: "As Marcus Tullius also shows most neatly . . . 'as it is fitting that all powers, authorities, and charges stem from the whole people . . . all the people choose one whom they think will most consult the interests of the people . . .' you see the true origin of parliaments" (Milton 1991, 206).[92] Like Nedham, Milton seems to take Cicero as the primary authority on this fundamental principle. Cicero provides the authoritative justification for parliamentary legitimacy. Milton deploys Cicero's *De oratore* and his speech *Pro Flacco* as proofs that "all the authority of a magistrate begins with the people" (Milton 1991, 118).[93] He also takes pains to show that even biblical kings owed their authority not only to the election of God but to the consent of the people (Milton 1991, 92).

Milton also incorporates an account of natural law into his doctrine of legitimacy that is somewhat more fleshed out than those offered by his fellow republicans. The principles of natural freedom and popular sovereignty are ultimately justified by a doctrine of natural law, a doctrine that trumps all human precedent (Milton 1991, 206–207). The legitimacy of consent depends on natural law. Milton's defense of tyrannicide includes a claim that the law a tyrant is judged against is the natural law, for which he appeals to Cicero again (Milton 1991, 9, 189). Milton draws his definition of natural law from Cicero but reinterprets Cicero's version in a Christian direction:

> As Cicero says in *Phil.* 12, "none other than right reason drawn from the power of the gods, commanding what is honourable, and forbidding the opposite" . . . so from God comes the establishment of magistrates . . . but the freedom to choose this or that form of government, these or those magistrates, has always been in the power of the free nations of men. (Milton 1991, 114)

In his blending of Ciceronian natural law with a Christian ethics of freedom, Milton makes an argument that strikingly anticipates Locke. He begins by raising the point that human beings are created in the image of God, and he reaffirms the Christian notion that we are God's property. He then infers: "since then we belong to God, that is, we are truly free and on that

---

[92] Milton's quotation of Cicero comes from *Leg. agr.* 2.7, 2.17.

[93] Milton quotes Cicero's *Tenth Philippic* again to prove that all coercive power derives ultimately from consent (Milton 1991, 221).

account to be rendered to God alone, surely we cannot, without sin . . . hand ourselves over in slavery to Caesar, that is to a man" (Milton 1991, 108).[94] Here Milton argues that, as the workmanship and property of God, it is, in fact, contrary to divine and natural law (Milton does not substantially distinguish the two) for us to give up all of our rights to a sovereign. Milton's point runs directly contrary to Grotius, who had claimed that just such a total alienation of rights was permissible and possibly even advisable. Thus, Milton's version of natural law not only legitimates the principle of consent, but it also limits it in a way that Grotius had not. Even free consent would not legitimate a people's choice to forsake their sovereignty indefinitely.

In this way, Milton follows Cicero in seeking universally applicable standards of right valid across time and space, principles that still sit uneasily with Milton's firm commitment to the people's sovereignty (Milton 1991, 18, 32–33, 206).[95] As Zuckert points out, Milton's doctrine of popular sovereignty, with its emphasis on the people's omnipresent option to change magistrates and governmental forms, offers a fairly unstable vision of politics, in which the people's whims might turn this way today and that way tomorrow.[96] Although Milton does not address this possibility, it seems that the people might well freely choose a form of government that does demand the surrender of too much of their rights.

Although Milton's and Nedham's accounts go furthest in elaborating the theoretical basis—and classical inspiration—for the doctrine of popular sovereignty, the basic logic recurs throughout many of the other significant works of this period. Harrington's Oceana is governed on the principle of popular sovereignty, where ultimate authority is lodged in the people, transmitted through their representatives. The epigraph to *The Commonwealth of Oceana* consists of a passage from the third book of Cicero's *De re publica* that affirms the people's ownership of the polity and condemns as tyrannical any attempt to deprive them of it. Sidney declares in a chapter title that "the contracts made between magistrates, and the nations that created them, were real, solemn, and obligatory" (Sidney 1996, 2.32.309).[97] He also justifies his position using Cicero's argument of natural human freedom: "every man is

---

[94] Although there is some scholarship on the relationship between Locke's and Milton's notions of freedom and slavery (Nyquist 2008; Binney 2010), I cannot find anyone who has noticed the striking similarity between this passage from Milton and Locke's workmanship argument. I elaborate on Locke's workmanship argument in chapter 5.

[95] In each instance, Cicero is either directly quoted or closely paraphrased.

[96] Zuckert 1994, 80–81.

[97] See Sullivan 2004, 218–219.

king till he divest himself of his right" (Sidney 1996, 1.7.25). Moyle agrees, and, like Nedham and Milton, he attributes the principle to Cicero: "in the people's hands, says Tully, the supreme power of all things is placed" (Neville and Moyle 1969, 214).[98]

None of the other major republicans makes so thorough an attempt as Milton to reconcile this principle of popular sovereignty with a doctrine of natural law, the latter often appearing as an underdeveloped concept, if it does at all. In this, English republicanism seems most like a mirror image of Grotius and Pufendorf. Harrington implies that the law of nature mandates equal human freedom (Harrington 1977, 11), but he does not elaborate on it. He shows an affinity for Grotius's doctrine of natural law, although he deploys it to defend popular government as the best possible form (something Grotius would not have countenanced) (Harrington 1977, 12). Nedham describes the alternative to Machiavellian reason of state as "the Law of God, or the law of common honest and of Nations," and says that we are taught by "the light of nature" to be self-determining and free (Nedham 2011, 39, 106). In every case, the appeal to natural law functions primarily to justify or ground the principle of popular sovereignty.

The Liberty of the Citizen in a Large Republic

In justifying their overthrow of a king in the name of popular sovereignty, the English republicans necessarily had to articulate an account of the role of freedom in politics. As mentioned, Pocock, Skinner, and others see the English republicans as drawing their conception of liberty from a tradition that traces back to Aristotle (Pocock) or the Romans (Skinner), crystallized and modernized by Machiavelli.

But the Cambridge School tends to ascribe a similar ideal of liberty to all of these writers, one based around a fundamental dichotomy of freeman and slave. As I have shown in previous chapters, however, there is little grounds to believe in this alleged similarity. Nevertheless, it is worth briefly summarizing the various positions. The Machiavellian concept of liberty concerns exclusively a political community undominated by an outside force but does little to guarantee individual liberty (free speech, free movement, bodily

---

[98] Moyle is especially interested in using Cicero's authority on popular sovereignty to deny the priestly class any special political rights.

security, secure private property) to citizens within the community. Internal conflict, rather than peaceful order, characterizes healthy political life.[99] As for Aristotle, liberty is not really an ideal at all. Citizens of the good regime must be free (in the sense of not being slaves), but this is one of the many necessary (but not sufficient) conditions to the actual end of the regime: the good life. Neither Machiavelli nor Aristotle shares with Cicero an ideal of liberty, "the mark of which is to live just as one pleases" and in which one enjoys security in one's body and property (*Off.* 1.70).[100]

Now, as discussed, one key way in which the doctrine of liberty entered into English republican discourse was through the idea that natural human freedom is the source of the principles of consent and popular sovereignty. But a pre-political state of natural liberty is incompatible with the doctrines of liberty found in Aristotle and Machiavelli. As we have seen, some (at least) of the English republicans saw the origins of such an idea in Cicero. The English republicans were also deeply concerned to preserve freedom within political society. For this reason, they rejected the Grotian option of total alienation of rights and power to the regime.

The English republicans evince an awareness that their republic covers a substantial territory; it is not limited to the confines of a single city, as the Greek or Renaissance Italian republics were. This is one of the many reasons they preferred to look to Rome as a model, which realized citizens' freedom far beyond the narrow bounds of a city's walls. Freedom must lie in something other than regular, meaningful, and direct participation in governing, since so large a polity makes that impossible. Nedham, for instance, cites book 1 of *De officiis* to prove that the Romans managed to extend liberty along with citizenship to the peoples they incorporated into their empire (Nedham 2011, 180).

The question for these writers, then, is what can liberty be within civil society and how can it be safeguarded? In part, that original sovereign freedom is preserved, albeit transformed, in the people's regular choosing of representatives. Thus, Nedham writes that "an uninterrupted course of successive parliaments or assemblies of the people" and "free election of members" are essential constitutional conditions of freedom (Nedham 2011, 10). Likewise, Harrington draws on Cicero by name to establish a fundamental link

<hr>

[99] See chapter 3.
[100] Recall again that Aristotle goes so far as to call "tyrannical" the democratic habit of "tolerating everyone living as he wants." He laments that "living in a disorderly way is more pleasant to the many than living with moderation" (*Politics* 6.2).

between popular elections and the people's liberty: "the election or suffrage of the people is freest [when secret, so that it does not] impair a man's liberty" (Harrington 1977, 181). In choosing our governors and assenting to the laws, we exercise collectively the freedom of self-determination that individuals had in the pre-political state.

But the English republicans' support for free political institutions should not be mistaken for an embrace of contestation for its own sake or an endorsement of Machiavellian tumults. Many of the leading English republicans view faction and tumults as a serious problem for the stability of a commonwealth. Nedham blames the division into factions for the demise of the Roman Republic (Nedham 2011, 22, 95, 118). Harrington goes further to show his opposition to this essential component of Machiavellian republicanism. Like Cicero, Harrington envisions a large role for elites to guide the people without dominating them. After approvingly citing Cicero's views, he writes, "The balance I have laid down, though unseen by Machiavel . . . Wherefore, as in this place I agree with Machiavel that a nobility or gentry, overbalancing a popular government; so I shall show in another that a nobility or gentry in a popular government, not overbalancing it, is the very life and soul of it" (Harrington 1977, 39).

Many of these writers suggest that the rule of law and the presence of faction are incompatible. Harrington's vision of a republic resembles Machiavelli's in some important ways, especially in the central role that an armed citizenry plays in it. But Harrington also expresses a strong preference for the rule of laws and not men (Harrington 1977, 162). Harrington cites Cicero as an authority to show that having a few simple laws is the best way to be governed (Harrington 1977, 187). Nedham agrees, also calling on Cicero as authority for his claim that Roman liberty lasted as long as the Romans were ruled by laws and ended once the rule of law was replaced by the will of individual men (Nedham 2011, 110).[101]

This rule of law can be achieved in part through a mixed regime. Harrington includes an element of kingship in his ideal political system, represented in *Oceana* by the position of archon.[102] He proposes a form of mixed or composite government that includes monarchic, aristocratic, and democratic elements, with a preponderance of power placed in this last. Nedham takes a similar view of mixed government, looking especially to the Roman example

---

[101] Adams cites this passage from Nedham approvingly, including his appeal to Cicero's authority.
[102] For more on Harrington's toleration of monarchy, see Hammersley 2013.

(Nedham 2011, 49). Milton, too, credits Cicero with showing that the Roman constitution admirably distributed powers and offices (Milton 1991, 187).

But a citizen's liberty cannot be entirely reduced to his participation in elections and the form of government under which he lives. After all, while the people as a body retain ultimate political sovereignty and must consent to the laws, in such a large state any individual person's say over the direction of the government will be quite small. The various schemes for representation proposed by Milton, Nedham, Harrington, Sidney, and others reflect the fact that the people themselves will not do much of the actual ruling in such a commonwealth. Where, then, is the real liberty of the citizen?

There is a tendency among some scholars to conflate republican liberty with power. Skinner connects Cicero in particular to this idea, quoting a passage from the *Fourth Philippic* that was especially popular among English republicans:

> Do you call servitude peace? Our ancestors took up arms not only to be free but also to win power. You think that our arms should now be thrown away in order that we should become slaves. But what cause of waging war can be more just than that of repudiating slavery? For the most miserable feature of this condition is that, even if the master happens not to be oppressive, he can be so should he wish. (*Phil.* 4)[103]

Milton reproduces this passage verbatim in his *Defense*, and the sentiment expressed in it can be found in nearly all the English republicans who contrasted a condition of liberty with the tyranny of a monarchy. However, a close reading of the passage reveals that for Cicero, freedom and power are distinct: "not only to be free, *but also* to win power" (emphasis added). As discussed in chapter 2, Cicero understands freedom as characteristic of one who can do as he wishes, secure in body and property. Some element of political power is essential to making that freedom secure, as this passage demonstrates, but it is not the same thing as freedom itself.[104] Milton demonstrates that he perceives the same relationship between the two

---

[103] As translated in Skinner 2002, 314.

[104] Milton comes closer than any of the other English republicans to the views of Grotius and Pufendorf. He asserts that human beings are born naturally free and that they must have yielded this freedom only through a contract. Like Grotius and Pufendorf (and unlike Hobbes), he argues that such a contract exists between governors and governed and that the latter may rise up if the former fail to adequately serve the common good (Milton 2014, 11, 12, 15). See also Skinner 2002, 298.

positions as Cicero does, writing that when someone has absolute control over "our lives and estates," we would be slaves, deprived of "that power, which is the root and source of all liberty" (Milton 1991, 32). That is to say, the people's power, protected by republican institutions, functions primarily to *ensure* their liberty but is not the same thing as liberty itself. In a world filled with morally corrupt and fallen creatures such as men, yielding up the safeguards of one's liberty is a sure way to lose it. For this reason, Milton continues, any social contract of the Hobbesian variety in which nearly all liberties are given up is nonsensical, "a violation of their natural birthright" and "a kinde of treason against the dignitie of mankind" (Milton 2014, 299–300). Sidney seems to agree, writing that "man is naturally free . . . equality of right and exemption from the domination of any other is called liberty" (Sidney 1996, 2.31.304).

The distinction alleged by Pettit, Skinner, and others between liberty as the absence of interference and liberty as the absence of the *possibility* of interference (i.e., non-domination) may seem trivial, but it is at the very core of the neo-republican attempt to distinguish liberalism from republicanism as ideals. In a representative argument, Pettit claims that the ideal of non-interference can be satisfied in precarious situations. You might be the slave of a benevolent or indulgent master who lets you do whatever you want, but the master could at any time change his mind; whereas the ideal of non-domination is satisfied only when you enjoy the "absence of interference by arbitrary powers, not just in the actual world, but in the range of possible worlds."[105] The arguments of Milton and Cicero show why this distinction is meaningless. In a world of fallen human beings who are inclined to vice, there is no such thing as a reliably benevolent slave master. Nedham begins the *Excellencie* with an appeal to Cicero to establish this as his starting assumption: "as Cicero saith, there is a natural desire of power and sovereignty in every man, so that if any have once an opportunity to seize, they seldom neglect it; and if they are told it is their due, they venture life and all to attain it" (Nedham 2011, 8). The liberty of the English republicans is at its base the same liberty as Cicero's: the security of life and property against harm or interference, ensured by having some say in political rule.

The English republicans recognized that this goal of an individual safe from interference and harm can only be achieved by political institutions

---

[105] Pettit 1997, 24–25.

that give individuals power to protect themselves from such violations.[106] The English republicans thus reveal the implausibility of a sharp distinction between classical Roman republican liberty and modern liberal freedom. Even on the issue of protecting private property—which some scholars take to be anathema to the civic republican mindset—the English republicans follow Cicero in making it central. Harrington's commonwealth is based on the idea that distributions of property must be protected and reflected in the regime. Nedham insists that the republican form of government is better in part because it protects the private possessions of the people, their "propriety," better than arbitrary rule (Nedham 2011, 48–49). Neville ascribes the origins of commonwealths to the desire to protect private holdings in a way that echoes Cicero's claims closely (Neville and Moyle 1969, 85).

Therefore, free institutions—suffrage, rule of law, some elements of popular government—are essential to having freedom as citizens. Harrington argues precisely this and suggests, using the Ciceronian logic of popular ownership, that magistrates who usurp authority have, in fact, stolen something rightfully possessed by the people (Harrington 1977, 170–250).[107] The English republicans follow Cicero in seeking an analogous and mutually supporting liberty for the citizen and the commonwealth.

These figures place little emphasis on Cicero's complex natural law doctrine, mostly mining it for arguments that justify popular government. However, as a theorist and rhetorician of liberty, Cicero was invaluable to them.[108] As this chapter demonstrates, they seem in general to have preferred Cicero's doctrine of liberty to those found in Aristotle or Machiavelli (or, for that matter, Hobbes). Here and there, we may find an appeal to Aristotelian rotation of offices or a Machiavellian citizen army. But only in Cicero could these republicans find support for an ideal of freedom in which individuals enjoy bodily protection, secure private property, and the liberty to move and speak as they will. Moreover, Cicero provides the logic to connect this personal liberty to a version of political liberty. Only free institutions, in which citizens have a real say, can ensure that such liberty is protected—the rule of laws and not of men. In this way, the liberty of the state and the liberty of

---

[106] For the additional alleged innovation of neo-republicanism—the distinction between arbitrary and non-arbitrary interference—see the earlier discussion on Pettit's attempt to differentiate a state of "non-freedom" from "unfreedom."

[107] See the discussion of Cicero's *In Verrem* in chapter 2.

[108] The English republicans more closely conform to Fox's vision of Cicero during this period less as a resource for systematic thinking and more as a republican inspiration (Fox 2013). However, even here, we see they often forged a reasonably coherent republican theory with his help.

citizens are mutually dependent. Liberty thus becomes perhaps the central *goal* of a just regime, not a mere presupposition as it is in Aristotle.

An Abortive Convergence

Aside from their near simultaneity, there appears little on the surface to link the new natural law philosophy of Grotius and Pufendorf with the republican project of figures such as Harrington, Milton, Neville, and Nedham. The systematic, legalistic, and predominantly monarchical doctrines of the former seem to be thoroughly at odds with the polemical, inconsistent, and enthusiastically republican writings of the latter. In this light, their mutual dependence on Cicero might appear to be coincidence, a case of both selectively drawing on a reputable classical author for support of arguments he would have had little to do with.

The evidence presented in this chapter challenges such a view. Examined closely, we see both groups taking Cicero's thought seriously and depending heavily on the conceptual resources and arguments he provides. In Cicero's philosophy, we find a compatibility between natural law and popular sovereignty. In both of these seventeenth-century movements, the two Ciceronian pillars are present, but each strongly prioritizes one pillar at the expense of the other. Cicero's legacy appeared to produce two different and increasingly opposed traditions of thought. But this cleavage was not to last.

With the Restoration in 1660 and a king again on the throne, English republicanism was defeated as an open political force. The heirs of its tradition of political thought, the Whigs, had to be far more circumspect and moderate about popular sovereignty and liberty, and anti-monarchical writing all but vanished. The values of liberty and the people's say in government were adjusted to be more compatible with a monarchical mixed regime. In some ways, this development reflected ideas present in the earlier overtly republican works. Milton had argued that the English monarchy, even before the Civil War, had been a part of a mixed regime (Milton 1991, 215).

After the Restoration, a number of Whig writers would follow Milton's logic of arguing from ancient precedent about the ancestral rights of the English people and Parliament against the king. The most influential of these was Sidney, who makes this case in his *Discourses Concerning Government*. There Sidney makes arguments similar to those of the earlier republicans about the naturalness of freedom and the people's sovereignty, but he goes to great lengths to establish that, as a matter of historical record, the prerogative of English kings was limited and balanced against Parliament. In this effort, he explores the Magna Carta, the manner and rights of English royal succession, and much else.

Defending English liberty through an appeal to English precedent—claiming, in other words, that the rightful limits and distributions of political authority in England depend on the original political decisions and compacts—opened up the possibility of a reconciliation between the Whig heirs of English republicans and Grotian natural law. Although he does not develop this possibility, Grotius's emphasis on the binding nature of an original contract entails the possibility that a people might reserve to themselves a whole range of rights and privileges that they do not grant to the sovereign. So on Grotian grounds, English Whigs could defend the prerogatives of Parliament and the rights of the people through a discourse that remained fundamentally within the tradition of English history and common law.[109] By placing emphasis on the binding nature of the original political compact, Grotian natural law could be pressed into service defending the Whigs' claims for a balance of power between Parliament and the king. In this way, Grotius became the "master of Whig thought" in the second half of the seventeenth century.[110]

But this reunification of the two strands of the Ciceronian doctrine of political legitimacy ultimately undermines the very purpose the doctrines were originally meant to hold: to provide a universally valid set of moral principles for government that would ensure the liberty of the people. Ironically, this Whig synthesis enlists Cicero and Grotius to defend (practically, if not in theory) the Carnedean position both had opposed: that all law is positive law. If natural law only serves to make eternally binding the original compact, then people have no greater claim to freedom than whatever their ancestors reserved for them. Grotius had accepted the legitimacy of revolt against a monarch if that monarch had been granted only limited powers in the original compact and was exceeding those limits: "if a King should have but one Part of the sovereign Power and the Senate or the People the other, if such a King shall invade that Part which is not his own, he may be justly resisted" (*De iure belli* 1.4.13). Following him, the Whig writer Gilbert Burnet argues,

---

[109] An example of such thinking is Gilbert Burnet's *An Enquiry into the Measure of Submission to the Supream Authority* (1689).

[110] See Zuckert 1994, 104–139, for a discussion of his role in shaping the thought of the heirs of the English republican tradition.

"bodies of men can give themselves upon different degrees to the conduct of others" and only revolt if those given such power exceed their trust (Burnet 1689, 3–4).[111] This formulation abolishes the idea that there is some universally valid standard of liberty in political society, to which people might appeal regardless of local precedent.

However, as we shall see in chapter 5, this particular attempt to reconcile natural law with popular sovereignty would not win out. But it is probably not a coincidence that the modern thinker who read and followed Cicero most closely also happened to stand at the intersection of the two traditions explored in this chapter: Locke. An unorthodox Whig, Locke would articulate a vision of popular sovereignty based in Ciceronian natural law that delineated precisely how much liberty the individual could rightly claim in society. The Lockean reconciliation of popular sovereignty with natural law would draw upon English republicanism and the natural law of Grotius and Pufendorf but unite them in a different way from his precedent-obsessed Whig rivals. In doing so, he would achieve a far more faithfully Ciceronian synthesis than either of the preceding intellectual movements. Precisely because his version returned to the ideal of universally applicable standards of liberty, it could transcend national limitations and sidestep the historical debates over precedent. Perhaps most significantly, Locke's project would come to culmination in the American founding, which realized this political vision of liberal republicanism in an actual regime.

---

[111] See Zuckert 1994, 148–149, for the Grotian element in Whig thought and in Burnet in particular.

5

Locke's Ciceronian Liberalism

> John Locke . . . must be confest to be the greatest Philosopher
> after Cicero in the Universe; for he's throly acquainted with human
> Nature, well vers'd in the usual Affairs of the World, a great
> Master of Eloquence (Qualities in which the *Roman* Consul excel'd)
> and like him also a hearty lover of his Country, as appears by his
> Treatises of *Government* and *Education*, not inferior in their kind to
> the divinest Pieces of Tully.
>
> —John Toland, 1699

A Curious Recommendation

In *Some Thoughts Concerning Education*, John Locke writes of the education
of a young gentleman:

> I know not whether he should read any other discourses of morality but
> what he finds in the Bible; or have any system of ethics put into his hand
> till he can read Tully's *Offices* not as a school-boy to learn Latin, but as one
> that would be informed in the principles and precepts of virtue for the con-
> duct of his life. (*Thoughts* 185)

The near-total silence of scholars on the relationship between Locke and
Cicero might lead a reader to assume that this passage is insignificant and
that Locke really did not mean to rank Cicero's *De officiis* next to the Bible
as a moral instructor.[1] Indeed, in citing *De officiis*, Locke may appear to be
simply following convention: Cicero's work had formed the core of a tradition of moral education for centuries. It had been the centerpiece of many
Renaissance Italian school curricula and had shaped the moral educational
program of Oxford for a long time before Locke had arrived. Yet evidence

---

[1] A few notable exceptions to this silence will be discussed at length.

Natural Law Republicanism. Michael C. Hawley, Oxford University Press. © Oxford University Press 2022.
DOI: 10.1093/oso/9780197582336.003.0005

suggests that Locke's recommendation is sincere and considered. Locke persists, both in private correspondence to friends and in other published works, repeatedly listing Cicero's work—and only Cicero's work—along with the Bible as the foundational texts for teaching morality or ethics (he uses the terms interchangeably in his recommendations).[2]

This link is significant because, in a sense, Locke's entire political philosophy derives from his ethics. A methodological and ontological individualist, Locke treats political societies as the creations of consenting individuals, who form governments in order to vindicate the natural law that binds them *as* individuals and determines their duties and obligations to their fellows. Government has no power or obligation that the individuals who made it up did not have first. Thus, all normative political questions depend, at bottom, on ethical questions.[3] Taking Locke's claims about the nature of ethics seriously means that Cicero's philosophy might well be central to Locke's political project.

In this chapter, I illustrate the ways in which we can understand Locke's thought much more clearly when we see its fundamental connection to Cicero. Moreover, looking both forward and backward from Locke, we see how Locke's thought represents the crucial penultimate step in establishing modern liberal republicanism. This liberal republican framework proves to be Ciceronian at its core and to owe much of its modern formulation to Locke's reception and adaptation of Cicero.

To suggest that Cicero plays a central role in Locke's political philosophy is to upend nearly every one of the great historical accounts of Western political thought. To those who point to a fundamental break between ancients and moderns, Locke and Cicero allegedly stand on opposite sides, with Locke a central figure in the development of modern liberalism or liberal republicanism that emerges over and against classical (if not Machiavellian) political philosophy. For the Cambridge School and neo-republican scholars, the crucial distinction is not between ancients and moderns but between liberals and republicans. Locke's philosophy of natural rights, property, and self-interest stands as a mortal enemy of their construed republican tradition of civic virtue.

Indeed, in nearly all accounts that depict liberalism and republicanism as separate camps, Locke appears at the forefront of the list of classical liberal

---

[2] See Marshall 1994, 301.
[3] More on this claim will follow.

thinkers.[4] If indeed there were a contest (or a later synthesis) between liberalism and republicanism during the seventeenth and eighteenth centuries, Locke *must* be a liberal, or else no one is. A few intrepid scholars have attempted to assert that latter alternative, arguing that even Lockean liberalism is an outgrowth of Machiavelli's republicanism.[5] The difficulty with such a position is the absence of any evidence at all that Machiavelli had a direct influence on Locke.[6]

Thus, Locke appears not to be a republican. Yet biographically, Locke had strong connections with the English commonwealth men. Locke's personal links to English republicans, the Whigs, and the Earl of Shaftesbury in particular, as well as the circumstances of his exile and return after the Glorious Revolution are well known. Locke's biography also connects him with the new natural law tradition of Grotius and Pufendorf. Besides owning and reading the works of both Grotius and Pufendorf, Locke may even have met Pufendorf in France, and at the very least, he moved in similar circles to his while in exile.[7] In fact, immediately following the passage in *Some Thoughts Concerning Education* where he recommends reading Cicero, Locke goes on to suggest both Pufendorf and Grotius as further reading on the subject (*Thoughts* 186). Locke thus stands at the intersection of the two Ciceronian traditions discussed in chapter 4. His political thought shows the influence of both.

Like the English republicans and their Whig successors, he supported free parliamentary government, while placing a high value on the freedom of the individual from interference. However, Locke also disapproved of the tendency of English republicans (and later the Whigs) to advocate absolute parliamentary sovereignty. He similarly rejected the positivist attitude that accepted no limits to parliamentary authority. In addition, Locke opposed the historicism in Whig arguments that grounded themselves on the "ancient constitution" or inherited rights. In short, Locke felt that the English

---

[4] On this, at least, figures as diverse as Quentin Skinner, Bernard Bailyn, Gordon Wood, Vickie Sullivan, Ruth Grant, and Leo Strauss can agree.

[5] For instance, Viroli describes liberalism as "incoherent republicanism" (Viroli 2002, 61), although he provides almost no evidence to support his view of liberalism.

[6] The clearest example of this conundrum is the case of Margaret Michelle Barnes Smith's chapter on Locke in Rahe 2006. Barnes Smith's entire purpose is to show the importance of Machiavelli to Locke's thought, yet she is forced to admit at the outset that Locke never cites Machiavelli, nor does he refer to him in private correspondence. Her strongest piece of evidence for a link is the fact that Locke owned Machiavelli's works and quotes from a passage in Livy *adjacent* to one that Machiavelli was fond of repeating. This is hardly better than no evidence at all.

[7] Marshall 1994, 202.

republican tradition and its heirs lacked a universal, supra-historical principle on which to ground political norms or by which to limit the power of government.

Locke finds just such a principle in the newly rearticulated natural law doctrine of Grotius and Pufendorf. As we saw in chapter 4, the natural law theory advanced by Grotius and Pufendorf rejected the teleological elements that discredited Aristotelian-Thomistic natural law and assumed human beings to be naturally free and equal. It addressed all human beings across religious affiliation, historical circumstance, and political situation. It aspired to serve as a standard by which all political arrangements could be judged, and it presented a theory of rights to structure just relationships in a decent political society. Yet the political arrangements defended by Grotius and Pufendorf came close to absolute monarchy and did nothing to ensure a place for participatory politics or for safeguards for the rights they ascribed to human beings in their natural state to be protected once humans entered societies.

Locke brings both of these Ciceronian traditions together in a manner that draws on each to correct for the deficits of both. Building on the natural law arguments of Grotius and Pufendorf, Locke establishes a universal normative and theoretical ground for popular sovereignty and a conception of natural rights. Locke unites both the logic of natural law and the logic of the people's sovereignty in the concept of natural rights. The just political system grounded in the natural law does not abolish natural human liberty; it protects and extends it.

Locke and "Tully"

If the argument for Locke's Ciceronianism lay solely in Locke's location at the convergence of two other Ciceronian traditions, it would suffer from the same fatal flaw that characterizes the voluminous literature on Machiavelli's posthumous influence criticized earlier. Both the Cambridge School and its critics are frequently forced to deploy dubious claims of indirect influence and often implausible intertextual connections to show that Machiavelli's influence lies behind developments in political thought after the zenith of English republicanism in the mid-seventeenth century. This is because few of the great eighteenth-century political thinkers in the English-speaking world show anything more than a dim awareness of Machiavelli's existence.[8] Here it is worthwhile to compare Pocock's *Machiavellian Moment* (2009) with the collection of essays in Rahe's *Machiavelli's Liberal Republican Legacy* (2006). Although the latter is explicitly a critique of the former's account of Machiavelli's influence in the "Atlantic Republican Tradition," it still endeavors to show that Machiavelli stands behind the development of liberal republicanism in England and America. Yet there is a feature common to many of the essays in it devoted to thinkers after the subsidence of the English republican movement: several begin with an acknowledgment that there is little or no evidence that the thinker in question even read Machiavelli.[9]

In contrast, there is abundant evidence that Locke's reconciliation of the two Ciceronian traditions takes place on the basis of deeply intimate and direct confrontation with the work of Cicero himself. In fact, Locke's interest in Cicero at times seems to border on obsession. As mentioned above, few scholars take any note of this relationship. Some important exceptions are Benjamin Straumann, Emily Nacol, Phillip Mitsis, and a short but rich portion of John Marshall's *John Locke: Resistance, Religion, and Responsibility*. In the epilogue to *Crisis and Constitutionalism*, Straumann touches on Locke's debt to the constitutionalist tradition Straumann identifies with Cicero. Mitsis and Marshall concentrate on Cicero's relevance to Locke's social milieu and focus on Cicero's potential contribution to Locke's ethical and social thought. Nacol focuses on Locke's theory of property.

Mitsis and Marshall are especially valuable in uncovering Locke's personal concern for Cicero's ideas. Mitsis draws out Locke's fascination with Cicero's view of praise and the role of social approval in teaching us moral virtue. Mitsis argues, however, that Locke's attraction to Cicero caused certain theoretical problems for Locke. According to Mitsis, Cicero's classical rationalism was ultimately incompatible with Locke's Christianity. In Marshall's view, Cicero was centrally important for how Locke thought about teaching the qualities of character proper to a gentleman. Marshall notes that Cicero may have been especially valuable to Locke because his work in reconciling the *honestum* and the *utile* proved to be of great help to Locke in his struggle to reconcile his hedonic premises about human motivation with our duty to

---

[8] There are some exceptions to this, of course, including Hume and Adams.

[9] See especially the chapters in Rahe 2006 on Locke, Madison, and Jefferson. This critique does not apply to those essays in the work devoted to English republicans proper, where Machiavelli's influence is clear and direct, or to the essays on Adams and Hume, who also did read Machiavelli.

do good to our fellows.[10] This last point is important and will be revisited. Neither Mitsis nor Marshall delves much into the political dimension of the connection between Locke and Cicero. But both do impressive work in providing evidence of the extent of Locke's personal interest in Cicero, to which the following discussion is indebted.

First, it is valuable to note the ubiquity of Cicero's thought in the general intellectual atmosphere in which Locke was educated and later wrote. As noted in chapter 4, numerous editions and translations of Cicero's work, especially of *De officiis*, were circulating in England (and across Europe) in the seventeenth century, in numbers that continued to rise through the eighteenth century. It was, as Marshall notes, "a basic text at schools such as Westminster and Eton, and at various Cambridge and Oxford colleges."[11] Locke's own education featured *De officiis* in its curriculum, and as a censor of moral philosophy at Christ Church, Oxford, he appears to have taught the text to students himself. Locke's friend John Toland describes it as a "common fashion at schooles" to begin the moral education of young gentlemen with *De officiis*.[12] In this respect, then, Locke's recommendation to start with Cicero in teaching ethics reflects his acceptance of a common educational practice.

In chapter 4, we saw that Cicero's ideas featured prominently in many of the major works of political thought of the seventeenth century, including those of Grotius and Pufendorf, who significantly influenced Locke. In exile in Holland, Locke found himself "living in an environment where Cicero's thought was as clearly at the center of moral discussion and of the conceptualisation of social relationships of friendship as it was in England."[13] Locke's intellectual companions, such as Toland and Jean Barbeyrac, acknowledge Cicero's ubiquity and praise his work profusely. Indeed, Neal Wood goes so far as to say that Cicero was to this early modern Europe "what Aristotle had been to the late medieval world of ideas: an inspiring, informative, and illuminating preceptor."[14]

Yet even in a time and place in which Cicero's thought was widely available, Locke's deep interest in Cicero was unusual. By the age of nineteen, Locke was already peppering his personal correspondence with quotations

---

[10] Marshall 1994, xvii.

[11] Marshall 1994, 162.

[12] Marshall 1994, 162.

[13] Marshall 1994, 300.

[14] Wood 1988, 1. Similar evidence of influence has been found on French thinkers of this period. See Sharpe 2015; Gawlick 1936. Fox illustrates how Cicero's ideas were not restricted to leading thinkers but were also ubiquitous among literati and scholars (Fox 2016).

from Cicero.[15] This tendency only intensified with maturity. Among Locke's friends in Holland was a Dutch bookseller and editor of an edition of Cicero's letters. Mitsis identifies in their correspondence "an escalating attempt on the part of both men to outdo each other both in their mastery of Ciceronian style and in the breadth of their Ciceronian references."[16] Marshall uncovers a similar dynamic in Locke's letters to his closest Dutch friend, where both men conceptualized their relationship as one of Ciceronian *amicitia*.[17] In *Some Thoughts Concerning Education*, Locke makes a rule out of this habit, where he recommends that young men model their letters—in Latin or English—on "Tully's Epistles, as the best pattern whether for business or conversation" (*Thoughts* 189).

The contents of Locke's library reflect his interest; there the Bible is the only book we find more copies of than *De officiis*. Locke's library contains multiple editions of many of Cicero's other works, as well as volumes of Cicero's letters to his friends and family.[18] After Locke himself, the author whose work features most prominently in his library is Cicero.[19] Noting Locke's meticulous recording of his opinions on the quality and value of these books, Mitsis writes: "the extent of Locke's knowledge as well as his passionate interest in the details of various editions would, I think, be sobering to even the most bookish of contemporary classical scholars."[20]

Locke's published and unpublished works also show clear signs of his attitude toward Cicero. He chose for the frontispiece of *An Essay Concerning Human Understanding* a quotation from *De natura deorum*.[21] The epigraph for the *Second Treatise of Government* comes from *De legibus*.[22] An unpublished essay called "Venditio," on certain questions of commercial ethics, is modeled overtly on a discussion from the third book of *De officiis*. Perhaps most telling is a discovery among Locke's papers from the later part of his life, several pages on which he was working out an exact chronology of Cicero's life and works. This is notable because Locke is known to have attempted

[15] Mitsis 2003, 52.
[16] Mitsis 2003, 53.
[17] Marshall 1994, 300.
[18] Harrison, and Laslett 1971, 108–109.
[19] Or possibly the second-most, depending on how one counts entries. Compare Mitsis 2003, 55, with Marshall 1994, 301.
[20] Mitsis also notes that Locke apparently so valued these possessions that "as an aged bachelor, Locke gave an expensive copy of *De finibus* to his young sweetie" (Mitsis 2003, 53).
[21] Although it is beyond the scope of this chapter to dwell on epistemology, Wood is persuasive in suggesting that Locke's skepticism about human knowledge and preference for speaking in terms of probability are connected to Cicero's moderate skepticism (Wood 1988, 60).
[22] This will be revisited.

such a timeline project for only one other individual: Jesus Christ.[23] Harking back to the opening discussion of this chapter, we are again confronted with the fact that the significance of Cicero to Locke's thought may be second only to that of Christianity.

Such a suggestion, of course, can only be demonstrated by an examination of Locke's works. But at the very least, this evidence for Locke's interest in Cicero makes all the more surprising the lack of attention this relationship has received from scholars. Given the Herculean detective work performed by many scholars to demonstrate the importance of Machiavelli to Enlightenment political thinkers, even in cases where there is no reason to think that the latter actually read the former, one can only wonder what they would make of such straightforward evidence of a direct connection to Cicero. Even before any analysis of Locke's texts, it is clear from these biographical details that Locke was deeply engaged with Cicero's thought and that this engagement influenced not only his work as a scholar but also his social life as a person. It would, in fact, be far more surprising if this influence did *not* also extend to Locke's political thought. In what follows, I will demonstrate that Locke's political thought was, in fact, deeply indebted to Cicero. In blending together English republicanism and the "new" natural law of Grotius and Pufendorf, Locke reunites two modern Ciceronian traditions that had appeared opposed to each other. Locke achieves such a synthesis by returning to the source, to Cicero's own thought. Cicero is thus, in a sense, both father and grandfather of Lockean liberalism.

The Conundrum of Locke's Natural Law

One of the pieces of evidence just mentioned provides perhaps the clearest sign that Locke's political thought owes a great deal to Cicero.[24] He chooses for the epigraph of his greatest political work, the *Second Treatise of Government*, Cicero's famous declaration, *salus populi suprema lex esto* ("the welfare of the people shall be the highest law"). *De legibus* is noteworthy in part as the location of Cicero's most extensive elaboration of his doctrine of natural law. Locke also makes it clear from the very beginning of his own political magnum opus that his philosophy rests on a doctrine of natural law.

---

[23] Marshall 1994, 301; Mitsis 2003, 53.

[24] Much of the discussion of Locke's natural law in this chapter is derived from Hawley 2021c.

In the *Second Treatise*, Locke refers to natural law almost immediately, in the first few lines of the first chapter. Reiterating his argument from the *First Treatise*, Locke writes that Adam's heirs lacked a right to dominion over the world and adds that even if they had such a right, there is "no law of nature nor positive law of God that determines which is the right heir in all cases" (II 1).[25] Here—as it appears frequently, natural law seems to have priority over natural rights—the right in question has to derive from natural law (or positive divine law) to be legitimate.

Throughout the *Second Treatise*, Locke continues to appeal to the law of nature for his argument. It forms the basis for his claims about our rights, our conduct in the state of nature, and the powers and purposes of government. Yet nowhere in this work does Locke define substantively the law of nature or explain what it is, where it comes from, or how we know its content. He is equally unforthcoming in the *First Treatise*, where he also refers repeatedly (although less often than in the *Second Treatise*) to the law of nature. He identifies the law of nature with "the law of reason" (I 101), but this is hardly illuminating.[26]

The absence of a clear definition of natural law seems to be a major problem for Locke, since his entire argument appears to rest on the content of this law.[27] How can a reader evaluate Locke's claims without access to the premises of the argument? How do we know that the natural law enjoins what Locke says it does? For some readers, the solution to this problem is easy: we are not meant to take Locke's assertions about natural law at face value.

There are, in fact, a number of influential scholars who deny that Locke really is a natural law philosopher at all. More precisely, they deny that Locke himself believed in any natural law and claim that his references to it were a rhetorical ploy to seduce readers into accepting his political prescriptions. The most notable of these is Leo Strauss, who argues in *Natural Right and*

---

[25] References for the *Two Treatises* are drawn from Locke 1988 but cited parenthetically.

[26] In the *Second Treatise*, he says that reason "is that law" (II 6).

[27] Indeed, nearly every modern scholar of Locke in one way or another encounters the problem that Locke never fully works out a doctrine of natural law, despite seeming to rest the entire weight of his political theory upon it. Zuckert compellingly suggests that scholarly responses can be grouped into three broad categories. The first group argues that the difficulties of Locke's natural law doctrine are only apparent and can be resolved by close examination of the text. Among these are Grant 1987; Polin 1969; and Aarsleff 1969. A second set, influenced by Strauss, believes that the tensions in Locke's written work are real but that they do not imply problems for Locke's *thought*; rather, they serve to illustrate Locke's more radical esoteric teaching. In this group, we find not only Strauss but also Zuckert himself. Finally, there are those such as Laslett 1988 and Dunn 1982, who argue that we must simply accept that Locke himself could not work out all the problems with his own doctrine. See Zuckert 1975 for more on this typology.

History that Locke intentionally left tensions in his work that could only be resolved by abandoning natural law as chimerical. Strauss focuses in particular on Locke's claim that the natural law is supported by sanctions of reward and punishment in the afterlife for obedience and disobedience. Yet, Strauss points out, Locke acknowledges the insufficiency of reason to prove that an afterlife exists. Since natural law must be accessible to unaided human reason, Strauss argues that Locke has on his own terms disproven natural law's existence.[28] According to Strauss, Locke's true natural law teaching is hardly different from that of Hobbes, who reduced the natural law to prudent calculation of self-interest.[29] For Strauss, the divergence between Locke and Hobbes is relatively small and takes place on the grounds of deep agreement about the nature of human beings and the normative issues of politics.

Strauss's discussion is relatively cursory. Zuckert offers a similar but more thorough argument in *Natural Rights and the New Republicanism*. Zuckert proceeds through a number of apparent tensions in Locke's work, including the role of reason, human self-ownership versus divine ownership, and the role of natural rights. Zuckert resolves these tensions by arguing that Locke himself is leveling a sophisticated critique of natural law, particularly of the sort advanced by Pufendorf and Grotius. Zuckert argues that once natural law and its theistic premises are jettisoned, all that remains are the natural rights that constitute Locke's real political agenda.[30] As this chapter continues, I will respond more fully to the arguments presented by Strauss and Zuckert. But as the logic of this chapter requires us to begin with Locke's natural law theory, some preliminary answer to Strauss and Zuckert seems necessary.

First, it is important to reiterate the frequency with which Locke appeals to natural law, especially in the *Second Treatise*. This fact alone establishes a presumption that Locke is serious about the natural law, and it places the burden of proof on those arguing that Locke does not mean what he repeatedly says.[31] Second, it turns out that Locke's theory of natural rights is inextricably

[28] Strauss 1953, 203–204.

[29] Strauss 1953, 220–231.

[30] Zuckert 1994, 258–259. In *Launching Liberalism*, Zuckert offers something of a restatement, in which he distinguishes two separate strains of Locke's argument for natural rights, one deriving straightforwardly from his natural law and the other arriving at natural rights independently from a principle of self-ownership (Zuckert 2002). But Zuckert still maintains that the former argument ultimately cannot withstand scrutiny, so that most of the weight of Locke's natural rights falls upon his self-ownership argument. This leaves the natural law doctrine somewhat vestigial; its primary function appears as a rhetorical device designed to convince people to accept the natural rights doctrine.

[31] Moreover, in *An Essay Concerning Human Understanding*, Locke denounces those who write or speak in such a way as to deliberately mislead: "he that designedly does it [misuses language] ought

dependent on a theory of natural law. Thus, to remove the latter to allow the former to stand on its own is to destroy the foundation of the very structure Locke appears to be building.

We will find that recognizing Locke as relying on a Ciceronian idea of natural law enables us to resolve many of the tensions that form the crux of the Zuckert-Strauss reading.[32] For the purposes of this book, there remains one other reason for viewing Locke as a theorist of natural law, even *if* the skeptical reading of it is true: the Americans who based their new regime in large part on Locke's political philosophy saw him as such.[33] In an overt echo of Locke's language, they famously appealed to "the Laws of Nature and of Nature's God."[34] Thus, even if Locke *did not* truly believe in his natural law arguments, the natural law was a central part of the doctrine he bequeathed to those who followed him.[35] We will revisit some of the arguments for the Strauss-Zuckert position throughout this chapter, but it is important at the outset to provide some provisional reasons an examination of Locke's thought can operate on the assumption that Locke was in earnest about natural law.

Returning to Locke's *Two Treatises*, we find that after systematically rebutting Robert Filmer's theological argument for the divine right of kings in his *First Treatise*, Locke turns in the *Second Treatise* to establishing his positive account of the nature, origins, and limits of political power. Whereas in the earlier work, Locke had engaged Filmer on his own ground (historically and theologically), in the latter, he makes no such appeals. Locke's argument in the *Second Treatise* is almost completely ahistorical and does not appeal

to be looked on as an enemy to truth and knowledge" (*ECHU* 3.1.5). Zuckert argues that Locke's real view on the matter is "almost the opposite" of what he says here (Zuckert 1974, 555). However, Zuckert arrives at this view by claiming that Locke ultimately denies the possibility of using words without some misleading quality. But this does not undermine Locke's previous denunciation, which applies only to "designedly" abusing language. Thus, Locke only demands that one *try one's best* to be clear. It seems only fair, then, to read Locke as *trying* to be straightforward—and not intentionally obscuring his own meaning.

[32] As Zuckert makes clear in *Launching Liberalism*, he disagrees strongly with Strauss that Locke's view eventually reduces to Hobbesianism. However, they do agree that Locke deliberately obscures his own views about the knowability of God's existence and the implications that has for a doctrine of natural law (Zuckert 2002).

[33] A version of this last point is made by Steven Dworetz, even though he himself finds the theistic natural law interpretation of Locke untenable (Dworetz 1990, 33–34).

[34] It may be worth pointing out that the Declaration of Independence, in fact, appeals to the "Laws of Nature and of Nature's God" *before* moving on to rights, just as Locke does.

[35] An even more extreme version of Dworetz's point comes from Thomas Pangle, who argues that some of the American founders, too, held esoterically skeptical views about the God of natural law (Pangle 1988, 289n17).

to any particular religious view (beyond positing the existence of a creator god, which is not offered as an assumption but rather as a deduction by unaided reason).[36] In this, Locke differs substantially from most other Whig thinkers, whose arguments often depended heavily on Protestant theology or claims about historically inherited rights of Englishmen.[37] Peter Laslett argues that Locke's decision to abstract away from the historical enabled his work to retain its relevance better than that of other writers (e.g., Sidney) who reached similar conclusions.[38] This is undoubtedly true. But that does not mean we should see Locke's ahistorical approach as primarily a tactical choice.[39] Locke finds historical appeals inadequate to the task of finding the truly just political order, not least because he understands that "is" (or, in the case of historical arguments, "was") cannot straightforwardly yield any "ought."[40] The existence of tyrants in the past does not justify contemporary tyranny. Instead, Locke follows Grotius and Pufendorf by seeking a normative standard for politics that transcends any particular circumstance. Also like Grotius and Pufendorf, he locates such a standard in the natural law.

Locke begins his most detailed published discussion of the law of nature in the second chapter of the *Second Treatise*, simultaneously with his introduction of the state of nature. According to Locke, we can only understand the true nature of political power if we "consider what state all men are naturally in, and that is a state of perfect freedom to order their actions and dispose of their possessions and persons as they think fit, within the bounds of the law of nature, without asking leave or depending upon the will of any other man" (II 4). Human beings are thus also naturally equal to one another in the sense that there is no "subordination or subjection" between any of them (II 4). All powers and claims human beings naturally have with respect to one another are reciprocal. The most prominent of these reciprocal powers is the

---

[36] There is some speculative discussion of the early history of government. But nearly all of this is explanatory, rather than normative argument, as Locke attempts to account for the worldwide prevalence of monarchy.

[37] For comparison, consider Sidney's *Discourses Concerning Government*, also highly influential among American colonists, which delves in painstaking detail into the specifics of the development of the English constitution to prove the author's claims. Cf. Pangle 1988, 289.

[38] Laslett in Locke 1988, 79.

[39] In fact, Locke paid a price for his frame of argument in the shorter term. Even after the Glorious Revolution, the ascendant Whigs wanted to emphasize the continuity of the new regime with English history, rather than accept Locke's more radical interpretation. As a result, they "went to considerable lengths to disassociate themselves" from Locke's views (Ashcraft 1986, 184). See also Zuckert 1994, 101–102.

[40] Locke writes: "at best an argument from what has been, to what should of right be, has no great force" (II 103).

right to enforce the law of nature by punishing those who violate it. This law wills "the peace and preservation of all mankind." It forbids us from harming the "life, health, liberty, or possessions" of anyone without provocation and commands us to preserve ourselves and—where this is not threatened—to preserve others as well (II 6, 7).

There are a few immediately striking features of this law of nature, which Locke claims is identical with the law of reason, that is, the principles of action that reason alone would discover for us. First, although Locke does not define the law in any further detail, nor does he explain how we come to know it, it is clear that this law bears almost no resemblance to Aristotelian-Thomistic natural law. There are no inherent ends or intrinsic purposes. This law is much more like a law in the ordinary sense: it commands and prohibits certain actions and behaviors and is backed by the threat of punishment and the promise of reward. Moreover, this law denies natural slavery and instead vindicates natural liberty and equality.

It is equally clear that this law differs significantly from Hobbes's account of the same topic—even if both do posit natural human equality. For Hobbes, our equality rests on our mutual ability to kill each other (Hobbes 1994, chapter 13). In contrast, Locke grounds natural equality in our equal human dignity as creations and possessions of God: "for men, being all the workmanship of one omnipotent and infinitely wise maker . . . whose workmanship they are, made to last during his, not one another's pleasure . . . furnished with like faculties, sharing all in one community of nature, there cannot be supposed any such subordination among us" (II 6). This difference from Hobbes forms an important explanation for why the commonwealths of Locke and Hobbes diverge so greatly in their characteristics. For Hobbes, our natural equality is a dumb fact, a practical rather than moral constraint. As a result, it raises no problem for Hobbes if his proposed political solution limits liberty and abolishes equality. Locke's position places great normative weight on our equality and liberty, and thus any decent political arrangement will have to somehow justify itself against this standard. In all of these respects (as well as identifying natural law with reason), the content of Locke's law of nature seems closely connected to the Ciceronian natural law of Grotius and Pufendorf.

Moreover, the idea of freedom found here shows a blending of the allegedly distinct liberal and republican conceptions of liberty. Locke repeatedly emphasizes the importance of non-domination. Yet this non-domination appears valuable because it ensures that we are not interfered with by others as we go about our business. Still, all of these claims about freedom, equality, and justice advanced by Locke depend on his assertion that they are supported by the law of nature—a law of nature he has outlined but still not adequately explained or defended.

Some of Locke's contemporary readers were no less perplexed by his reticence to explain what he meant by "the law of nature" than are many modern scholars. Some readers, professing a similar view to that later offered by Strauss, read Locke's *Treatises* (along with his *Essay Concerning Human Understanding*) and concluded that Locke was, in fact, following Hobbes. They could point to passages in the *Essay* where Locke argues—citing Cicero for his authority—that our sense of virtue and vice is determined by public approbation and blame, which obviously vary according to time and place (*ECHU* 2.28.13). They charged him with transforming the law of nature into prudential calculation of self-interest, abolishing natural standards of right and wrong, virtue and vice, in favor of conventionalism. Locke denied not only this view but also that he himself had ever even read the "justly decried" "monster of Malmesbury."[41] With respect to his argument in the *Essay*, Locke insists that readers misinterpreted his position. He claims that the passage shows where our ideas come from, not their correctness according to "the Law of Nature, which is that standing and unalterable Rule, by which they ought to judge" (*ECHU* 2.28.11, note). But despite these specific rebuttals about what his natural law is *not*, Locke nevertheless continued to refuse to offer a positive account of precisely what natural law is or where it comes from.

James Tyrrell, Locke's friend, begged him repeatedly to respond to these charges, to explain what he meant by natural law, its relationship to divine law, and whether the divine rewards and punishments allegedly underpinning it could be demonstrated by the light of reason alone.[42] Locke's continued refusal to do so further perplexed Tyrrell, since Tyrrell appears to have closely read an unpublished manuscript by Locke devoted entirely to natural law. Tyrrell could not understand why Locke would not vindicate himself by publishing it—nor did Locke explain his reasons for refusing. This work, which was only rediscovered and published in the mid-twentieth century,

---

[41] It is, of course, difficult to say how Locke could know Hobbes to be "justly decried" without having read him. For more on these controversies, see Horwitz's introduction to Locke 1990, 6–9.

[42] Locke 1990, 20–29. That contemporaries should have leveled these concerns certainly adds plausibility to the Strauss-Zuckert thesis.

was written in Latin and consists of a number of questions relating to the law of nature, which Locke proceeds to answer in turn. The contents of this manuscript go a long way toward helping us understand what Locke conceives the natural law to be.

The Natural Law of *Questions*: Reconciling *Honestum* and *Utile*

It is hazardous to attempt to interpret an author in light of unpublished writings—after all, writings usually go unpublished for a reason. Nevertheless, this particular work was clearly more than an idle essay for Locke. He produced three copies of the manuscript and even used an amanuensis to prepare a more polished version, which Locke himself then carefully read over and edited. According to Jenny Strauss Clay, the treatment of these manuscripts suggests the strong possibility that Locke—at least for some period—intended to publish the work.[43] For these reasons, it seems legitimate to look to these *Questions Concerning the Law of Nature* for clarity about Locke's views on the concept.

It may be that Locke chose not to publish because he found that he could not resolve some of the very problems identified by critics of his doctrine. But it is also possible that Locke had more benign reasons for not publishing. It may be that he felt the job of explaining natural law had already been adequately done. In *Some Thoughts Concerning Education*, immediately after recommending Cicero's "*Offices*" as the basic text (with the Bible) for educating a young man, he writes:

> When he has pretty well digested Tully's *Offices*, and added to it, *Puffendorf de Officio Hominis & Civis*, it may be seasonable to set him upon *Grotius de Jure Belli & Pacis*, or, which perhaps is the better of the two, *Puffendorf de Jure naturali & Gentium*; wherein he will be instructed in the natural rights of men, and the original and foundations of society, and the duties resulting from thence. This general part of civil-law and history, are studies which a gentleman should not barely touch at, but constantly dwell upon, and never have done with. (*Thoughts* 186)

[43] Locke 1990, 69.

Striking about this passage is that Locke connects Cicero with Grotius and Pufendorf and lists these three as the teachers both of individual duty and of the principles of political society. Locke has clearly identified the Ciceronian tradition with which this book is concerned and has implicitly enrolled himself in it.

Ruth Grant points to the same passage as evidence that Locke saw his project in the *Second Treatise* as the same as that undertaken by Grotius and Pufendorf.[44] When we examine Locke's unpublished *Questions Concerning the Law of Nature*, we find very close similarities between it and the accounts found in Grotius's and Pufendorf's work. More important for our immediate purpose, we find its argument compatible with arguments made in Locke's published works. For this reason, it makes sense to use it to help us shed light on the greatest lacunae of the *Second Treatise*: what the natural law is and how we come to know it.

The fact that *Questions* went unpublished is not the only feature that makes the work hard to interpret. The manner in which Locke writes also makes the task difficult. Unlike most of Locke's other works, *Questions* does not take the form of a straightforward, linear argument. It more closely resembles scholastic writings, in which questions are put forward and answers in the form of contending arguments are produced. Occasionally, Locke will refute one argument only several "questions" later, which can make it difficult to determine whether any particular argument is Locke's final position. Nevertheless, a relatively coherent account of natural law can be drawn out of the work.

Locke's first question—"Is there given a rule of conduct or a law of nature?"—seems to get straight to the heart of the matter.[45] In his framing of the question, Locke implies that for him, the law of nature is identical to a universal rule of conduct.[46] Locke explains that such a rule has been referred to in different terms, all of which he finds acceptable if properly construed. Cicero's formulations feature prominently in the vocabulary Locke uses: the law of nature is known as the "morally upright" (*honestum*) or "right reason" (*recta ratio*).[47] In the latter case, Locke specifies that this cannot mean simply the faculty of the mind by which we speak and calculate but rather "definite

---

[44] Grant 1987, 21–22.

[45] Locke 1990, 95. Diskin Clay translates the verb as "exist," but the word Locke uses is *detur*. Given the importance of Locke's argument that the law does not simply "exist" but is rather "given" by God, it is important to capture his sense here.

[46] Here we begin to see how Locke's ethics stand behind his politics.

[47] Horwitz notes the connection to Cicero's views expressed in *De legibus* and *De re publica*, as well as the modernized version of the same concept in Grotius's work (in Locke 1990, 97n6).

practical principles from which flow the sources of all virtues . . . what is rightly deduced from these principles is properly said to conform to right reason" (Locke 1990, 99). This description fits with Locke's claims in other works that the reason he endorses is not substantive (in the way that Plato's reason establishes ends for human life) but rather deductive, proceeding from established premises to draw correct conclusions (*ECHU* 2.1.34).[48] Finally, Locke gives his most comprehensive definition of natural law: "a law which each individual can discover by that light alone which is in us implanted by nature; to which too he ought to show himself obedient in everything . . . demanding a rational account of his duty; and this is that famous precept 'live according to nature' which the Stoics urge upon us" (Q1).[49]

Locke finds this last definition most satisfactory and uses it to distinguish natural law from any natural right: "for right [*ius*] consists in the fact that we have free use of something, but law [*lex*] is that which either commands or forbids some action" (Q1.11). Locke explains that this law is not a "dictate of reason," as Grotius puts it (*De iure* 1.1.10), because reason does not lay down the law but merely discovers it. In this correction, Locke follows Cicero rather than Grotius's innovation. His definition recalls Cicero's discussion in *De legibus*, where the latter, too, defines law as "right reason in commanding and forbidding" and separates natural law from natural right (*Leg.* 1.23, 1.33). The obligatoriness of the law derives from both the fact that its dictates are consonant with our rational nature *and* the fact that they are simply commanded by God. Locke's project thus more closely resembles Cicero's own in *De officiis* of demonstrating the fundamental unity of the *honestum* and the *utile* than Grotius's had done.

This dynamic—that natural law expresses both what is conformable to us as reasoning beings and what is ordered by God—is at the bottom of Locke's rationalism. It is how Locke resolves the tension between theistic and rational morality. The ultimate moral claims on us have a kind of double grounding, one deriving from our reason, the other from divine command. As we go along, we will see that this relationship can also help us to understand how Locke is able to describe obedience to natural law both as something in our self-interest and as something that supersedes our self-interest.

---

[48] See also Grant 1987, 6–7, 21, for further discussion of this feature of Locke's understanding of reason.

[49] Here it is worth remembering that Cicero was (wrongly) often numbered among the Stoics.

Having established what natural law is, Locke then must prove its existence and account for how we know it. Locke explains that the "natural" feature of natural law means that it must be perceivable by human beings on their own, that is, without hearsay or special revelation. In this way, Locke distinguishes natural law from divine positive law (the spoken commands of God that one might find in the Bible and that most of us can only know through the testimony of others)—but not, of course, from divine law simply; both natural law and divine positive law depend on God's rewards and punishments for their sanction.[50] To know such rules as law, Locke follows the definition of Grotius and Pufendorf and insists that law must be the known (or at least knowable) will of a superior, and the rewards and punishments for obedience must also be known, since no one can obligate us without first having power over us (Q1, Q8).

Locke considers a number of accounts to prove the existence and knowability of the law, including Aristotle's intrinsic ends, Grotius's appeal to universal human consensus, and the Christian idea of an innate conscience. He rejects all of these. Locke's critique of innate ideas, the same in *Questions* and in the *Essay*, rules out any natural human conscience. Our ideas of right and wrong are taught to us by others; they are not innate. Locke refutes Aristotle and Grotius together by pointing out that an empirical look at human behavior reveals no such universal rules of behavior or ends. This refutation echoes Pufendorf's argument against Grotius, and it likewise echoes Cicero's rejection of relativism in *Leg.* 1.42 and 2.13.[51]

But this raises a difficulty, which Locke acknowledges: if, in order to be binding, the law of nature must somehow be promulgated to humanity, how is it that the vast majority of humanity seem ignorant of all or at least some of it? Locke explains that the law of nature is in this respect like the principles of geometry. We do not need to rely on hearsay or revelation to understand the relationship of sides and angles in a triangle, yet few people have actually figured out those truths for themselves. As Locke puts it, using yet another analogy:

---

[50] In this, Locke follows a long-standing tradition in Christian natural law thought that has its most influential expression in Aquinas (*Summa* 1.91). This is not to say, as W. von Leyden does, that Locke felt that all laws, including human positive law, were divine (in Locke 1954, 28). For further critique of von Leyden's position, see Horwitz in Locke 1990, 49.

[51] In fact, Locke adopts one of Cicero's more peculiar arguments by claiming that the intensity of human disagreement is, in fact, evidence of the existence of natural law: the disagreement shows that we feel the importance of the universal rule but differ on interpreting it (Q1.17); compare to *Leg.* 1.47.

Good, rich veins of gold and silver lie hidden in the bowels of the earth, and moreover arms and hands and reason, the inventor of machines, are given to men, with which they can dig them out. Yet from this we do not conclude that all men are wealthy. First they must gird themselves for work and that wealth which has been hidden in the darkness must be excavated with great labor. It does not offer itself up to the idle and indolent. (Q2.34)

For Locke, our vices—particularly our laziness and myopic concern for our narrow self-interest—prevent most of us from even bothering to try to figure out the true law of nature, contenting ourselves at most with what others tell us is right and just.

How, then, should we reason rightly to understand the natural law? For Locke, all knowledge derives from sense experience, and knowledge of the natural law is no different. Locke begins with a relatively orthodox proof of the existence of God: the orderliness of the universe, the need for a first cause, and the fact that we are not the makers of ourselves leads us to recognize that there must be "some superior authority to which we are rightly subject, god, that is who holds over us a just and ineluctable power, who as he thinks proper [can raise us] to the heights of blessedness or thrust [us] down into wretchedness and punishment. From this . . . a knowledge of a legislator, or some superior power, to whom we are necessarily subject" (Q5.56).

Thus, Locke argues, reason establishes the essential criterion for a natural law: the existence of a superior, capable of rewarding and punishing us for obedience or disobedience to his will.[52] Later, in the *Essay Concerning Human Understanding*, Locke offers a still more extensive proof of God's existence that also appeals to the idea of a first cause, as well as to the idea that human intelligence must have proceeded from some higher intelligence. For support there, Locke appeals not to Aquinas or any of the other Christian natural law thinkers but to Cicero, saying:

---

[52] Horwitz notes that when discussing the divine in this manuscript, Locke deliberately writes *deus* rather than the Christian *Deus* and occasionally refers to God in the pagan Roman manner reserved for Jupiter: *optimus, maximus*. For Horwitz, this is evidence that Locke's manuscript contains contending voices: a pious Christian voice and an irreverent pagan one (in Locke 1990, 49). However, in fact, Locke is simply following the terminology used by Pufendorf. See chapter 4, note 45. It seems that Locke is merely attempting to confine himself to what is accessible to all, without the Christian revelation; he is adopting those references to the divine that would seem compatible with a natural religious mind, one that is likely to refer to the omnipotent as "the best and greatest."

If, nevertheless, any one should be found so senselessly arrogant, as to suppose man alone knowing and wise, but yet the product of mere ignorance
and chance; and that all the rest of the universe acted only by that blind haphazard; I shall leave with him that very rational and emphatical rebuke of
Tully (I. ii. De Leg.), to be considered at his leisure: "What can be more sil-
lily arrogant and misbecoming, than for a man to think that he has a mind
and understanding in him, but yet in all the universe beside there is no such
thing? Or that those things, which with the utmost stretch of his reason he
can scarce comprehend, should be moved and managed without any reason
at all? (*ECHU* 4.10.6)

Locke thus grounds the theistic basis of his natural law on the pagan Cicero!

But it is still necessary for Locke's argument that reason also tell us what
the divine will is. In language almost identical to that deployed by Grotius
and Pufendorf, Locke argues that the same features in the observable world
that point toward God's existence illustrate also his will. Since God does not
create idly, we must be intended to use our faculties—especially reason—for
God's glory (Locke does not specify quite what this would entail, expressing
his hope that there would be some later opportunity to discuss it). But we
certainly recognize ourselves as God's creation and therefore God's property, with an attendant duty to ensure our own preservation and even flourishing (Q5.58–61).[53] Our own strongest natural impulses reinforce this
same sense—and once again, God's command and our rational self-interest
coincide.

We would likewise recognize that God has also created all other human
beings and endowed them with reason, too. They are therefore the property
and creation of God as well as we. Just as we are compelled to preserve ourselves as God's property, so, too, we ought to preserve others whenever doing
so does not conflict with our primary duty to ourselves. As a result, the first
command of natural law with respect to others is the Ciceronian imperative to preserve human sociality: "[man] is impelled to form and preserve
a union of his life with other men, not only by needs and necessities of life,
but [also] . . . by a certain propensity to enter society, and is fitted to preserve
it by the gift of speech and the commerce of language" (Q5.61). Such a view

---

[53] Locke describes God as a "powerful and wise being who has jurisdiction and power over men
themselves. Who, indeed, will say that clay is not subject to the potter's will and that the pot cannot
be destroyed by the same hand that shaped it?" This is a fairly straightforward claim that as God's
creations, we belong to him.

precisely follows Cicero's account in *De officiis* of our duty derived from nature to preserve human sociality. There, too, Cicero bases the duty upon our capacity for speech and reason, which compels us to associate both to acquire necessities of life and because we have a spontaneous desire for fellowship (*Off*. 1.12). It also echoes Cicero's claim that the sovereignty of God over all of us places us in a community of law with all other rational beings, united in our shared capacity for reason and our shared subjection to the creator (*Leg*. 1.22–23; *Fin*. 285).

Zuckert contends that the view expressed here amounts to Aristotle's claim that human beings are by nature political animals, which he traces through Cicero and Grotius.[54] But, in fact, this position places Locke in the Ciceronian camp *against* Aristotle. Aristotle's claim that we are political animals is a consequence of his argument that the city is natural. This he shows by arguing that the city achieves the end at which other associations aim: self-sufficiency.[55] The Lockean-Ciceronian position holds that society forms only partly to satisfy natural needs; we also desire company for its own sake.[56] We are in that sense naturally *social*, but precisely because we can gain some measure of self-sufficiency and even society without establishing political communities, we are not naturally political. Political life comes to be through contingent circumstances and human will.[57]

Drawing this theory of natural law from *Questions* allows us to see Locke's apparently abrupt pronouncements on the content of the natural law in the *Second Treatise* in a new light. We find the content of the natural law there identical to that found in *Questions*. This fact alone is strong evidence for treating Locke as earnest in his discussions of the natural law. More important, we can now understand the reasoning whereby Locke arrives at his claims about what the natural law entails. What appears in the *Second Treatise* as a series of bald assertions about the content of natural law's commands does have a theoretical grounding. Moreover, the strong resemblance of Locke's reasoning in *Questions* to the natural law theories of Grotius, Pufendorf, and Cicero—coupled with Locke's recommendation of

---

[54] Zuckert 1994, 136. However, as mentioned, Zuckert believes that Locke ultimately rejects the entire idea of natural law discussed here.

[55] Cf. book 1 of the *Politics*.

[56] Pufendorf clarifies this very distinction. See Pufendorf 1991, 133.

[57] Nor is there any sense in Locke that political life is natural in the other Aristotelian sense, according to which the human telos is found in the exercise of practical reason in the experience of ruling and being ruled in turn. Cicero's pronouncements on the same subject are open to a wider variety of interpretations, but see Hawley 2020a for my argument that Cicero, in fact, rejects this Aristotelian thesis as well, preferring to embrace a diversity of natural human ends.

those writers in the *Essay*, among other places—might explain why Locke felt it unnecessary to run through the argument again in the *Second Treatise*. Anyone who had been educated in this tradition and had read their works (or anyone who had taken Locke's advice and mastered Cicero, Grotius, and Pufendorf) would see immediately why human beings have obligations to preserve themselves and others. His readers would likewise see immediately how our common condition as God's creations subject to his sovereignty means that there is no natural justification for any of us to rule another—thus grounding our freedom and equality in the same source.

The Problem of Punishment: A Natural Law for the Skeptic

But Locke's formulation leaves out one final component necessary for establishing the validity of natural law: the existence of rewards and punishments to back up that law. According to the Strauss-Zuckert thesis, this is where the Lockean version of natural law falls apart. They point to Locke's statement in the *Essay* that God has the power to uphold "divine law" with "Rewards and Punishments, of infinite duration, in another Life" (*ECHU* 2.28.8), and connect it with Locke's statements elsewhere in the *Essay* and in *The Reasonableness of Christianity*, where he claims that reason cannot establish the existence of an afterlife.[58] If, in fact, our unaided reason cannot establish the rewards and punishments attendant on the natural law, it would seem that it no longer qualifies as *natural* law (i.e., accessible to unaided reason), and Locke's project of establishing a normative ground for politics accessible to all regardless of denomination has failed (or, in the Strauss-Zuckert reading, has rightly fallen away, revealing Locke's true political teaching).

However, the crucial passage in the *Essay* can be read in a more generous way that can preserve Locke's doctrine as it stands. After pointing out how the prospect of eternal reward or punishment changes a person's calculation of good and evil, Locke says: "for if there be no prospect beyond the grave the inference is certainly right, 'let us eat and drink,' let us enjoy what we delight in, 'for tomorrow we shall die'" (*ECHU* 2.21.60). Here Locke is not stating that certain knowledge of rewards and punishments is necessary to

---

[58] See, for instance, Strauss 1953, 202; Zuckert 1994, 211.

preserve morality and natural law; the mere *prospect* of the afterlife is suffi-cient. For earthly hedonism to be justified, the burden of certainty is on the atheist to prove that there is no afterlife. Moreover, elsewhere in the *Essay*, Locke presents his proof of the existence of God, a proof that attributes om-nipotence to God. Therefore, Locke seems to have demonstrated, if not the certainty, then at least the possibility of divine reward and punishment.

Thus, Locke, in fact, explicitly denies that sure *knowledge* of rewards and punishments in the afterlife is necessary for the viability of natural law as law. This is what makes Locke's adaptation of Ciceronian natural law such a theo-retical advance. As was discussed in chapter 1 of this book, the fact that Cicero was a philosophical skeptic poses a certain puzzle for his natural law doc-trine: how can one reconcile a general attitude of doubt and uncertainty with the apparently dogmatic claims of natural law? Cicero himself never offers a solution to this problem, but Locke offers a version of this natural law that does not require such certain knowledge, at least on the most dubious of the requirements of the doctrine: rewards and punishments. While Locke insists that our reason is able to establish on its own the existence of the lawgiver and the content of his will, the epistemological task for reason is considerably more modest when it comes to the rewards and punishments attendant on the law. Here it is not necessary to prove that those rewards and punishments *will*, in fact, occur, only that they *might*: "the rewards and punishments of another life, which the Almighty has established as the enforcements of his law, are of weight enough to determine the choice, against whatever pleasure or pain this life can show, *when the eternal state is considered but in its bare possibility*, which nobody can make any doubt of" (*ECHU* 2.21.70; emphasis added).[59]

This is not an underhanded attempt to move the goalposts.[60] If one were to make the *certainty* of reward and punishment a requirement for true law, then not only natural but all civil laws would fail the test.[61] After all, even in a well-governed commonwealth, a criminal can at most expect that he will be caught and punished. But he does not know for certain. This does not un-dermine civil law's claim to being true law. Furthermore, given that Locke believes reason *can* establish the existence of God and discover what he wills

---

[59] Cicero offers a similar vision in the dream of Scipio, where those who obey the will of the su-preme deity best are those who most advance the primary obligation of natural law: human socia-bility. They are rewarded most richly in heaven after their deaths (*Rep.* 6.13).

[60] However, it is a slight modification of the unpublished view of *Questions*.

[61] Cicero himself makes a general rule of avoiding claims to certainty, preferring the more episte-mologically modest "more probable or less probable" (*Off.* 2.7).

for man, it seems not merely possible but even very probable that God would reward those who obey and punish those who do not.

It may seem as though all of this is contradicted by a striking statement Locke makes in *The Reasonableness of Christianity*. Speaking of the classical philosophers (including "Tully") who attempted to establish the moral law on the basis of reason alone, Locke says:

> Those just measures of right and wrong, which necessity had anywhere introduced, the civil laws prescribed, or philosophy recommended, stood on their true foundations. . . . But where was it that their obligation was thoroughly known and allowed, and they received as precepts of a law; of the highest law, the law of nature? That could not be, without a clear knowledge and acknowledgment of the law-maker, and the great rewards and punishments, for those that would, or would not obey him. (*Reasonableness* 243)

Read in isolation, this passage seems to contradict Locke's claims in the *Essay*, suggesting now instead that sure knowledge of the afterlife *is* necessary for obedience to the divine law. But, in fact, as Locke continues, it becomes clear that he is not setting out a rigorous epistemological standard for the law of nature but rather talking about the practical and historical challenges of making the great mass of people actually obey the moral law. "Thoroughly known and allowed" here refers to the general practice of human beings and not to rare philosophic exceptions. Indeed, in the previous paragraph, Locke had reaffirmed the existence of the natural law, despite admitting that no philosopher before Christ had managed to get it exactly right. Locke claims that the real problem with the natural law (and hence also the real reason for the needfulness of Christianity) is that even a completely sound proof of the natural law will not succeed in making most people obey it: "The greatest part of mankind want leisure or capacity for demonstration; nor can carry a train of proofs. . . . And you may as soon hope to have all the day-labourers and tradesmen, the spinsters and dairy-maids, perfect mathematicians, as to have them perfect in ethics this way. Hearing plain commands, is the sure and only course to bring them to obedience and practice" (*Reasonableness* 246). In other words, revelation and the certainty it provides about reward and punishment are not strictly necessary to the establishment of natural law as a binding standard for the discerning; but they are necessary to make most ordinary people actually obedient to their moral duties. It is thus possible to harmonize Locke's apparently contradictory claims in *Reasonableness* and the *Essay* while also preserving intact his logic of natural law and his own philosophical commitment to epistemic modesty.

So now, according to Locke, we can say that the coherence of natural law would collapse only if reason could disprove the "bare possibility" of an afterlife of reward and punishment, which Locke quite plausibly denies that reason is capable of doing. Skepticism now works *for* Locke's argument rather than against it. It is quite hard for reason to prove the *non*-existence of posthumous rewards and punishments. Locke explains the purely naturalistic, hedonic logic of this claim: "he that will allow exquisite and endless happiness to be but *the possible consequence* of a good life here, and the contrary state *the possible reward* of a bad one; must own himself to judge very much amiss" if he does not conclude that he ought to choose virtue (*ECHU* 2.21.70; emphasis added). Locke here follows the logic of Pascal's wager; he elaborates that reason alone is sufficient to show that as long as infinite happiness and infinite suffering in the afterlife are *possibilities*, they should rationally outweigh any earthly pleasure or pain. The worst-case scenario for a good man (no afterlife and thus no sensation after death at all) corresponds to the best-case scenario for the villain (his alternative being an eternity of punishment). Given this, reason can confidently commend the life of virtue on hedonistic grounds, no matter whether the earthly rewards and punishments favor a life of vice.[62]

Yet Locke is not prepared to concede even on this last point. According to him, the balance of pleasure and pain—even if one only considers consequences in this life—favors obedience to the natural law (*ECHU* 2.21.70). The just profit more often than the wicked. The natural law thus *is* backed by sanction we can see with our own eyes. Locke presents a second, connected account of the rewards and punishments attending the natural law which illustrates both his indebtedness to Cicero's ethical-political thought and his innovation on that Ciceronian foundation as he attempts his own reconciliation of *honestum* with *utile*.

---

[62] At another point in the *Essay*, Locke seems almost exasperated with the kind of misreading later posited by Strauss: "I would not here be mistaken, as if, because I deny an innate law, I thought there were none but positive laws. There is a great deal of difference between an innate law, and a law of nature; between something imprinted on our minds in their very original, and something that we being ignorant of may attain to the knowledge of, by the use and due application of our natural faculties. And I think they equally forsake the truth, who, running into the contrary extremes, either affirm an innate law, or deny that there is a law knowable by the light of nature, i. e. without the help of positive revelation" (*ECHU* 1.3.13).

Returning to *Questions*, in the final section, Locke asks whether the foundation for the law of nature is each individual's self-interest, and he almost immediately denies that it is. As a stalking horse for his argument, Locke chooses the same target as Cicero and Grotius had done before him: Carneades. Using language taken almost verbatim from Cicero and Grotius, Locke attributes to Carneades the view that all decisions should be referred to the immediate self-interest of the individual agent.[63]

In rejecting Carneades, Locke clarifies that he does not mean that the natural law and private interest are opposed to each other—in fact, the law is the "greatest defense" of the private good of individuals (Q12.107). Locke asserts that "nothing is as conducive to the common advantage of the individual, nothing so protective of the safety and security of men's possessions, as the observance of the law of nature" (Q12.108). The *general following* of the law of nature is in our interest because human cooperation and society can only persist if people deal fairly with one another. Without the natural law to provide a stable standard, our conceptions of virtue and vice would disintegrate, and, with it, our ability to live together (Q1.20).[64] Developing an argument that is prominent in the *Second Treatise*, Locke insists that we are liable to be biased judges in our own case—that in many individual instances, we would be tempted to violate the law of nature. But if people generally followed this immoral principle, human society would become impossible, and all the benefits we accrue from it would be lost. The immediate gain of violating the law of nature is thus outweighed by the high costs of making our "immediate" self-interest our standing rule of action. Thus, Locke says boldly, "in truth, you want the decision of what is useful and what is not to reside in the power of another" (Q12.108).

In this, Locke seems to follow Cicero closely. In *De officiis*, Cicero argues that after the divine, the greatest benefactors of man are other men (*Off.* 2.10). Nearly all the good things of this life come into being because of

---

[63] Regardless of whether this is a fair depiction of Carneades's view, Locke uses him as Cicero does to serve as the standard-bearer for total immorality. See Locke 1990, 235nn94–95, for the several different places in which Locke appears to lift wholesale Grotius's and Cicero's descriptions of Carneades's views.

[64] Jeremy Waldron mentions that it is a central hope of modern secular liberalism that one can surgically remove (or "bracket") the theistic claims from Locke's argument and still retain the rest of his liberal theory (Waldron 2002). A. John Simmons, in his attempt to do just that, points to this kind of argument as Locke's "rule-consequentialism," the possible secular warrant for a Lockean view (Simmons 1992, 50). Eleanor Curran convincingly shows how God indirectly stands behind even this element of Locke's theory (Curran 2013).

human society. For this reason, violating the natural law for our own short-term benefit harms us more generally because it undermines "the common life and fellowship of men." It would be as if "every limb of the body thought it could profit by seizing the strength of its neighbor; necessarily the body as a whole would weaken and perish" (*Off.* 3.21). For his part, Locke brings Cicero himself into the argument, asserting that if we accept the Carneadean alternative, we must judge that Catiline "was a True Born son of nature and, since he invaded Rome, he was more deserving of empire over the world than Tully who defended it" (Q12.112).

From this discussion, we see that Locke does believe that there are at least very obvious rewards for obedience to the natural law that can be discerned by unaided reason. Thus, "the rightness of an action does not depend on interest, but interest follows from rectitude" (Q12.119). In other words, our self-interest is not the source of rightness, but we will ultimately benefit from behaving rightly. Punishments are discernible as well, at least on the level of society (the collapse of cooperation harms everyone). But it is still not quite clear whether there is any rationally deducible, this-worldly punishment for the *individual* for breaking the natural law. After all, I can easily see how I benefit from a society in which people respect one another's rights and property, but that does not give me a reason to do the same if I believe I could gain by being the only (undetected) violator.

Locke recognizes this and concludes *Questions* with a reiteration of the importance of punishment as a sanction for all law. Yet he does not offer there an answer to the problem. We find that solution, however, in the *Second Treatise*'s discussion of the state of nature, to which it is necessary to turn. There, immediately after summarizing the law of nature, Locke discusses who will enforce the law of nature and punish offenders in this life: other human beings:

> And that all men may be restrained from invading others' rights, and from doing hurt to one another, and the law of nature be observed, which willeth the peace and preservation of all mankind, the execution of the law of nature is, in that state, put into every man's hands, whereby every one has a right to punish the transgressors of that law to such a degree, as may hinder its violation: *for the law of nature would, as all other laws that concern men in this world, be in vain, if there were no body that in the state of nature had a power to execute that law, and thereby preserve the innocent and restrain offenders.* (II 7; emphasis added)

Locke here responds in advance to the Strauss-Zuckert critique about the absence of specific, worldly punishment for violations of the natural law He acknowledges that the law of nature *would* be "vain" without punishment and offers each person's own jealous defense of his own interest as the source of that punishment. As we are all God's property, one can see how God's authority as lawgiver can be credited behind such sanctions. It seems that Locke's natural law does indeed satisfy the third and last requirement of a true law.

Once again, the sure knowledge of punishment for any particular violation does not seem to be a requirement of legitimate law for Locke. It is enough that humans generally do avenge wrongs done to themselves and tend also to want to restrain those who wantonly harm others as well. Locke uses a Ciceronian analogy in relation to this punishment. Cicero had likened those who violate the rules of justice by using force to beasts, who only appear as men and have, in fact, placed themselves outside the community of human beings (*Off.* 1.105, 3.82; *Leg.* 1.30; etc.). So Locke says about an aggressor: "having quitted reason, which God hath give to be the rule betwixt man and man, and the common bond whereby human kind is united into one fellowship and society . . . so revolting to his own kind to that of beasts by making force, which is theirs, to be his rule of right, he renders himself liable to be destroyed" (II 15).[65]

Locke's construal of violators thus far conforms closely to Cicero's claims in book 1 of *De officiis*. Recall that Cicero asserted that the two principles of justice were that no one should harm anyone else unless provoked by wrongdoing and that one should respect the property of others (*Off.* 1.21). When we are provoked by wrongdoing, we are entitled to deal out punishment to the offenders sufficient to restrain them and to deter others from following their example (*Off.* 1.33). Moreover, in *Pro Milone*, Cicero had articulated the permissive logic of self-defense in a condition like the state of nature, where no authority is immediately available for protection: "there is, o judges, a law—not written, but natural—which we did not read, or learn, or acquire, but which we took and drank in from nature itself . . . namely if our life is endangered by certain plots, or by force and weapons of criminals and enemies, all means of achieving our safety are morally upright" (*Mil.* 10). Locke echoes this language, saying that we have

---

[65] See further Grant 1987, 71.

the right to use any force necessary against anyone who seeks to put us in their power: "and hence it is that he who attempts to get another man into his absolute power, does thereby put himself into a state of war with him . . . for I have reason to conclude, that he would get me into his power without my consent, would use me as he please when he had got me there" (II 17). If the threat is overcome and the guilty captured, Locke also follows Cicero in arguing that the right of punishment extends "to that degree, and with so much severity, as will suffice to make it an ill bargain to the offender, give him cause to repent, and terrify others from doing the like" (II 8). With this final addition, Locke appears to have established the grounds for his understanding of the law of nature.

The final picture resembles very closely the Ciceronian version of natural law, although, like Grotius and Pufendorf, Locke expands and systematizes the role of the divine power standing behind the law. Recalling Locke's own recommendations about teaching duty through *De officiis* and the Bible, we might see that his natural law theory consists of Ciceronian moral philosophy supported by a more overtly monotheistic natural theology.

However, Locke also picks up a challenge offered by Cicero that Grotius and Pufendorf had sidestepped: how a skeptical epistemology, which cannot possibly establish the *certainty* of divine reward and punishment, could yield a clearly binding doctrine of natural law backed by rewards and punishments. Grotius had gone so far as to dodge this problem altogether by claiming that we could know the natural law merely by the universal behavior of the nations. Locke takes the problem much more seriously and presents a way in which someone who shares a Ciceronian skepticism about the capacity for sure human knowledge could nevertheless come to endorse a natural law backed by the undeniable *possibility* of punishment and reward. This new systematic grounding for the natural law under the condition of epistemic modesty is one of Locke's great contributions to the Ciceronian tradition.

Rights and the State of Nature: Locke contra Hobbes

This understanding of Locke's natural law also helps us to better understand his contribution to the Ciceronian tradition's theory of rights, especially as it relates to the other early modern theorist sometimes acclaimed as the founder of liberalism: Hobbes. Many scholars of various outlooks take

Hobbes to be the crucial figure in the development of liberalism.[66] Insofar as both Hobbes and Locke present theories of pre-political natural rights and contracts in which Hobbes comes chronologically first, this view is clearly true. It is beyond the scope of this book to attempt to adjudicate whether Hobbes or Locke deserves more credit (or blame) for inaugurating modern liberalism. However, by recognizing the Ciceronian structure of Locke's natural law, we can better understand his theory of rights and see how Locke's rights differ in their nature and grounding from Hobbes's. From here, we can also see finally how this difference can explain why Locke derives a theory of free and limited government from his premises about natural law and rights while Hobbes does not.

A. John Simmons, expressing a common opinion, complains that Locke "offers no definition of a 'right' generally, nor does he ever say clearly what a right is."[67] We have already seen that Locke offers at least the beginning of a definition in *Questions*, where he explains that a "right [*jus*] consists in the fact that we have a free use of something, but law [*lex*] is that which either commands or forbids some action" (Q1.11). In addition, Locke's language there has sometimes before implied that natural rights are derivative of natural law. Locke confirms this view in the *Second Treatise*: "man being born . . . with a title to perfect freedom, and an uncontrolled enjoyment of all the rights and privileges of the law of nature, hath by nature a power to preserve his property, that is his life, liberty, and estate, against the injuries and attempts of other men" (II 87). The famous Lockean rights to "life, liberty, and estate" are simply the mirror image of those things that the law of nature forbids us to harm or interfere with when they belong to others. They exist (in a sense) in the negative space created by the duties of all individuals with respect to one another. To say that I have a right to something is to say that you have a corresponding duty not to interfere with me over it. Pufendorf put this most succinctly: a right "in the strict sense" entails that there be a

---

[66] Strauss (1953), Patrick Deneen (2019), and others take Locke to be essentially Hobbesian in his basic premises, even if he draws different immediate political conclusions. C. B. Macpherson's famous argument about liberalism's possessive individualism likewise places Hobbes and Locke in the same camp (MacPherson 2011). Skinner, Pocock, and others see Hobbes as the great opponent of their republican tradition, giving rise to the liberalism that would ultimately supplant it. In Sullivan's account of the emergence of liberal republicanism in England, Hobbes provides the strain of liberalism that mixes with Machiavelli's republicanism (Sullivan 2004). Of course, not everyone accepts this view. Judith Shklar claims that "Hobbes is not the father of liberalism" because "No theory that gives public authorities the unconditional right to impose beliefs and even a vocabulary as they may see fit upon the citizenry can be described as even remotely liberal" (Shklar 1989, 24). On this side, we also have Locke's repeated denunciations of Hobbes.

[67] Simmons 1992, 92.

corresponding "obligation in another" (*De iure naturae* 3.5.3).[68] This understanding of the relationship between rights and duties might well account for the initial affinity of Locke the rights theorist for Cicero the famous theorist of duties (*officiis*). To be a rights theorist in this way automatically makes one a theorist of duties as well.

Pufendorf's statement regarding the relationship between rights and duties is aimed explicitly at the theory of Hobbes. It is worth turning to Hobbes's theory briefly, not only because Locke's becomes clearer by contrast but also because the differences in their views help to explain how Locke is the only one of the two to draw liberal political conclusions from what at first appear to be common liberal premises. In doing so, we can also see Locke's innovation on the Ciceronian tradition, giving rise to the powerful strain of liberal theory that begins with Locke and continues through the American founding.

Hobbes is quite clear about what he means by a right. Like Locke, he distinguishes right/*jus* from law/*lex*: "For though they that speak of this subject, use to confound *Jus*, and *Lex*, *Right* and *Law*; yet they ought to be distinguished; because RIGHT, consisteth in liberty to do, or to forbear; Whereas LAW, determineth, and bindeth to one of them." Thus far, Hobbes and Locke appear similar. Their first fundamental right also at first appears to be the same, the right to life: "the right of nature, which writers commonly call jus naturale, is the liberty each man hath to use his own power as he will himself for the preservation of his own nature." But then Hobbes explains what he means by liberty: "By liberty is understood, according to the proper signification of the word, the absence of external impediments" (*Leviathan* 14). Elsewhere, Hobbes calls this condition in the state of nature a "blameless liberty" (*De corpore*, 1.14.6).[69] This liberty is blameless, because, as we have noted before, Hobbes denies that there are natural standards of justice and injustice; thus, there is no reason for blaming any action taken in the state of nature (except perhaps on prudential, rather than moral, grounds). But for the same reason, our apparently expansive rights come with no corresponding obligations for others to respect them. In the state of nature, each man is only "governed by his own reason"—which for Hobbes simply calculates the appropriate means to chosen ends. The laws of nature, Hobbes clarifies, "are not properly Lawes"; they only become so once a sovereign comes into being that "obliges men to obey them" (*Leviathan* 14). Until then,

---

[68] See on this Zuckert 1994, 275.
[69] See further on this Spragens 1973, 179.

our right to life gives us a right to do or use anything we see fit for aiding our self-preservation, including the bodies of others.

For this reason, Hobbes's state of nature is a state of war: "that right of all men to all things, is in effect no better than if no man had right to any thing. For there is little use and benefit of the right a man hath, when another as strong, or stronger than himself hath right to the same" (*Elements of Law* 80). Thus, the Hobbesian solution is to give up our rights and enter political society, and only then do obligations come into being: "when a man hath . . . abandoned or granted away his right, then he is said to be obliged, or bound" (*Leviathan* 14). Whereas for Locke, rights and duties appear together, for Hobbes, the presence of one entails the absence of the other.

Locke may indeed have Hobbes in mind in *Questions* when he rails against the followers of Carneades, who think that "all right . . . should be determined by the interest of each individual" (Q12.106). Locke even presents a powerful critique of Hobbes's solution to the problem of the state of war that ensues from his premises. Hobbes suggests that we have an obligation not to break our covenant once we have agreed to give up our rights. But Locke notes that there is no place to derive such an obligation from if our self-interest would be served by breaking it: "men under the law of nature are [as these writers say] in a state of war. All society and trust, the bond of society, are destroyed. What reason for keeping promises, what force for the preservation of so-ciety . . . when all justice and equity is what is useful?" (Q12.15).

Locke's solution avoids this problem by drawing a conclusion from prem-ises deeply embedded in the Ciceronian natural law tradition, which the tradition itself had nevertheless not developed. For all the cosmopolitan elements of the Ciceronian tradition as it appears not only in Cicero's writings but also in those of Grotius and Pufendorf, rights appear meaningfully only among those in political society with one another. Rights are the structure of just relationships and are reflected in law. Following the Ciceronian tradi-tion, we have seen that Locke takes the law of nature (contra Hobbes) to be a true law, binding, obligatory to all regardless of situation by virtue of the uni-versal sovereign, God. Locke recognizes that it follows from this that the state of nature—even though it lacks political societies of human construction—is nevertheless a political society in one respect: it is under the sovereignty of God.[70] There is thus already the basis in Locke for a kind of natural cosmo-politanism of rights and duties.

---

[70] Not unlike the cosmopolis ruled by the highest god in Scipio's dream.

The universal sovereignty of God means that the state of nature is not without law in Hobbes's "proper" sense, and human beings therefore are all in relationship with one another as subjects of this same sovereign.[71] This gives Lockean rights (and concomitant obligations) a firm grounding even before the rise of human political life. It also means that these rights, while strict in forbidding the interference of others, do not give us carte blanche to act as we will. We are forbidden to harm ourselves—or even to wantonly destroy animals or inanimate objects, since these, too, derive their dignity from being part of God's creation.

For Hobbes, rights have no ultimate moral justification and are in a fundamental sense an obstacle to the establishment of peaceful political society. For Locke, rights have real normative weight as the obverse side of real duties that are commanded to us by the highest law. Not only does this make our entrance into political society easier to explain for Locke (as it avoids the Hobbesian problem with covenant keeping), but, more important, it means that any just political society will have to accommodate itself to rights by making them the central focus of the regime.[72] Rights are now grounded directly in the law of nature, yet they also provide the foundation for the people's corporate claim to sovereignty. This might reasonably be taken as the essence of the liberal innovation in early modernity, which Locke draws from Ciceronian premises, even if Cicero and his heirs until Locke did not draw it themselves.[73]

Property

Before we move on to see how Locke's liberal political vision reflects this innovation, it is important to consider one peculiar right among those that Locke considers natural: property. As we have already seen, Locke and Cicero share

---

[71] Since we are also social creatures—and not naturally asocial, as Hobbes has us—we may have also considerably more substantial relationships with one another.

[72] It may seem as though Hobbes's commonwealth is also structured and fundamentally constrained by the right to life. After all, we form such commonwealths solely for the protection of our lives. Yet Hobbes's sovereign is not constrained in this way. Because the social contract takes place only between the subjects and not between the subjects and the sovereign, the sovereign is not bound and can therefore kill any of its subjects (although the subjects may resist such attempts) or commit any other offense against them, because justice is only ever what the sovereign decrees. Once again, rights entail no obligations in the Hobbesian construal of them.

[73] It is certainly one of the defining Lockean features of the new American regime.

a great deal, but thematically, their concern for property and its relationship to the ends of political life may be the most obvious and striking of their commonalities. This makes it nearly shocking that so few scholars have attended to the link between them.[74] Both face the same theoretical conundrum. Both assume that, as Cicero puts it, "no property is originally private by nature" (*Off.* 1.21). In Locke's words, God "has given the earth to men in common" (II 26). Yet not only do both accept the natural justice of holding private property, but both go so far as to conclude that the protection of property is a primary goal of political society. In Cicero's words, "political communities and commonwealths were established particularly so that people could hold on to their property; true, nature first guided human beings to congregate, but it was in hope of protecting their possessions that they sought the protection of cities" (*Off.* 2.73). In noticeably similar terms, Locke writes: "the great and chief end, therefore, of men's uniting into commonwealths, and putting themselves under government, is the preservation of their property" (II 124).[75]

Thus, both Cicero and Locke begin from the same premise and arrive at the same somewhat counterintuitive conclusion. As discussed in chapter 1, Cicero never presents a single unified argument to account for either the *just* development of private property or why its protection is such a priority for a just society. Locke does. Although he depends on elements of Ciceronian logic throughout, he nevertheless offers a far more systematic account that achieves a major theoretical objective of Cicero's political thought, which Cicero himself never quite managed.

In chapter 1, we encountered Nussbaum's critique of Cicero's theory of private property, but it is worth revisiting briefly what Nussbaum finds so problematic about Cicero's account, since it is precisely this difficulty that Locke in an innovative manner attempts to solve. Cicero uses the Stoic analogy of the theater: "just as, though the theater is a public place, yet it is correct to say that the particular seat a man has taken belongs to him, so in the state or in the universe, though these are common to all, no principle of justice militates against the possession of private property" (*Fin.* 3.67).[76] But this

---

[74] Only Nacol seems to devote sustained attention to this link, and even she hesitates before attributing to Cicero real influence on Locke. She says, more modestly, "Cicero's thought *may* have shaped Locke's well-known views" on property (Nacol 2021, 141; emphasis added).

[75] Locke offers there a capacious definition of property that includes all of a person's natural rights to life and liberty as well. But at other points, he emphasizes the importance of actual physical property in the creation of political societies.

[76] This analogy did not originate with Cicero, despite the fact that Grotius, Pufendorf, and others attribute it to him. Garnsey points out that the tendency to treat Cicero as the originator of this image is so pervasive that it even affects contemporary scholars such as Waldron (Garnsey 2007, 113).

appealing analogy glosses over important facts: that in reality not everyone seems to have a "seat" and that some of those "seats" were acquired unjustly. Cicero's account of the origins of property in *De officiis* seems to recognize these features but presents them without comment or acknowledgment that they pose a normative problem. There, Cicero lists among the original ways in which property was acquired both settlement in vacant land and conquest (*Off.* 1.21). As discussed in chapter 1, Cicero's apparent unconcern with these problems can be explained once we recognize that his interest lies in the role property plays in facilitating justice within existing societies more than in its legitimate origins. Yet if we subscribe to the notion that anything held justly must also have been acquired justly, Cicero's position is open to Nussbaum's critique that property originating in conquest and property originating in peaceful settlement "look morally different," and there is no reason to expect that "there is any close relationship between existing distributions and the property rights justice would assign."[77]

Locke's account of the origins of property is one of the most famous aspects of his political thought and has been covered extensively by other scholars.[78] My purpose here is to show how Locke begins from Cicero's principles and reaches Cicero's conclusion by a new route—yet a route that depends on a number of Ciceronian insights. Locke accepts the view of Cicero (and Grotius and Pufendorf) that the world originally belonged to humanity in common. Locke explicitly rejects the Grotius-Pufendorf solution that there must have been some tacit agreement among humankind to allow the divvying up of the earth.[79] If such a universal agreement were necessary from the start, Locke says, humanity would have starved (II 28). Instead, Locke argues that the principle of self-ownership (or self-usufruct, as God is truly our owner) is sufficient to explain just appropriation from the original commons. Since we already have property in ourselves, the mere act of mixing that property with something previously unowned makes it ours. Locke admits some initial limitations to this right: our duties to avoid waste and to refrain from disadvantaging anyone else (by leaving "as much and as good" for others). These limitations, however, flow from the first insights of natural law: that the earth is the property of God, who has given it to all humanity in common (so we

[77] Nussbaum 2000, 182.
[78] Including, but by no means limited to, Dunn 1982; Macpherson 2011; Garnsey 2007; Zuckert 1994; Zuckert 2002 Grant 1987; Tully 1980; Waldron 2002.
[79] See chapter 4. See also Garnsey 2007, 142–143.

must not harm it by wasting its fruits), and that all other humans are likewise subjects of God (so we must respect their interests as well).

The intuitive logic of Locke's argument relies on a view of the world that Cicero regularly emphasized. As explored in chapter 1, Cicero interprets the natural world as simultaneously bountiful and barren. On one hand, the entire earth exists for human benefit and consumption, and much that is useful can be extracted from it (*Leg.* 1.25). On the other hand, while other animals naturally acquire with relative ease all their basic necessities of life, we humans "supply ourselves with food barely—or not even barely—with great labor" (*Fin.* 2.111). The earth is perhaps best described as *potentially* abundant and can be made *actually* abundant only through the application of human reason and industry.

Locke expresses a similar view when he argues that uncultivated land produces one-tenth or even one-hundredth of what could be produced once it is cultivated by human industry (II 40). Our reason provides us with this ability to make land far more productive: "God gave the world to men in common . . . he gave it to the use of the industrious and the rational . . . not to the fancy or covetousness of the quarrelsome and contentious" (II 34). The multiplying effect of human labor on the productivity of land helps Locke once again reconcile individual self-interest with our duty to preserve our fellows. Locke explains:

> he who appropriates land to himself by his labor, does not lessen, but in-crease the common stock of mankind: for the provisions serving to the sup-port of human life, produced by one acre of enclosed and cultivated land, are (to speak much with compass) ten times more than those which are yieled by an acres of land . . . lying waste in common. And therefore he that encloses [ten acres] may truly be said to give ninety acres to mankind. (II 37)

By applying our reason and industry to serve ourselves, we have, in fact, created a surplus that benefits the rest of humanity. In this way, the collective ownership right of humanity over the world is not destroyed by individual appropriation; it is enhanced. The introduction of money by the tacit consent of all allows individuals to acquire and produce far more than they need without violating the prohibition on waste, and it only intensifies the effect of this dynamic. Producers thus become benefactors of the community.

The classical republican tradition is often viewed as essentially opposed to commerce.[80] As a result, Cicero might not appear as a likely source for Locke's view that increasing wealth is a component of our duty.[81] Yet Locke's own papers suggest otherwise. Marshall points to one of the earlier references Locke makes to Cicero in his notes, taken from book 2 of *De officiis*, "which declared that it was 'a duty to make money, but only by honourable means, and a duty to save and increase it by care and thrift.'"[82] Locke's illustration of the benefits of rationally directed labor and cooperation (from loaves of bread to ships, irrigation, buildings, trade, etc.) strongly resembles Cicero's list of all the benefits of human cooperation in *De officiis*.[83]

Locke at times expands his use of the term *property* to include all of a person's natural rights: "his property, that is, his life, liberty, and estate" (II 87). In bringing the ideas of property and rights closer together and in describing rights as something a person *owns*, Locke makes explicit and memorable something already present in the Ciceronian tradition. As we saw in chapter 4, Grotius and Pufendorf write of rights as something an individual possesses. In chapter 2, we saw that Cicero's concept of rights also entails an element of ownership, such that the rights citizens claim as part of the commonwealth are, in a sense, ownership rights. However, Locke's language concerning rights in the *Second Treatise* places a new emphasis on this aspect. This emphasis comes at the expense of the other sense in which the Ciceronian tradition construes rights: as the manifestations of justly structured relationships. This is why Pufendorf denies that rights exist in the state of nature, because rights only make sense in relationships with other people. We see from his *Questions* that Locke himself largely agrees with this view of rights, deriving them from the natural law and from our insight that we and others are all connected as subjects of God. In other words, for Locke, too, rights make no sense except in relation to others. But this facet or foundation of rights is far less evident in (although, again, completely compatible with and, in fact, the grounds for) Locke's treatment of them in the *Second Treatise*, where they are introduced largely without the theoretical grounding

---

[80] Machiavelli's claim that arms acquire gold better than gold can acquire arms (*Discourses* 2.10.1) undoubtedly looms large in this interpretation.

[81] But, as noted in chapter 2, Cicero, in fact, approves of commercial life, as long as it is carried out on a sufficiently large scale.

[82] Marshall 1994, 300. Cf. *Off.* 2.87, where Cicero goes on to refer readers to his own translation of Xenophon's *Oeconomicus*, which details how best to increase one's (agricultural) property.

[83] Cf. Strauss 1953, 237n110. Compare sections 40–44 of the *Second Treatise* to *Off.* 2.12–14.

provided in *Questions*.[84] Since the legacy of Locke's political philosophy is derived almost entirely from the *Second Treatise* and since *Questions* was not rediscovered until the mid-twentieth century, the rights-as-possessions aspect of Locke's theory came to dominate among those who followed him at the expense of rights-as-just-relations.[85] At the end of this book, I will return to discuss what conceptual difficulties in thinking about rights might be overcome if we recover what was lost in the latter formulation.

Natural Law and Limited Government

Having explored Cicero's importance in shaping the pre-political and super-political aspects of Locke's theory, it now remains to see how Locke's theory of government reflects those elements. From his deduction that no man has any superior by nature, Locke easily arrives at the conclusion that government is not natural. In this, he agrees not only with Hobbes but with the Ciceronian tradition as well (*Sest.* 42). Given all of their rights in the state of nature, it might at first be unclear why people would want to form political society.

Locke explains that the state of nature is no idyll. People in it do not enjoy the blissful ignorance that would characterize Rousseau's state of nature. It is characterized by "inconveniences" arising largely from the right of each individual to be the executor of the law of nature. Locke follows Cicero in recognizing that human beings feel far more strongly slights against themselves than against others, making us poor judges in our own cases (*Off.* 1.30). From this feature of our psychology, Locke imagines humans in the state of nature will be prone to overreact, to overpunish those who have injured them even when they want to merely give an equal return for an injury they have suffered and, as a result, to find themselves locked into cycles of revenge in the state of nature, as each individual avenges himself as he sees fit (II 7). These dynamics, coupled with the chaos caused by a few individuals who disregard the law of nature entirely (and are like beasts in human form), mean that the state of nature will suffer from ineradicable violence. Locke nevertheless insists against Hobbes that the state of nature is not a state of war

---

[84] A still more extreme version of this same dynamic can be found in Robert Nozick's opening lines of *Anarchy, State, and Utopia*, where Nozick (himself an avowed Lockean) simply presents individual rights-as-possessions as an unexamined starting assumption (Nozick 1974).

[85] Macpherson's critique of Locke's "possessive individualism" is perhaps the most famous expression of the view that takes this element of Locke's thought to be both central and deeply problematic (Macpherson 2011).

(II 19). Most people live at least roughly according to the law of nature: "men living together according to reason, without a common superior on earth, with the authority to judge between them," is the state of nature (II 19).[86] Yet the state of war constantly breaks out, also impeding the acquisition of property and the comfortable life most seek.

In this, Locke's state of nature resembles neither Hobbes's nor Rousseau's so much as Cicero's. Cicero describes the situation as follows:

> For who of you . . . does not know that the nature of things has been such that once, before there was any natural or civil law established, men wandered in a haphazard way over the land, holding just that property which they could either seize or keep by their own personal strength and vigor, by means of wounds and blood? Those men, therefore, who appeared to be most outstanding for virtue and wisdom . . . recognized the character of humanity's capacity for instruction and of their natural disposition, brought the formerly scattered men together, taking them from their old savage way of life and bringing them to justice and mildness of manners. Then came those associations devised for the good of man, called "commonwealths."
> (*Sest.* 42)

Like Locke's, Cicero's state of nature is not the hell Hobbes imagines. But it is extremely "inconvenient," and it lacks those comforts that come with human settlement and large-scale coordinated activity.

As a result, people find it far better to live under a common superior. Thus, they contract to form a commonwealth, and Locke arrives at the Ciceronian conclusion that we form political communities in order to preserve our property.[87] The consent of each individual is required for the newly established commonwealth to have any authority over them. It may seem that the centrality of consent places Locke firmly in line with Hobbes's new contractualist vision of politics. But instead, Locke is, in fact, developing an idea drawing on the Ciceronian tradition. Grotius and Pufendorf had concluded that some kind of consent was necessary to forming political society. Cicero's own definition of a commonwealth included the element of consent to the principles justice. Whereas Hobbes accepts that the "consent" to the contract can be

---

[86] Note that humanity's natural sociability is evident here. People in the state of nature are not—as Hobbes would have it—"solitary." They live together but without an authority over them.

[87] Whereas Cicero credits unnamed but outstanding individuals with seeing the benefits of political society, Locke's foundation takes place more democratically.

achieved by force, Locke follows Grotius and Pufendorf in requiring that the consent be given freely. More important, for Locke and Cicero, the agreement must be about true justice (i.e., the law of nature), which exists independently of human approval. This differs sharply from Hobbes's account, where justice comes into being only with the commands of the newly created sovereign and is determined by the content of those commands.[88] This far more substantive idea of consent also provides the basis for Locke's very un-Hobbesian theory of revolution.

On the terms of the contract, Locke once again departs widely from Hobbes. The parties to Hobbes's contract forfeit all the rights except one: their final right to self-preservation. In contrast, Locke's individuals only surrender one right absolutely: the right to be executors of the law of nature, the right to judge offenses and punish wrongdoers for themselves. Thus, "all private judgment of every particular member being excluded, the community comes to be umpire, by settled standing rules, indifference, and the same to all parties" (II 87).[89] We also give up *some* of our right to order our lives and property as we see fit but not the whole of it, only so much as is required for the legitimate functions of government. Government, as a result, is firmly limited in its power, as the people still retain most of their rights.

Part of this gulf between Hobbes and Locke might be derived from their differing views on human sociability. If, as Hobbes asserts, human beings are naturally asocial and unavoidably in the grip of their tendency toward pride, aggression, and other destructive passions, then it makes sense that the only way people can live together is under extreme constraint, of the sort provided by Hobbes's "mortall god" (*Leviathan* 17). But for Locke, human beings are naturally social; they want to live together and cooperate. Therefore, far less coercion would likely be needed to facilitate living together in security.

Still, at times, Locke's language leaves the impression that the power of government of the new commonwealth is nearly as unlimited as that of Hobbes's leviathan. Locke writes that "every man, by consenting with others to make one body politic under one government, puts himself under an obligation to every one of the society to submit to the determination of the majority and to be concluded by it" (II 150). But Locke clarifies that the amount of natural liberty that we give up here is only so much as is necessary for

---

[88] Compare to *Leviathan* 13–15.

[89] Elsewhere, Locke also grants that the individual gives up some of his natural liberty but by no means all of it, only "so far forth as the preservation of himself and the rest of society shall require" (II 128).

achieving the legitimate ends of the society: "he is to part also with *as much of his natural liberty*, in providing for himself, *as the good, prosperity, and safety of the society shall require*" (II 130; emphasis added). The "liberty of man in society" is still to live under these just laws and otherwise to dispose of himself and his possessions as he sees fit (II 22). Here we find the normative element of Locke's theory of limited government. Locke brings to its conclusion a train of thought running through Cicero and his heirs in Grotius and Pufendorf, opposed equally by Machiavelli and English republicans as well as Hobbesian absolutists: that legitimate government has fixed limitations on its just powers. According to Locke, we cannot transfer to another person or group any right that we do not hold ourselves. We cannot therefore give any government the kind of unlimited, arbitrary power we ourselves lacked in the state of nature.

This, in other words, is how Locke resolves more evenly the potential tension between popular sovereignty and natural law. The people's claim to ownership over the community is nothing more than the aggregation of the natural rights of each over himself. Those rights, in turn, are derived from the natural law. Thus, whenever people seek to use political power in a way that contravenes the law of nature, they are also contravening someone's natural rights, which are the original source of the people's sovereignty. There appears little daylight left between properly understood popular sovereignty and the natural law—natural (rather than merely political) rights make this linkage possible.

Locke thereby rules out absolute monarchy as a legitimate form of government (II 90). In giving any person absolute domination over myself, I am granting someone the right to kill me, which I do not have myself.[90] Like the English republicans, Locke accepts the dichotomy of liberty and slavery and

---

[90] Zuckert and Pangle deny this (Zuckert 1994, 242–243; Pangle 1988, 160). They acknowledge that Locke's explicit injunction against suicide would seem to confirm the idea that, as God's workmanship, we do not have total right over ourselves. But they argue that this prohibition is overturned by Locke's doctrine that a slave who tires of subjugation may rise up and, "by resisting the will of his master, draw on himself the death he desires" (II 23). Laslett agrees that Locke seems to have walked into a contradiction (Laslett's comment on II 23 in Locke 1988). For Zuckert and Pangle, the contradiction is resolved by recognizing that Locke *is* positing a far more radical self-ownership right that excludes God from consideration. However, they are too quick to dismiss the indirectness and (more important) the uncertainty of the slave's death. For one thing, no one would consider all actions that could likely end in one's own death a suicide (imagine the soldier who falls on the grenade to save his comrades). Second, Locke describes the slave's action as "resisting" the will of the master. This suggests that the slave does not passively refuse the master's orders and await death as punishment but rather puts up some sort of fight. Under such circumstances, one's life is at risk but not clearly and automatically forfeit. In short, Locke's acceptance that a slave may resist a master even at the risk of death does not establish radical self-ownership to the exclusion of God's ownership. The slave is not committing suicide by resisting.

accepts that the latter is characterized by domination, the presence of absolute and arbitrary power (II 23). At the same time, Locke shows how the distinction between republican and liberal freedom alleged by Pettit is incoherent. Locke rejects the legitimacy of domination as much as any republican, but he sees that domination as evil precisely because it empowers the dominator to violate the (negative) rights of those subject to him. Like Milton, Locke sees that our liberty to dispose of ourselves is never secure under conditions of domination. Pettit argues that liberalism's ideal of freedom is compatible with the idea of a benevolent absolute master. According to him, liberal freedom is achieved as long as the master does not make use of his power to interfere with his subject.[91] But such a counterfactual would make no sense to Locke. According to him, anyone who would try to get me into his absolute power must not have my interests at heart.

More compelling is the suggestion that Locke's contract places the property of all at the disposal of the community. James Tully points out that Locke insists that when one consents to the social contract, one "submits to the community, those possessions, which he has, or shall acquire" (II 120). Locke continues: "it would be a direct Contradiction, for any one, to enter into Society with others for the securing and regulating of Property: and yet to suppose his Land, whose Property is to be regulated by the Laws of the Society, should be exempt from the Jurisdiction of that Government" (II 120). From this, Tully concludes that the distribution of property is now entirely conventional.[92]

But this would be difficult to square with Locke's view expressed even in the quotation cited by Tully that we form governments in part to secure our property. It seems far less contradictory for Locke to view government's relationship to property in the same light as government's relationship to the freedom of its citizens. It has power over those things necessary to achieve its just ends or to execute the law of nature. That would give government the right to adjudicate in any disputes over property, to punish offenders, to compensate victims through the seizure of property, and to satisfy the duty under natural law that we preserve others commensurate with our own self-preservation. Locke, in fact, demonstrates that this alternative view is correct

---

[91] Pettit 1997, 12.

[92] See Tully 1980, 165. Tully views this as a kind of coming full circle of Locke's theory of acquisition, whereby we are free to acquire private property as long as "enough and as good" are left for others, yet when we come together and land becomes scarce, our rights conflict, and all property reverts to communal ownership.

when he explicitly denies government absolute authority in matters of property. In dealing with wrongdoers, Locke writes that magistrates have the right to punish or—when the good of society calls for it—refrain from punishing lawbreakers. But the same magistrate "yet cannot remit the satisfaction due to any private man for the damage he has received" (II 11). Since the right to reparation remains with the victims, they are entitled to demand compensation, and the agent of the government has no right to refuse them that, regardless of the benefits to society that might be had from forbearance. As is the case with an individual's liberty, the government is the unbiased "umpire," but it is firmly constrained by the law of nature and by those rights not yielded up to it in the social contract. Property rights are now subject to regulation, but they are not conventional, nor are they totally elastic.[93]

The fact that the law of nature demands that we preserve the lives of others when there is no threat to our own would seem to give the government some limited right of redistribution. Locke by no means construes this right in the state of nature to be anything like a right to equal property or even to comfortable living. But there is no reason to believe that we are relieved of our duty to keep others from extreme privation by joining society. Locke does not address this issue directly in the *Second Treatise*, but his *Essay on the Poor Law*, which endorses a very limited welfare (or we might call it "workfare") scheme, seems to follow logically from the premises found here.[94]

Locke's position on taxes likewise illustrates the natural limitations of government. Like Cicero, Locke accepts the theoretical principle that a wide variety of forms of government could satisfy the requirements of a legitimate commonwealth, even (hypothetically) simple monarchy (II 74).[95] But for any large or complex society, the only good practical form of government will be mixed. Governments of large territories require taxes to maintain themselves in a way that the king of a small clan would not. Yet Locke denies that all legitimate governments have the right to tax their people. Only those governments that can gain consent from their citizens either directly or through some body of representatives may take their property to support themselves:

---

[93] Straumann argues that the taking of property would be arbitrary and thus in violation of Locke's conception of the legitimate forms of power (Straumann 2016, 318–319).

[94] In "Venditio" as well, Locke outlines the responsibility we have in society to keep others from starving.

[95] Like Cicero, Locke assumes that simple monarchies were the first forms of government.

governments cannot be supported without great charge, and it is fit every one who enjoys his share of the protection, should pay out of his estate his proportion for the maintenance of it. But still it must be with his own consent, i.e., the consent of the majority, giving it either by themselves, or their representatives chosen by them: for if any one shall claim a power to lay and levy taxes on the people, by his own authority, and without such consent of the people, he thereby invades the fundamental law of property, and subverts the end of government: for what property have I in that, which another may by right take, when he pleases, to himself? (II 140)

Locke goes on to insist that mixed government ought to contain three elements. Although the branches he identifies do not correspond perfectly to those later enshrined in the American Constitution, the separation of powers serves a similar function: to protect by institutions the constraints on government that already exist by the law of nature. In other words, the separation of powers works to ensure that the theoretical normative limits on government are also actual practical limits. Locke distinguishes the legislative, executive, and federative powers of government (II 143–145). The first is the supreme power, emanating directly from the people. If the legislative power is held by a body of representatives rather than the people themselves, it is delegated to the former by the latter as a "trust." In this way, Locke remains faithful to the Ciceronian tradition of locating ultimate sovereignty in the people. But it places Locke opposite most of his contemporary Whigs, who located supreme authority in the Parliament. Moreover, the representatives may not exempt themselves from the laws that they make. Thus, a separate executive power must exist that ensures that the makers of law must also live under it. Here Locke again deviates from both Hobbes and the Machiavellian republican tradition, neither of which accepts that the makers of law should be limited by it. Finally, Locke identifies the federative power, which allows the government to marshal the resources of the state for the common defense (which Locke grants naturally also belongs with the holder of the executive office).

This arrangement, while not as developed a conception of constitutionalism as would later be elaborated by the American founders, nevertheless reveals that Locke shares with Cicero a commitment to divided government. Here again, we see how Locke provides a more authentically Ciceronian synthesis of the English republican and new natural law traditions. With the former, Locke opposes arbitrary authority and defends a conception of popular sovereignty reflected by the need for *continued* consent, and with the latter, he envisions politics limited by universal moral standards. Following Cicero, he proposes a solution endorsed by neither to ensure that those normative aims are reflected in the realities of government: division of powers.[96] While not quite Cicero's "blending of rights" (*Leg.* 3.28), Locke envisions a government where the separation of powers ensures that our rights are protected against "arbitrary power," which is at bottom always a form of slavery. As Straumann writes: "given human frailty and the temptation to 'grasp at Power' and to 'act contrary to the end of Society and of Government,' the various powers have to be limited by law and separated, that is they themselves have to be subject to a constitutional framework."[97]

Locke's recognition of the imperfection of any humanly arranged government leads him to present forcefully one final safeguard for our natural rights, the extraconstitutional right of revolution. Like Cicero, Locke understands tyranny not as particular to monarchical government; rather, tyranny arises whenever "the power, that is put in any hands for the government of the people, and the preservation of their properties, is applied to other ends, and made use of to impoverish, harass, or subdue them to the arbitrary and irregular commands" (II 201). Thus, governments of the few or the many may also be tyrannical when they abandon the rule of law: "Wherever law ends, tyranny begins" (II 202). Wood connects Locke's doctrine of revolution with Cicero's arguments for tyrannicide.[98] Locke's proposal for the division of powers is meant to thwart the development of tyranny, by ensuring the existence of a separate power that compels the lawmakers to obey the laws they enact. But the human tendency to "grasp at Power" and the contingencies arising from unpredictable political developments mean that we can never be sure that even a well-established government will not degenerate into tyranny.

In such an event, we have a natural right to rebel grounded in the fact that it is only our consent that makes any government legitimate. This

---

[96] As noted, English republicanism's conflicts with the crown had driven its leading proponents to argue for Parliament's absolute and undivided authority.

[97] Straumann 2016, 318. Thus, Straumann identifies Locke as following a Ciceronian tradition of constitutionalism.

[98] Wood 1988, 192. For Wood, this connection is lamentable. He sees both Cicero and Locke as mere apologists for landed ruling aristocracies, who invent imaginary distinctions to legitimate resistance to popular reformers, while prohibiting outbursts of violence from the truly oppressed classes. Although such a view may be demanded by a Marxist interpretation of both thinkers, certainly neither presented his own thought in such a way. For Locke and Cicero, all members of society benefit from the regularities of life brought about by the standing rules of law. In violating those rules, the tyrant wrongs rich and poor alike.

requirement of consent is not confined to a founding moment. Actually, according to Locke, those truly guilty of rebellion are those responsible for the government's violation of the "trust" placed in it by the governed. Since our natural right to our life is unalienable and since the arbitrariness of tyranny threatens that right just as all arbitrary power does, we have a right and duty to resist. In this, Locke builds upon one of the few common doctrinal points present in both the new natural law theorists and the English republican tradition. Unlike the latter, Locke does not justify revolution as a means to recover historical privileges. Unlike the former, Locke does not then layer over the right of resistance so many conditions and caveats as to make it a near practical impossibility.[99] Instead, he returns to a position much closer to Cicero's original: that the right of resistance is very real, based on unchanging principles rather than historical inheritance, but it remains a last resort.

Of course, Locke's Ciceronian theory of natural law places a high value on the preservation of human society. As a result, he makes it clear that his theory is not intended to justify constant eruptions of violence from the dissatisfied (II 228). The right to resist lies in all of us as individuals, but the occasional wrong against a particular member of society does not energize the mass to revolt. Locke's emphasis on humanity's natural sociality and even natural conservatism leads him to believe that most will bear a considerable amount of evil from their government before rising against it (II 223).[100] It would take "a long train of abuses, prevarications, and artifices, all tending the same way," subjecting the people to constant and unjust depredation to prompt a general revolt. When the people do rise, it is, in fact, as a defense of human society against governors whose actions place themselves outside it, becoming the animals in human guise who are liable—according to both Cicero and Locke—to be destroyed as threatening beasts.

Lockean Liberalism out of Cicero's Republicanism

A loyal subject of William and Mary, Locke in his political philosophy never approaches republicanism in Skinner's nominal sense of anti-monarchism. The American founders would accomplish that final task as they developed

---

[99] Tuck 1982, 79.
[100] At times, though, Locke appears to lament the fact that human beings are quite so stolid.

a far more sophisticated constitutional doctrine to protect the rights than Locke had elaborated. Nevertheless, Locke represents the penultimate (and by far the most significant) step in the development of the liberal republicanism that would come to greater perfection in the American founding. He had re-established the link between the negative rights of individuals and the idea of a self-governing political community. After Machiavelli's critique had prompted a division among followers of Cicero, a universal moral framework for politics no longer seemed easily compatible with the political freedom of popular sovereignty. It appeared necessary to the English republicans and the new natural law theorists alike to choose which of the two to emphasize. Drawing faithfully but creatively from Cicero, Locke illustrates that the Machiavellian choice is a false one. Meaningful liberty depends on the reconciliation of popular sovereignty and a fixed transcendent moral law.

From the foregoing analysis, we can see how deeply indebted Locke's project is to Cicero and how much clearer certain ambiguities in Locke's thought become once we are aware of this relationship. Not only did Locke bring together the two opposed traditions of English republicanism and new natural law, which were themselves in different respects indebted to Cicero, but Locke himself achieved their synthesis by returning to their common origin. At the core of Locke's political philosophy is a doctrine of natural law that is essentially drawn from Cicero. This natural law provides a standard outside of historical contingency to evaluate politics and to limit the just powers of government. But it also justifies the people's claim to be the ultimate authors of political action. Developing a concept of rights in line with Cicero's, Locke innovates by imagining these rights existing in our pre-political state and placing them at the center of the proper ends of government. Locke embraces an understanding of freedom that encompasses non-interference with the life or property of others, but he recognizes that such a freedom is completely incompatible with a situation of domination. In this way, Locke follows Cicero in rejecting the very liberal-republican dichotomy proposed by Pettit, Pocock, and others. Locke's similarities with Cicero on the importance of property, the value of human society and cooperation, mixed government, tyranny, and the right of revolution flow largely from this initial connection. In the same way that we might describe Aquinas as Aristotle made Christian, it might also be accurate to see Locke as Cicero made modern.

Most important of all, we can see how Locke uses the concept of rights to reconcile the principles of natural law and popular sovereignty or consent on a more equal footing than does Cicero himself. As we saw when examining

Cicero, while he never explicitly addresses this fundamental conflict between absolute moral laws and the people's claim to sovereignty over the political community, he strongly implies that the latter is ultimately subordinate to the former. For him, the people's claim to supremacy is grounded in natural law and thus becomes invalid when it conflicts with other precepts of that law. Locke, however, distills nearly all of the content of the natural law into rights that are thus likewise natural. These rights are, as we have seen, almost purely the reflection of the duties of Cicero's natural law: the duty to respect property yields the right to hold it, the duty to uphold justice yields the right against harm and to punish wrongdoers, and so on. This locates the origin of the people's sovereignty in the sovereignty of each individual over himself as expressed in these rights. There is in the state of nature a perfect fit between the commands of natural law and the sovereignty of each person as Locke understands it.

This fact also means that when individuals unite to form a commonwealth, it is both to vindicate the natural law and, by giving up a portion of their rights, to secure the rest. But if rights are an expression of the original sovereignty each had over himself, the rights retained by individuals in a commonwealth amount to a residuum of their personal sovereignty. Thus, those rights held by individuals in the new commonwealth reflect the continuing applicability of *both* the natural law and that original personal sovereignty. The sovereignty of the people as a body is derivative of the sovereignty each person originally had over himself (and thus subject to the same limitations). The state cannot (for instance) take its citizens' property arbitrarily, because doing so violates the commands of the natural law, or, put differently, it violates the citizens' natural right to property.

In this light, the tension between popular sovereignty and natural law as originally found in Cicero is drastically reduced. Recall that each of those principles served for Cicero as a standard by which to judge the legitimacy of political institutions and political acts. In Locke's case, they speak almost with the same voice. It is, of course, still possible for the *people as a corporate body* to act in a way that contradicts the natural law (again, for instance, by taking some citizen's property arbitrarily). But every conceivable instance of this is a violation of a justly retained right of a particular person, grounded in natural law—and this is the same thing as the person's primordial self-sovereignty. Thus, natural law (as manifest in natural rights) and the sovereign of the people (or, now, individual persons) amount to the same practical thing. Neither is clearly subordinate to the other, and the people's liberty lies equally in both.

It is not accidental that one of the early modern thinkers most engaged with Cicero's thought elaborates a comprehensive account of just government, for which the primary end is to secure the rights of the individual against harm and interference. Locke draws out the latent liberal elements of Cicero's theory of duties to build his system of rights. In this way, Cicero provides much of the logic that guides Locke's political thought as well as the central normative and practical concerns that motivate it. Locke integrates elements of Christian monotheism and modern epistemology and science with Cicero's political philosophy. But in this synthesis, the underlying moral-political concerns remain largely the same. In chapter 6, we will examine how the American founders built upon this Lockean system to construct liberal republican constitutions. But the theoretical work in describing a framework for connecting the concepts of rights, property, and just government had already been laid out in Locke's reception and adaptation of Cicero.

6

Adams, Wilson, and the American *Res Publica*

> [In Cicero's letters and orations] we see the true character of the times and the passions of all the actors on the stage. . . . Cicero had the most capacity and the most constant as well as the wisest and most persevering attachment to the republic. Almost fifty years ago I read Middleton's Life of this man . . . change the names and every anecdote will be applicable to us.
>
> —John Adams, letter to Benjamin Rush 1805[1]

James Otis and the *Salus Populi*

According to John Adams himself, the American Revolution began not with the signing of the Declaration of Independence nor with the battles at Lexington and Concord but, in fact, much earlier. It began during a 1761 speech by James Otis on the now-obscure *Paxton* case, which implicated the British writs of assistance. According to Adams, "the child independence was then and there born." Adams would continue to reaffirm for his entire life this view that the flame of revolution was lit by Otis in 1761.[2] Otis's speech offers an account of a Lockean state of nature, but it is also explicitly informed by Cicero, containing citations to Cicero's *Pro Archia*, among others.[3] An early figure in the revolutionary moment, Otis would go on to write a more theoretical work, *Rights*, which depends heavily and explicitly on Cicero's ideas to explain the state of nature, natural human sociability, and the relationship between popular sovereignty and natural law. In particular, Otis also accepts Cicero's doctrine of *salus populi suprema lex* as the fundamental justification

---

[1] For more on the way Conyers Middleton's *Life of Cicero* reflected a strain of Enlightenment views toward Cicero, see Fox 2013.

[2] See Somos 2019, 1.

[3] Somos 2019, 72.

Natural Law Republicanism. Michael C. Hawley, Oxford University Press. © Oxford University Press 2022.
DOI: 10.1093/oso/9780197582336.003.0006

for popular sovereignty and republican government (*Rights* 16).[4] Otis became more erratic later in life and played little direct role in events after 1769. But if Adams is correct, the spark the lit the flame of the American Revolution may have come from a Ciceronian ember.

Still, when the delegates at the Second Continental Congress voted to adopt the Declaration of Independence and to "dissolve the political bands" that had connected them with their mother country, they were deeply self-conscious that they were doing something profoundly novel. Both at the commencement of the Revolution and again during the crafting of the Constitution of 1787, many of the leading founders waxed almost poetic on the newness of the American enterprise. As Adams describes it in a letter to John Penn in 1776:

> a period, when the greatest philosophers and lawgivers of antiquity would have wished to live . . . of circumstances without example, has afforded to thirteen colonies, at once, an opportunity of beginning government anew from the foundation and building as they choose. How few of the human race have ever had any opportunity of choosing a system of government for themselves and their children! (Adams 1979, 78)

In 1782, they would choose for the Great Seal of the United States the motto *novus ordo seclorum* ("a new order for the ages").[5] James Madison likewise writes that it is the "glory of the people of America" that they "accomplished a revolution which has no parallel in the annals of human society" (*Fed.* 14). Yet, for all of this emphasis on newness, there was a simultaneous tendency among many of these same individuals to emphasize that what they were attempting was perfectly in keeping with commonly accepted—even ancient—views. For instance, Thomas Jefferson writes that his draft of the Declaration was based on the recognized authority of "Aristotle, Cicero, Locke, Sidney, &c." (Jefferson 1984).

How could the founders see themselves simultaneously as a radical break from and loyal adherents to an ancient truth? In part, this apparent paradox disappears if we recognize that the Americans saw themselves as innovating relatively little in the highest levels of political philosophy—in discerning the

---

[4] For more on this, see Somos 2019, 88–90.
[5] This motto is, ironically but tellingly, not new at all—as it clearly alludes to the fourth line of Virgil's *Fourth Eclogue*: *magnus ordo saeclorum* ("a great order for the ages").

nature of justice, determining the role of the state, and so on.[6] But to actually, self-consciously attempt to construct a government de novo on the basis of these principles? The founders could see no precedent for that.

Some of the most influential and learned members of the founding generation saw their project as an attempt to finally make real a long-hoped-for republican vision. The only large states in Europe of the time were monarchies—lending credence to the "small republics" thesis persuasively revived by Montesquieu. Cicero, as the expositor of the only successful large republic in history, becomes thus an obvious resource.[7] Two founders in particular—Adams and James Wilson—expressed clearly how much the new American endeavor was indebted to Cicero directly. Moreover, they saw the connection between Cicero and the Lockean liberalism that had become a kind of American political creed.

There are good reasons for concentrating on Adams and Wilson to understand the relationship between the American founding and the Ciceronian tradition considered in this book. For one thing, each was involved in both of the great founding moments: the Declaration of Independence and the construction of the new Constitution. They were thus in a position to speak to ideas behind both the Revolution and the Constitution. Wilson was a signer of the Declaration of Independence and a significant figure in the drafting of the Constitution. He also went on to serve in Congress and on the Supreme Court. Adams was by far the primary driving force behind the Second Continental Congress's decision to declare independence, and he sat on the committee that drafted the Declaration. Although he was abroad serving as envoy for the newly free United States during the drafting of the Constitution, he was the primary author of the Massachusetts Constitution. The latter was a model for many of the other state constitutions and one of the chief models for the US Constitution.[8] The drafters of the constitutions of North Carolina, Virginia, and New Jersey sought and generally followed his advice. Moreover, his *Defence of the Constitutions of the United States* was powerfully influential among the actual drafters of the Constitution,[9] and he heartily supported the Constitution once it was published.[10]

---

[6] However, they saw themselves as contributing something new in a few areas, such as the possible territorial size of republics.

[7] The following evidence runs sharply counter to Fox's argument that "it is fallacy to imagine that Cicero played a particularly prominent role in the founding values of the American constitution" (Fox 2013, 320).

[8] Gordon Wood calls it the "most significant" of the state constitutions (Wood 1998, 568).

[9] Thompson 1998, 40–41, 252–254.

[10] For a narrow but direct link between Cicero and these constitutional debates, see Cole 2019.

Moreover, even among such renowned peers, Wilson and Adams stood out for their erudition and were acknowledged as authorities well qualified to pronounce upon the theoretical underpinnings of the American founding. Starting in 1790, as the newly created professor of law at the College of Philadelphia (later the University of Pennsylvania), Wilson delivered and later published a series of "Lectures on Law." In these lectures, he intended to codify American law and aspired to be "an American Blackstone."[11] The augustness of his audience matched his aspirations; the lectures were attended by President George Washington, Vice President Adams, and many members of the new Congress.

As for Adams, Benjamin Rush said that there was a consensus among the founding generation that "Adams possessed more learning, probably, both ancient and modern, than any man who subscribed the Declaration of Independence."[12] Gordon Wood describes the *Defence of the Constitutions* as "the finest fruit of the American Enlightenment."[13] As mentioned, many of the framers of state constitutions considered Adams the expert in their craft.

Of course, as Wood also argues, Adams eventually fell out of step with the general views that came to dominate the ratification of the Constitution.[14] Among some of the drafters, his work certainly prompted resistance and even accusations of wanting to import European institutions of monarchy and nobility. Luke Mayville has demonstrated that much of this derived from a (sometimes deliberate) misconstrual of Adams's warnings about the dangers of oligarchy as advocacy for it.[15] At any rate, many of Adams's contemporaries took it to be the best expression of the philosophical underpinnings of *both* the Revolution and the Constitution, agreeing with Arthur Lee's statement that it was "the Work of the greatest Genius that had ever been written in this Country."[16] That the *Defence* was a powerful

[11] Mark Hall in Wilson 2007, 403–404.

[12] As quoted in Thompson 1998, xiii.

[13] Wood 1998, 568.

[14] Wood 1993, 592.

[15] See Mayville 2016. As Ryerson also demonstrates at length, the very motivation for Adams's advocacy for a strong central government stemmed from his fear that the rich and powerful might dominate everyone else in the new republic (Ryerson 2016).

[16] See Thompson's work for other testimonials to the essential accuracy of the *Defence* as an expression of American thought from Thomas Pinckney to Benjamin Franklin (Thompson 1998, 252–253, 274). Moreover, Adams's reputation was still good enough to get him elected the first vice president and the second president. It seems that much of the sense that Adams's ideas became passé during the founding really depends on the fall of Adams's popularity in the election of 1800. But by then, the founding itself had clearly been already accomplished, and the reasons for Adams's fall from grace then are—although beyond the scope of discussion here—at best loosely connected to his important ideas and contributions to the founding itself.

expression of the ideas undergirding the Constitution is testified as much by Adams's enemies as by his friends. John Taylor took twenty years to write a massive (five-hundred-page) rebuttal of it. As Bradley Thompson points out, the very fact that Taylor did this showed that he considered Adams's *Defence* sufficiently influential to warrant a refutation two decades later. According to Taylor, his targets were simultaneously the *Defence* and *The Federalist Papers*, but he considered the former more dangerous. The latter may have had a more "elegant style," but the former was distinguished by its "erudition."[17] Furthermore, this work appeared to many founders as a decisive influence on many important decisions. Despite Adams's being absent from the 1787 Constitutional Convention, his work so impressed its members that Rush wrote: "Mr. Adams's book has diffused such excellent principles among us, that there is little doubt of our adopting a vigorous and compounded federal legislature. . . . [Adams] has done us more service than if he had obtained alliances for us with all the nations of Europe."[18]

Thus, there are good reasons for looking to Adams and Wilson as providing at least a very compelling perspective on the way in which the American founding relates to earlier republican thought. Moreover, Wilson's "Lectures" and Adams's *Defence* differ in an important way from the source most frequently looked to on this subject, *The Federalist Papers*. While the third is an overtly polemical exercise to get ordinary voters to cast ballots for the new constitution, the first two are aimed at a learned audience of scholars, statesmen, and constitution makers (in Adams's case, also potential constitution makers in Europe). Such an audience could be expected to appreciate the relationship of the new American endeavor to the tradition of political philosophy with which they were all familiar and would want to know the theoretical underpinnings of it.

Both Wilson and Adams took the American founding to be indebted profoundly to the Ciceronian tradition's conception of a commonwealth, the role of justice, the nature of rights, the content of natural law, and the organization of political powers.[19] To recognize how significantly this connection might alter long-standing views of the intellectual spirit of the American founding, it is necessary briefly to re-examine some old but unresolved

---

[17] Cf. Thompson 1998, 255.

[18] As found in Straumann 2016, 337. Cf. Farrand 1911.

[19] Ryerson's otherwise compelling examination of Adams mentions in a note that Cicero was Adams's "hero" (Ryerson 2016, 496), but he does not pursue the consequences of this fact at all in the rest of his work.

debates over the role of classical republicanism and Lockean liberalism in the American founding.

The Contested Legacy of the American Founding

In addition to being an event of great historical importance to understanding American political thought and life, the American founding occupies a central place in the great debate over the relationship between liberalism and republicanism.[20] This scholarly focus might seem odd given that this period produced few philosophical works of the first rank.[21] But the importance of the American founding to this discourse makes sense once we recognize this event as a time when political life was organized in a self-conscious attempt to bring theory into practice. Thus, there is a special probative value for claims about the relationship between liberalism and republicanism as traditions (or families of ideals and concepts) when we can see how they relate in practice rather than merely on paper. Moreover, since the American founding issued in a written constitution, whatever settlement was achieved in this moment shapes the present in a more direct way than any purely intellectual movement. The United States is a country whose fundamental political arrangements and institutions (and, to at least some extent, values) are determined by the decisions and documents that came out of this moment.

In this light, it is then hardly surprising that the American founding would feature as the central point for many of the great scholarly works that make up both the historical and conceptual elements of the liberalism-republicanism discourse. There is, of course, a nearly endless amount of scholarly literature on other theoretical aspects of the founding as well. In this section, I focus

---

[20] For the purposes of brevity, I use the terms "founding" and "founders" to refer to the period stretching from the War of Independence through to the ratification of the Constitution of 1787 and the figures involved in both. I do not deny that we may speak of them as "two foundings" (Lim 2014), and there will be times when it is important to distinguish between the revolutionary period and the ratification of the Constitution. But I will argue that there is far greater unity to the two moments than is suggested by scholars such as Elvin Lim and Gordon Wood and that it is not essential to *always* distinguish between the two, especially given that many (although by no means all) of the actual individuals involved were the same.

[21] *The Federalist Papers* and Adams's *Defence of the Constitutions* are undisputedly the best theoretical products of this period, but they are rarely placed in the same category as Aristotle's *Politics*, Machiavelli's *Prince*, or Locke's *Second Treatise* in terms of originality or philosophical depth, even by those who specialize in studying them.

on the most important of those that are connected to the debates over the relationship between liberalism and republicanism, which in turn implicate debates over the relationship between ancient and modern political thought.

Louis Hartz articulated a powerful and still influential view of the American founding as the political expression par excellence of Lockean liberalism. According to Hartz, American society "begins with Locke, and thus transforms him, stays with Locke by virtue of an absolute and irrational attachment it develops for him."[22] However, this view of the American founding as predominantly Lockean spurred a great deal of debate, the first wave of which sought to overthrow Hartz's conclusion.

Much of the framework of this debate has been set by works of three important scholars who all broadly fit into the contemporary republican (or neo-Roman/civic humanism) camp: Gordon Wood, Bernard Bailyn, and J. G. A. Pocock. Each has had a powerful role in shaping the contemporary views of the American founding, seeking in one way or another to challenge Hartz's claim of the centrality of Locke. All three are influenced by one another's work, yet they all also offer slightly different interpretations of what took place between 1776 and 1789.

Chronologically first is Bailyn's *The Ideological Origins of the American Revolution* (1992). Bailyn does not accept that the Americans were "motivated" by the abstract arguments of philosophers and constitutional theorists.[23] However, he does argue that the American intellectual world was shaped by a number of different traditions of discourse. Bailyn identifies five such traditions: classical political thought, Puritanism (and Protestantism more broadly), English common law, Locke and other Enlightenment philosophers, and the English opposition tradition (including both English republicans and their intellectual heirs among the Whigs, such as John Trenchard and Thomas Gordon).

According to Bailyn, by far the dominant tradition for Americans was the English opposition, the vessel of English republican thought. Although Bailyn seems to acknowledge the ubiquity of Locke and admits that he is "cited often with precision on points of political theory," he takes Locke's role to be secondary by far to the tradition of English republicanism.[24] The true formative role belongs to English republicanism. Bailyn assigns a particularly

---

[22] Hartz 1991, 6.
[23] Bailyn 1992, 11.
[24] Bailyn 1992, 28.

important role to Algernon Sidney's *Discourses on Government* and the series of essays by Trenchard and Gordon, *Cato's Letters*.[25]

As for the classics, Bailyn acknowledges that they were "everywhere in the literature of the revolution, but are everywhere illustrative, not determinative of thought."[26] Bailyn suggests that Americans' classical learning was very broad and rhetorically useful to call upon for authority in political arguments but also essentially shallow. Bailyn notes one exception to this general superficiality of learning: "their detailed knowledge and engaged interest covered only one era and one small group of writers." "What gripped their minds, what they knew in detail," was the period surrounding the end of the Roman republic. According to Bailyn, "they had at hand and needed only, Plutarch, Livy, and above all Cicero, Sallust and Tacitus."[27] Yet, despite acknowledging the importance of at least these writers to the founders, he continues to insist that the classics were "not the source of political and social beliefs."[28] I will suggest a possible reason for Bailyn's decision to ignore the significance of his own evidence about the role of at least some classical ideas to the Americans' political understanding. But for the moment, the central relevant element is that Bailyn identified English republicanism (or "Opposition thought"), classical thought, and Lockeanism as separate intellectual traditions for the American founders, the influence of each group existing in uneasy tension with the others. Bailyn makes no claims about the eventual triumph of one strand to the exclusion of the others, but he does take English republicanism to be the predominant force that drove the American Revolution.

Following on Bailyn's treatment, Wood sharpened the distinction between the Lockean-liberal and Whig-republican strains identified by the former. Wood's depiction of the founding is stark in its portrayal of a showdown between the traditions of liberalism and republicanism. This starkness is moderated somewhat in Wood's later works.[29] For Wood, there were essentially two founding moments, the first in 1776 with the Declaration of Independence and the second in 1787 with the ratification of the new Constitution. This idea of two foundings would be further elaborated by Lim. For Wood and Lim, the second founding was essentially a betrayal of the first.

---

[25] Bailyn 1992, 34–35.
[26] Bailyn 1992, 26.
[27] Bailyn 1992, 25.
[28] Bailyn 1992, 26.
[29] Compare the two editions of Wood [1969] 1998.

Wood improves on Bailyn's treatment somewhat by seeing the connection between classical Roman republicanism and the modern expressions of English republicans. But, like Pocock (and, to a certain extent, Skinner), Wood lumps together as part of one great republican tradition Aristotle, Cicero, Machiavelli, Montesquieu, and the English Whigs. Moreover, it is on the implicit basis of this indiscriminate combination that Wood distinguishes far more sharply than Bailyn this republican tradition from Lockean liberalism.[30] Whereas Bailyn discusses "overlaps" between Locke and the republican sources (without, however, taking the next step and recognizing their fundamental connection), Wood sees totally incompatible alternatives.[31]

For Wood, classical republicanism promoted an idea of liberty that was entirely public, identical to "participation by the people in government."[32] Such a vision of liberty required the total commitment of citizens to sacrifice their own private interests to the public good. Wood writes that "ideally, republicanism obliterated the individual."[33] Wood sees this idea as the initial impetus to the American Revolution. The developments leading to the ratification of the Constitution were another revolution entirely—a modern liberal one that "shattered the classical Whig world of 1776" and "marked the end of the classical conception of politics."[34] In establishing a government that protected rights and supported the individual pursuit of self-interest over Spartan commitment to the community, Americans had allowed Lockean liberalism to triumph over republicanism.

Pocock occupies a distinct third position in this group. Like Wood, Pocock sees a fundamental connection between classical republicanism and its more modern expression. Pocock also agrees with Wood in drawing a very sharp line between liberalism and republicanism. But, unlike Wood, Pocock simply finds no place at all for Locke in the story of the American founding. Writing in the bluntly titled essay "The Myth of John Locke and the Obsession with Liberalism," Pocock rails against the "fiction of Locke." He insists that an

---

[30] Wood [1969] 1998, 29, 50.
[31] Compare to Bailyn 1992, 34.
[32] Wood [1969] 1998, 61.
[33] Wood [1969] 1998, 24. In this, Wood's view of republicanism seems to be shaped by Montesquieu's judgment of the classical republics, which he wrote were animated by a painful, self-forgetting virtue (*Spirit* 4. 5). Although Hannah Arendt wrote before the contemporary debate over liberalism and republicanism at the founding had truly erupted, she, too, believed "it was a question of whether the new government was to constitute a realm of its own for the 'public happiness' of its citizens, or whether it had been devised solely to serve and ensure their pursuit of private happiness more effectively than had the old regime" (Arendt 2006, 133).
[34] Wood [1969] 1998, 606.

understanding of the political debates of the eighteenth century "does not necessitate reference to Locke at all." For Pocock, the American founding was in a sense the last great gasp of Machiavellian republicanism, born in "the dread of modernity."[35] Opposed to the modernizing changes of commercial life and its apparently corrupting influence on Britain, Pocock's Americans sought to maintain their republican purity and virtue.

Thus, for Pocock (as for Bailyn), there is no essential rupture between the Revolution and the Constitution. In Bailyn's case, this is because both liberalism and republicanism were present in both cases.[36] In Pocock's view, there was no break, because there is no Lockean liberalism present at any point.

Although Bailyn, Wood, and Pocock disagree on several issues, all three are united in their view that Lockean liberalism is (a) fundamentally distinct from the republican tradition and (b) not the primary force that drove the American Revolution (and for Bailyn and Pocock, at least, it never achieves supremacy). Against this argument, a number of scholars have emerged to vindicate the importance of Locke (and Lockean liberalism) to the American founders, although not always in the manner put forth by Hartz. Foremost among these are Ronald Hamowy, Steven Dworetz, Bradley Thompson, Thomas Pangle, and Michael Zuckert. Hamowy, in particular, has detailed the near hegemonic place Locke occupied among the Americans prior to the Revolution. His thought was "so commonplace that little if any intellectual dispute surrounded it."[37] Zuckert even points to Bailyn's own account, noting the wealth of evidence for Locke's importance to the American founders and rightly pointing out that Bailyn provides no convincing reason to support his claim that the Americans' knowledge and use of Locke were superficial.[38]

For Zuckert, Thompson, Pangle, and Hamowy, the American founding was deeply Lockean. For them, this by no means entails that it was not republican. They reject the incompatible dichotomy advanced by Pocock and others. Pangle goes so far as to recognize that American republicanism is in an important respect anti-Machiavellian republicanism: "[the founders] reject Machiavelli's republicanism in the name of a more humane, liberal republicanism."[39] Zuckert criticizes Bailyn, Pocock, and Wood for postulating false

---

[35] Pocock 1908, as cited in Zuckert 1994, 162; see also Kramnick 1990, 167.

[36] See Bailyn's claim that the Constitution was the "fulfillment" of the Revolution (Bailyn 1992, 321).

[37] Hamowy 1979. See also Dunn 1982. For Dunn, Locke's importance to America emerges only later in the eighteenth century, although Zuckert 1994, 23, notes that there is almost no evidence to support Dunn's claim that Locke was not a significant figure in the first half of the century.

[38] Zuckert 1994, 153. See also chapter 1 of Thompson 2019.

[39] Pangle 1988, 52.

"'gog and magog' battles between liberals and republicans—of which . . . the alleged 'participants' were quite unaware."[40]

But Zuckert and Pangle go still further and argue that this liberal republicanism of the founders is a new synthesis. It may trace back to Locke but not substantially further. Pangle writes that Locke and his American followers adopt "a profoundly *anti*-classical conception of human nature and politics . . . the rallying cries of the new republicanism are the Natural Equality and Rights of Men."[41] Zuckert concurs: "no genuine partisan of the old republicanism, such as Plato, Aristotle, or Livy, would say what James Madison said, very much in the spirit of Locke's new 'natural law' teaching: 'the protection . . . of the diversity in the faculties of men, from which the rights of property originate . . . is the first object of government.'"[42] For these scholars, Locke and the American founding were the emergence of a completely new orientation toward political life that put the protection of rights and the self-interest of individuals at the center.

The Founding out of the Ciceronian Tradition

Pangle, Thompson, Hamowy, and Zuckert provide a powerful and necessary rebuttal to the revisionist claim that Locke was not centrally important to the American founders. Their arguments are supported by powerful evidence collected by others. By almost any test one might apply, Locke occupies the dominant place. H. Trevor Colbourn performed a survey of colonial libraries, which revealed that no political work appears as frequently in them as Locke's.[43] Donald Lutz's analysis of citations found that "Locke, by a very wide margin, was the most frequently cited author in the American political writings."[44] Dworetz points out that this outsize intellectual footprint only grows when we recognize that Locke's ideas were often echoed (sometimes verbatim) without attribution and that Locke's *political* ideas were as likely to reach an American mind from the pulpit as from a political pamphlet.[45]

[40] Zuckert 1994, 165.

[41] Pangle 1988, 35. Pangle singles out Locke's state of nature as an idea especially incompatible with classical republicanism.

[42] Zuckert 1994, 272. It should be quite clear from the foregoing analysis that such a claim misses the significance of Cicero entirely, who expresses almost the exact same sentiment as Madison. Cf. *Off.* 2.73.

[43] Colbourn 1965, 200–232.

[44] Lutz 1988, chapter 11.

[45] Dworetz 1990, 43–45.

The testimony of particularly important individuals likewise supports the claim of Locke's ubiquity. Zuckert relates that Jefferson was known to recommend Locke's *Treatises* "as a basic reading in politics to friends and relatives, as well as for the University of Virginia curriculum."[46] Thompson demonstrates that a young Adams likewise drew a substantial part of his own self-education from the work of Locke.[47] Similar evidence can be found concerning other leading figures, such as Madison (Madison 1973, xx–xxiv) or Wilson (Wilson 2007, xxi).

Even many of the examples from the English republican/Whig/opposition tradition held out by Bailyn, Wood, and Pocock as the conveyors of allegedly anti-Lockean republicanism were themselves, in fact, deeply connected to Locke's ideas. In particular, these three scholars claim that the influence of Sidney's *Discourses* and Gordon and Trenchard's *Cato's Letters* were far more important. Their works also appear frequently in Americans' libraries (although less frequently than Locke's).[48] But Hamowy and Sullivan have already demonstrated that both of these figures share with Locke fundamental agreement about concepts such as liberty and rights.[49] In turn, Margaret Jacob has illustrated how the republicanism of Gordon and Trenchard in particular is far from hostile to commercialism.[50] Thus, even the alleged alternatives to Locke are not always really incompatible rivals—which is perhaps why Jefferson and Adams often listed Locke together with Sidney and "Cato" as champions of liberty.

But perhaps the most significant evidence for Locke's importance comes from the great documents that were the cornerstone of the political acts themselves. For instance, it is almost cliché to point out that the theoretical structure of the Declaration of Independence is overtly Lockean. Just as Locke does, it appeals to the "Laws of Nature and of Nature's God." Like Locke, the Declaration asserts that the existence of this law means that human beings (or men) are naturally free and equal. They possess "unalienable" rights to life and liberty—with the pursuit of happiness substituting for property. The purpose of government is to vindicate this law and the rights it entails. Legitimacy for such government derives from the consent of the governed. This consent is formally instantiated in the right to have all taxes approved

[46] Zuckert 1994, 19.
[47] Thompson 1998, 11–17.
[48] See again Colbourn 1965, 200–232.
[49] See Sullivan 2004, chapters 6 and 7; Hamowy 1990.
[50] Jacob 2010.

by elected representatives. When government "becomes destructive" of its proper ends, the people are entitled to withdraw their consent; they retain an ultimate right of revolution against tyranny. It is on this final Lockean right that the American colonists base their justification for rebellion. The later Constitution likewise reflects these views. One of the chief debates between federalists and anti-federalists was over whether the protection of Lockean rights under the new frame of government was sufficiently obvious and implicit in the structure of the whole, or whether it was necessary to explicitly articulate them.[51]

If to draw out such obvious parallels between Locke's expression and the founding documents strikes the reader as elementary or even insulting, I only offer it here to illustrate how baffling Pocock's claims about "the fiction of John Locke" truly are. Hardly less perplexing is Wood's insistence that a revolution that began with such a Declaration could possibly have been betrayed by the infusion of Lockean liberalism at the ratification of the Constitution. The fact that the individuals most responsible for crafting the Declaration—Jefferson and Adams—both heartily approved the Constitution only confirms that from the subjective standpoint of the actors involved, the "second founding" was not a betrayal of the first.[52]

For these reasons, we cannot but agree with the critique of Zuckert, Pangle, and others that the founding was, in fact, shot through with Locke's political philosophy. Locke's logic undergirds both the Americans' justifications for rebellion (the right of revolution) and the ideas for the government that they sought to erect in place of British rule: a government based on representation, consent, and the division of powers—all organized to protect natural rights. Yet in correcting the republican revisionist view of the founding, these critics make a similar error. By characterizing Locke and the American founders as breaking radically with the classical tradition—and, in particular, classical republicanism—they accept too much the terms of the argument offered by their opponents. Just as Bailyn and Pocock ignore (or explain away) the

---

[51] And in choosing the latter course, the protection of that last Lockean right—to property—against arbitrary seizure by the state is made explicit. The Fifth Amendment echoes precisely Locke's three great rights: life, liberty, and property.

[52] Those anti-federalists who did claim such a betrayal certainly did not rest their objections on the grounds that the Constitution was too Lockean. If anything, the threat its concentration of powers posed to natural rights meant it was not Lockean enough for them. The objections to the Constitution of Patrick Henry and Samuel Adams illustrate their concern that insufficient protections of rights were incorporated into its structure.

constant American appeals to Locke, Pangle and others cannot account for the Americans' obsession with classical Rome.[53]

These writers are correct to say, as Pangle does, that the ideas of the founders were anti-Machiavellian.[54] Although there is little evidence that most Americans were even familiar with Machiavelli, it would be fair to say that their principles were incompatible with much of Machiavelli's teaching.[55] The founders' views of natural law—particularly their rejection of teleological ends and natural hierarchy—likewise provide compelling evidence that the Americans were not fundamentally Aristotelian.[56] As for Plato, Adams and Jefferson were actively appalled by the lack of freedom (as they understood it) in his *Republic*.[57] On the basis of these rejections, Zuckert and Pangle thus conclude that the American founding is a break with classical republicanism precisely because of its Lockeanism. In short, they largely accept the Pocockian story about what classical republicanism is and its essentially irreconcilable relationship to liberalism.

The entire thrust of this book is that such a story is incompatible with the reality of Cicero's importance in the development of liberalism. I will not here belabor the points made in the previous chapters. I will only summarize my argument that Locke's liberalism is born out of Ciceronian thought. His natural law teaching, his conception of rights, his ideal of liberty, his understanding of justice, his defense of property, and his constitutionalism all point to an account of liberalism that arises from engagement with Cicero's classical republicanism. Thus, precisely because the American founders were so Lockean, they were operating according to principles and assumptions that derive from Cicero's philosophy. In short, the Lockeanism of the American founders was indeed incompatible with central features of Machiavelli's and Aristotle's thought. But that does not make the founding's ideals hostile to

---

[53] In a kind of perverse even-handedness, Bailyn counts American references to *both* Locke and the classics as largely insignificant, despite the enormous number of them that he himself uncovers. Cf. Wood 2011; Straumann 2016, epilogue.

[54] Pangle 1988, 52. Strauss's *Thoughts on Machiavelli* likewise begins with the assertion that America was founded on anti-Machiavellian principles (Strauss 1995, 13).

[55] One exception to this is John Adams, probably the most widely read of the founders. He admires the clear insights of the Florentine, but he parts company with him precisely because his politics are not morally grounded. He is therefore wont to refer to the "machiavellian dissimulation" of the British governor of Massachusetts. He likewise warned that a failure to pay public officials would introduce "a universal system of Machiavellian hypocrisy into popular elections." See Thompson 1998, 224; Bailyn 1992, 121–122.

[56] Zuckert 1994 argues persuasively for the divergence between Locke and Aristotle.

[57] Bailyn relates that Adams was, in fact, so aghast to discover the actual details of Plato's City in Speech that he concluded the book must have been a satire (Bailyn 1992, 24–25).

the particular version of classical republicanism we find in Cicero and in the tradition Cicero inspired in early modernity. In fact, the former are derived from the latter.

Moreover, it turns out that Cicero is, in fact, a common link among nearly all of the other major thinkers often suggested as theoretical sources for Americans' ideals. Sidney's *Discourses* and *Cato's Letters*—the works pointed to by Pocock and Bailyn—evince their authors' close familiarity with Cicero. As chapter 4 of this book has demonstrated, Cicero also loomed large for their English republican predecessors—such as Nedham and Harrington, whom the Americans also cited often. Bailyn himself reports that American pamphlets regularly also appealed to Grotius and Pufendorf about the laws of nature.[58] Some scholars, such as Garry Wills, have also pointed to the Scottish Enlightenment as a source of Americans' political ideas.[59] The importance of figures such as Francis Hutcheson, David Hume, and Adam Smith to the founding is hotly disputed.[60] Regardless, all three acknowledged important intellectual debts to Cicero. Hume, for instance, wrote to a friend that he had Cicero's *De officiis* "in my Eye in all my reasonings." Nor did Hume think he was alone in his interest: "the fame of Cicero flourishes at present, while that of Aristotle is utterly decayed" (Hume 2011, 34). Smith copied nearly verbatim large passages of Cicero in his *Theory of Moral Sentiments*, including those in which he expressed his understanding of justice and propriety.[61]

Most significantly, there is Montesquieu, whose *The Spirit of the Laws* was often appealed to by federalists and anti-federalists alike as an authority on liberty, constitutionalism, republics, and the possibilities of freedom in territorially extensive commonwealths.[62] For his part, Montesquieu was sufficiently moved by Cicero's thought that he wrote a "Discourse on Cicero." There he writes: "Cicero is, of all the ancients, the one who had the most personal merit, and whom I would prefer to resemble." He specifies that although Cicero deserves admiration for his rhetoric, his true genius lay in his philosophy: "he deserves the title of philosopher no less than Roman orator. One can even say that he has distinguished himself more in the Lyceum than

---

[58] Bailyn 1992, 27.

[59] Wills 2017.

[60] Hamowy provides a compelling refutation of Wills's particular theory that the Declaration of Independence was inspired by Hutcheson and not Locke (Hamowy 1979).

[61] Cf. Hawley 2019.

[62] In a variety of ways, Cicero's thought permeated the French Enlightenment, including figures ranging from Rousseau to Denis Diderot and Voltaire. See Gawlick 1936; Sharpe 2015. Sharpe shows that Cicero may well have served as Voltaire's model of an enlightened man.

on the platform: he is original in his books of philosophy, but he had many rivals in his eloquence" (Montesquieu 2002).[63]

For these reasons, Montesquieu might then seem a prime candidate to be a transmitter of this Ciceronian tradition to the Americans, meriting a more sustained direct treatment in the present exploration. However, Montesquieu was neither *clearly* a republican nor *clearly* an adherent to natural law in the sense meant by the Ciceronian tradition. This is not to say that Montesquieu was not, in fact, either of those things. But the ambiguity of Montesquieu's positions on both natural law and popular sovereignty meant that his contributions to the thought of the founders lay primarily in other areas.

Montesquieu's magisterial *Spirit of the Laws* does begin with an account of the various types of laws, which he calls "the necessary relations deriving from the nature of things." Within this category, Montesquieu finds not only "natural laws" but also divine laws, laws of matter, positive laws, and more (*Spirit* 1.1). Montesquieu's account of those natural laws bears some resemblance to the Ciceronian-Lockean construal: human beings perceive the existence of a supreme creator, intuit the basics of justice and relations of fairness, are primarily concerned with their own preservation and comfort, but are also drawn to one another once the initial fear of strangers is alleviated (1.1). But Montesquieu makes few appeals to these natural laws throughout the rest of his work, and he does not seem to make any great effort to use them as a clear standard by which to judge political communities. As Sullivan puts it, "although Montesquieu notes the existence of 'civil laws that are contrary to natural law'(26.3, 496), he himself does not denounce any law, among any people, as 'unjust' in the entirety of the work."[64] There is some scholarly debate over what to make of Montesquieu's natural law—some arguing that its function undergirds the whole argument of *The Spirit of the Laws*, others that it is meant primarily to refute Hobbes.[65] However, for our purposes, the significant fact is that Montesquieu's natural law doctrine seems to have made little direct impact on the American founders, who rarely appealed to him for support or guidance on this subject.[66]

---

[63] Thus, we can see that the view of later scholars such as Theodor Mommsen or Moses Finley that Cicero was unoriginal or "unphilosophical" (Finley 1983, 128) was not at all shared by the leading lights of the eighteenth century. The lingering influence of Finley's evaluation may also help to explain contemporary scholarship's failure to see Cicero's role in the great theoretical developments of this period.

[64] Sullivan 2017, 51.

[65] See, among others, Waddicor 1970; Zuckert 2009; Pangle 2020.

[66] Indeed, I could find no evidence of either Adams or Wilson ever drawing explicitly from Montesquieu on this topic.

Montesquieu's status as a republican is even more complicated than his position on natural law, spawning a diverse set of interpretations both among scholars and among the American founders themselves.[67] Anne Cohler compellingly demonstrates the deference Americans gave Montesquieu on matters of constitutional design especially.[68] However, that deference was not absolute. Montesquieu had taken Rome to be perhaps the archetypal republic but had attributed the loss of its republican freedom in large part to its failure to remain small (*Spirit* 2.2).[69]

Anti-federalists took Montesquieu to support their view that republics could never grow beyond very strict limits in territory and in population. The anti-federalist writer known as "Brutus" captures this attitude when he quotes Montesquieu in his first letter: "It is natural to a republic to have only a small territory, otherwise it cannot long subsist. . . . In a large republic, the public good is sacrificed to a thousand views. . . . In a small one, the interest of the public is easier perceived, better understood, and more within the reach of every citizen."[70] Brutus goes on to draw the conclusion from this: no republic had ever been as large as the United States, and when Rome grew to such a size, "their governments were changed from that of free governments to those of the most tyrannical that ever existed in the world" (*Brutus* 1). Anti-federalists sought to draw on Montesquieu's solution to the small-republic problem: federation. Montesquieu had argued that small republics could federate to overcome their security vulnerability without losing their liberty (*Spirit* 9.1).

Against this, federalists such as "Publius" took a more authentically Ciceronian view. As explored above, Cicero did not object to the size of Rome's polity and did not blame it for the collapse of the republic. In *Federalist* 9 and *Federalist* 10, Publius (Alexander Hamilton and Madison, respectively) argues that even individual American states are too large to remain free by Montesquieu's principle. Publius prefers to draw on Montesquieu's ideas for the separation of powers—as well as new mechanisms to alleviate the ills of factionalism—to preserve liberty in the absence of the small homogeneous society Montesquieu had elsewhere claimed was essential.

---

[67] On the debate over Montesquieu's republicanism among scholars, see Pangle 2020; Douglass 2012; Levy 2006; Shklar 1991; Spector 2003; Radasanu 2010; Rahe 2009.
[68] Cohler 1988.
[69] See further Gilmore 2020, 364–365.
[70] Cf. *Spirit* 8.16.

But it was not even clear to Americans that Montesquieu was, in fact, a republican. He certainly offered analysis of republican government and proposed solutions to the problems it faced—but he did so likewise with monarchies and even despotism. Indeed, he gave some (again ambiguous) evidence that he preferred monarchical government or the English hybrid model where "a republic hides under the form of a monarchy" (*Spirit* 5.19). Whatever else one may say about Montesquieu, he nowhere insists that republics are the only legitimate form of government or that the people are the rightful holders of sovereign authority. This ambiguity was not lost on some of the founders. Thus, Adams refers to him in the following way: "Montesquieu, who will scarcely be denominated a republican writer" (*Defence* 403).

It cannot be denied that Montesquieu was deeply important to the founders' debates over the possible size of the new republic and over the constitutional question of the separation of powers, both of which implicate certain features of Ciceronian republicanism. Thus, he certainly serves as a conduit for Ciceronian ideas to America. But given the evidence noted here, it is unsurprising that a thinker with such an ambiguous connection to both natural law and republicanism would not offer the founders much in the way of reconciling the two principles. On both issues, as we will see, the founders preferred to go to Locke or straight to Cicero himself.

Indeed, it would require perhaps another entire book to fully explore the ways in which Montesquieu or figures such as Sidney, Gordon, Trenchard, Hutcheson, Hume, and Smith in their own manner adapted and responded to Cicero's political philosophy. They are all in different ways connected to the emergence of the liberal republican doctrine in the eighteenth century, and they all also were part of the intellectual world of ideas in which the American founders were immersed. It must suffice for now simply to note that Cicero's indirect influence carried forward through them as well as through Locke and the figures explored in chapter 4. Cicero is—as far as I can discern—the only classical common link who connects all of these figures. Although he provided little evidence for his claim, Neal Wood was essentially correct when he said that Cicero's relationship to early modern thinkers was analogous to Aristotle's relationship to medieval scholastics. To try to approach the web of interrelated political ideas about justice, rights, liberty, and government in which the American founding took place without recognizing the ubiquity of Ciceronian themes is to miss a massive part of the story.

Cicero, though, is not simply an indirect source of themes for the founding generation. He was also regularly engaged in his own right. As noted above, the educational curriculum in America featured Cicero prominently, such that Madison and Hamilton had to translate extensive passages from his works (among others) as part of the entrance exams for the College of New Jersey and King's College (later Princeton and Columbia). Hamilton would later adopt Cicero's anglicized nickname, "Tully," as his pseudonym when writing against the Whiskey Rebellion (thus likening the rebels to the Catilinarian conspirators). Adams spent many nights of his youth obsessively memorizing Cicero's orations against Catiline.[71] He would later write in the preface to his *Defence of the Constitutions* that "ages of the world have not produced a greater statesman and philosopher united in the same character" than Cicero (*Defence* pr.). His cousin Samuel Adams made a slogan out of Cicero's *cedant arma togae* to oppose the principle of standing armies. According to D. L. Wilson, Jefferson also first encountered Cicero as a schoolboy, but he "continued to read his letters and discourses throughout his life. He admired him as a patriot, valued his opinions as a moral philosopher, and there is little doubt that he looked upon Cicero's life, with his love of study and aristocratic country life, as a model for his own." According to Jefferson, Cicero was "the father of eloquence and philosophy" (in Jefferson 1989, 159–161). Likewise, John Witherspoon so admired Cicero's rhetorical ability and his political principles that he named his own home, Tusculum, after Cicero's villa.

Now, since the founders did have a broad classical education, we might expect that Cicero would at least be among those they cited, imitated, and invoked. The evidence noted here already suggests a more central place for Cicero than is often credited, but this alone would not demonstrate that Cicero's thought was close to the center of the founding project—although the language of some of the endorsements here is suggestive. But we might recall that even Bailyn, who argues that Americans' engagement with their classical heritage was generally superficial, acknowledges an exception to this trend: the authors who wrote just before and after the collapse of the Roman Republic—particularly Tacitus, Sallust, and Cicero.[72] Wood concurs, identifying the same authors as particularly important.[73] But perhaps the reason

---

[71] Bailyn 1992, 26. See also Richard 2015, 124–126.
[72] Bailyn 1992, 24.
[73] Wood 1993, 100.

Bailyn *and* the anti-revisionist critics such as Pangle and Zuckert fail to see the special importance of Cicero lies in what Bailyn claims these Roman authors offered the founding generation. According to Bailyn, these writers were fundamentally moved by the calamity of the lost Roman Republic, and they were animated by an almost despairing nostalgia for the vigor and virtue of the imagined past:

> They had hated and feared the trends of their own time, and in their writing had contrasted the present with a better past, which they endowed with qualities absent from their own, corrupt era. The earlier age had been full of virtue: simplicity, patriotism, integrity, a love of justice and of liberty.... [For the colonists] the analogies to their own times were compelling. They saw their own provincial virtues—rustic and old-fashioned, sturdy and effective—challenged by the corruption at the center of power. (Bailyn 1992, 26)

Thus, in Bailyn's account, Cicero, Tacitus, and Sallust gave the Americans an image and a vocabulary of simple honest virtue threatened by corrupt monarchism. For Wood, too, this is the "classical" element of the classical republican legacy present during the Revolution and betrayed by the constitutional ratification.

But Cicero is, of course, a different writer from Tacitus or Sallust (or Livy, for that matter). Not only were his works written during the period when the republic still stood (or during which there were at least vigorous armed attempts to revive it), but he is also not a historian; he is a political philosopher. True, Cicero, too, occasionally looked to the past as a time of greater virtue than the present, and his moral theory was certainly a powerful influence on the founding generation, but he also offered—as we have seen—a powerful aspirational vision of republican politics, justice, and natural law. If the founders drew substantially from this element of Cicero's thought, it would be wrong to lump him in with the nostalgic Roman historians as having the same *type* of contribution to the founders' thought. Correcting this error would enable us to see what is truly "classical" about the republicanism—and liberalism—of the founding. The founders' ideas of what a commonwealth is (and is for), the nature of justice and rights, the role of property, and the significance of a mixed constitution all derive in large part from this Ciceronian tradition—that is to say, both through the indirect sources discussed here and from Cicero's own writings directly.

Adams and Wilson

I do not mean to suggest that all of the significant figures of the founding saw themselves as participating in a tradition of which Cicero is the central figure or that they all recognized that Cicero stood behind many of the ideas of Locke and others that formed the orthodoxy of the Revolution. But some of them did, especially John Adams and James Wilson, to whom is it now necessary to return, for reasons discussed earlier.

It is worth beginning with the decisive question, what is the nature of a republic? As already mentioned, Adams's preface to the *Defence* includes an appeal to the authority of Cicero as history's greatest "statesman and philosopher." But the extent of Adams's reliance on Cicero for the full meaning of this concept is worth presenting in full:

> The word *res*, everyone knows, signified in the Roman language wealth, riches, property . . . *res publica*, therefore was *publica res*, the wealth, riches or property of the people. . . . *Res populi*, and the original meaning of the word republic could be no other than a government in which the property of the people predominated and governed . . . it signified a government, in which the property of the public, or people, and of every one of them, was secured and protected by law. This idea, indeed, implies liberty; because property cannot be secure unless the man be at liberty to acquire, use, or part with it, at his discretion, and unless he have his personal liberty of life and limb, motion and rest, for that purpose. It implies, moreover, that the property and liberty of all men, not merely of a majority, should be safe . . . as each citizen is part of the public . . . the property, therefore of every man has a share in government . . . it is governed only by the law.[74]

Here Adams shows that his understanding of the idea of a republic is strictly Ciceronian. Adams captures the sense that the term implies joint ownership of the citizenry over the regime, that they have a kind of property right in it, just as we saw Cicero does. He shows also that such a regime exists in large part to protect the property of individual citizens, even against majoritarian tyranny. The *res publica* is the property of the people as a corporate body *and* as individuals. Finally, Adams follows Cicero in his way of conceiving the relationship of the liberty of the community to the liberty of individuals—that

---

[74] For a compelling analysis of this passage, see Thompson 1998, 190–191.

the former exists for the sake of and as a guard for the latter. Not virtue or the good life but justice—understood as the protection of rights and property—is the ultimate goal of the regime.

Wilson likewise depends on Cicero to explain this central concept of republicanism—the republic itself. He quotes from *De re publica* and goes on to describe "a body of free persons, united together for common benefit, to enjoy peaceably what is their own, and to do justice to others" (Wilson 2007, 635). For both Adams and Wilson, the rule of law is characteristic of republics, essential to their justness. The very epigraph of Wilson's published version of his lectures shows his derivation of this from Cicero, drawn from *Clu.* 146: *Lex fundamentum est libertatis, qua fruimur. Legum omnes servi sumus, ut liberi esse possimus* ("Law is the foundation of the liberty which we enjoy. Let us all be slaves of the law, that we might be free") (Wilson 2007, 415; translation mine). Adams writes that the hallmark of free government is the "rule of laws and not of men." A republic is where laws "are the only possible rule," and he similarly cites Cicero's *De re publica* as his authority (*Defence* pr.).[75]

Moreover, this republic was not to be—as Machiavelli's republic was—an amoral vehicle for collective selfishness. Ethics and politics are to be governed by natural law. The doctrine of natural law had permeated American discourse by the outbreak of the Revolution. As noted, Locke's ideas had permeated the American colonies by this time, and figures such as Grotius, Pufendorf, and even lesser (and derivative from these) natural law thinkers such as Jean-Jacques Burlamaqui and Emer de Vattel gained substantial readership as well.[76] Moreover, the founders tended to see that rights grounded in natural law hold the key to reconciling natural law with the concept of popular sovereignty and liberty.[77]

Here, too, Adams and Wilson are illustrative. Adams accepts that human beings are distinct because of their rationality and that they are naturally social ("gregarious"). According to him, we are rationally able to deduce the existence of a divine creator. From all of this, we can further deduce the fundamental laws of nature ("which is Reason"), which teach us first our obligation

[75] For all of Adams's and Wilson's dependence on Cicero, *De re publica* was only available to them only in fragments, a fact that Adams repeatedly lamented. Yet those fragments, many of them large and crucial, were preserved by Augustine and Lactantius (see chapter 1). Those fragments had been collected into volumes to which Adams and Wilson had access. In addition, they did have access to Cicero's extant works.

[76] Cohen 1978 illustrates how this natural law doctrine even shaped the way the less theoretically and politically important revolutionary historians interpreted contemporary events.

[77] Most famously, there is the formula of the Declaration of Independence, which grounds the Americans' right to independence on "the laws of Nature and of Nature's God."

to care for our own preservation and next our obligation for "promoting the good, as well as respecting the rights of mankind." These rights are supported by naturally deducible rewards and punishments.[78] The rights of liberty, to resist tyranny, and to "the preservation not only of my person, my limbs and life, but of my property" derive from the law of nature.[79] Thus, for Adams, as for Locke, natural rights are grounded in natural law but also amount to a kind of personal sovereignty that each originally has over himself.

When he wrote the Massachusetts Constitution, Adams made the centrality of this idea clear by beginning with a Declaration of Rights, article 1 of which reads: "All men are born free and equal, and have certain natural, essential, and unalienable rights; among which may be reckoned the right of enjoying and defending their lives and liberties; that of acquiring, possessing, and protecting property; in fine, that of seeking and obtaining their safety and happiness."[80] Finally, Adams also accepts the idea of a state of nature, which we leave to better secure these rights but against which we can judge political institutions.

Adams's reasoning is almost identical to Locke's. Both see humans as rational, their underlying selfishness moderated by a natural sociality. Both describe natural law and its derivative natural rights in the same way, and both conceive of just government as a way of upholding them. That Adams gets much of this directly from Locke is clear—he was effusive in his praise of him. But as we saw in chapter 5, much of the crucial logical steps made by Locke appear only in *Questions*, yet Adams follows Locke's reasoning there as much as that available in the *Two Treatises* or the *Essay*. Moreover, Adams's view of human equality—as an equality of moral obligation to natural law and not equality of abilities or merit—is overtly Ciceronian.[81] It is unclear whether Adams independently made the same logical leaps or whether he relied—as Locke himself did—on Cicero and the Ciceronian law teaching of Grotius and Pufendorf (whom he also studied well).

For Wilson, however, there is no ambiguity. If anything, he appeals even more to Cicero directly than to Locke (or Grotius and Pufendorf) to explain the law of nature. Here again, it is worth quoting at length to illustrate the point:

---

[78] For an excellent exploration of this line of Adams's thought, see Thompson 1998, 151–154.

[79] As quoted in Thompson 1998, 47.

[80] This right would only a few years later prove the basis of Massachusetts's abolition of slavery.

[81] Mayville illustrates how Adams thus rejected absolutely Aristotle's idea of natural slavery, while nevertheless equally rejecting the idea of general egalitarianism (Mayville 2016, 77–80).

The law of nature is universal. For it is true, not only that all men are equally subject to the command of their Maker, but it is true also, that the law of nature . . . has an essential fitness for all mankind. . . . This law, or right reason, as Cicero calls it, is thus beautifully described by that eloquent philosopher. "It is, indeed," says he, "a true law, conformable to nature, diffused among all men, unchangeable, eternal. By its commands, it calls men to their duty; by its prohibitions, it deters them from vice. To diminish, to alter, much more to abolish this law, is a vain attempt. Neither by the senate, nor by the people, can its powerful obligation be dissolved. . . . It is the same eternal and immutable law, given at all times to all nations: for God, who is its author and promulgator, is always the sole master and sovereign of mankind." (Wilson 2007, 523)[82]

Wilson thus takes wholesale from Cicero his conception of natural law and uses the quotation from *De re publica* to emphasize both its support from our own self-interest and the divine sovereign's rewards and punishments. He appeals to Cicero again to support his understanding of God as the source of moral obligation and his view that the rules of moral conduct can be demonstrated from first principles such as mathematics (Wilson 2007, 508).[83] Wilson also sees natural law as meant to guide man-made political laws, and its commands do not vary according to circumstance—it is universal and cosmopolitan.

Wilson further cites Cicero to derive from this natural law our right to preserve ourselves, our liberty, and our property (and those of others) (Wilson 2007, 1082–1083). Wilson follows Locke, but appeals to Cicero by name, when explaining that we leave the state of nature to achieve the security offered by standing rules to defend our rights (Wilson 2007, 690). Wilson makes clear that he sees the Ciceronian origins of the founders' apparent Lockeanism when he even cites Cicero in support of the famously Lockean doctrine that consent (at least, tacit consent) is essential to the legitimacy of free government—that, in other words, the right of free exit is indispensable to liberty. He quotes from *Pro Balbo*: " 'The power of retaining and of renouncing our rights of citizenship, is the most stable foundation of our liberties' " (Wilson 2007, 642).[84] Wilson's habit of using Cicero in this way

---

[82] Wilson is translating accurately from *Rep.* 3.33. Thompson argues that Wilson's view expressed here "sums up the view of an entire generation" (Thompson 2019, 57).

[83] In the prolegomena of *De iure belli*, Grotius makes a similar analogy.

[84] Cf. Cicero's *Balb.* 13.

(where it would seem to us far more intuitive to cite Locke) suggests that he may have grasped better than any of his contemporaries or any modern scholar the close relationship between Locke's natural law teaching and Cicero's.[85] He thus also sees that Locke's way of reconciling natural law with the principles of popular sovereignty and consent is grounded in Ciceronian principles.

Wilson and Adams both also look to Cicero to illustrate the special protections for property that ought to exist in a just regime. We already saw that Adams drew heavily from Cicero's understanding of a *res publica* to argue that property was, in fact, the basis of the liberty found in a republic. He elaborates (rather hyperbolically) that "the moment the idea is admitted into society, that property is not as sacred as the laws of God, and that there is not a force of law and public justice to protect it, anarchy and tyranny commence."[86] As for Wilson, he tells a story remarkably similar to Locke's account of the just origins of property:

> while men were few, and supplies of every thing were abundant, it is probable that many things were possessed and used in common. With regard to the possession and use of some things, however, this could never be strictly the case. In the fruit plucked or gathered by one for his subsistence; in the spot which he occupied for his shelter . . . in the skin which he has obtained by his skill . . . he gains a high degree of exclusive right, and of this right he cannot be dispossessed without a proportioned degree of injustice. (Wilson 2007, 388)

But after (and before) this discussion, which is nearly a paraphrase of Locke, Wilson does not even mention Locke; instead, he quotes for support Cicero's example of the property in the theater![87]

To defend the property, liberty, and other rights of the just republican regime, the American founders were nearly unanimous in their belief that mixed government and a division of powers were necessary. Adams, for

[85] He and Adams, though, were hardly alone in depending on Cicero for the contours of natural law. Others include Samuel Adams, Benjamin Rush, Thomas Paine, and Thomas Jefferson. See Richard 2015, 137–142.

[86] Thompson 1998, 191. Like Zuckert and Pangle, Thompson believes that Adams's concern for the rights of property marks his departure from the classical republican tradition (Thompson 1998, 197). But the arguments of this book illustrate why this is not the case once one recognizes Cicero's significance. Ciceronian republicanism is deeply concerned with property.

[87] As I have noted, Cicero is not the true originator of the example, but Wilson (along with nearly everyone else) attributes it to him.

instance, criticizes English republicans such as Nedham for supporting absolute parliamentary supremacy, arguing that simple forms of government degenerate easily into tyranny.[88] In *The Federalist*, Madison credits Montesquieu as the expositor of the fundamental truth that "the legislative, executive, and judiciary departments ought to be separate and distinct" (47). Straumann has suggested that Cicero stands behind this element of Montesquieu's constitutionalism.[89] This is likely true. But Adams and Wilson derive the principle from Cicero directly, as Straumann also notes.[90]

In the preface of his *Defence*, when Adams first appeals to the authority of history's best "statesman and philosopher," he does so in citing the argument from *De re publica* that the best commonwealth contains a mixture of monarchy, aristocracy, and democracy in its constitution. Adams appeals to Cicero's authority that there should be both a mixture of these three elements in the regime and a division of powers into different branches of government. As *Fed.* 51 explains, the checks and balances arising from this division would help prevent any one element of government or society from achieving a position to dominate the rest. Adams explores this same theme by updating the musical analogy in Cicero's story of the "blending" and "harmony" of the mixture of rights and powers outlined in *De re publica*:

> [Cicero] was so far from apprehending "disputes" from a variety of orders, that he affirms it to be the firmest bond of justice, and the strongest anchor of safety to the community. As the treble, the tenor, and the bass exist in nature, they will be heard in the concert: if they are arranged by Handel, in a skilful composition, they produce rapture the most exquisite that harmony can excite; but if they are confused together without order, they will "Rend with tremendous sound your ears asunder." (*Defence* pref.)

Not to be outdone by Adams in his poetic praise of Cicero's idea of a mixed constitution, Wilson writes that Rome was "adorned and enriched by the exquisite genius of Cicero, which like the touch of Midas, converts every object

---

[88] Thompson 1998, 130.

[89] Straumann 2016, 321.

[90] Straumann insists that the approved regime is "tempered" but not "mixed." However, following the usage established in chapter 1, Adams follows Cicero in endorsing both. Adams's ideal regime certainly includes at least a mixture of aristocratic principles and democratic ones, as well as a distinct division of powers. Carl Richard also illustrates the ways in which the founders drew from Cicero to develop their understanding of mixed government, including a notable speech by Hamilton during the Constitutional Convention, in which he cites Cicero (with Aristotle and Montesquieu) directly (Richard 2015).

into gold. . . . He composed a republick: and for the use of his republick, formed a system of laws. In this system, he expatiates on the wisdom and excellency of the Roman constitution" (Wilson 2007, 760). Wilson believed that Cicero was unique among the ancients in discovering this great idea of mixed government.[91] He says that the ancients imagined only simple governments or governments that could be reduced to one of these at bottom, despite superficial elements of the others. But "Cicero, indeed, seems to have indulged a fond speculative opinion, that a government formed of the three kinds, properly blended and tempered, would of all, be the best constituted. But this opinion was treated as visionary by his countrymen, and by Tacitus, one of the wisest of them." Wilson thus takes Cicero to be the true discoverer of the modern principle of mixed government, and he suggests that the example of Great Britain moves in the direction of bringing Cicero's vision into reality: "the example of Great Britain, however, has evinced that the sentiments of Cicero merited a very different opinion [from Tacitus]; and that, if they did not point to the highest degree of excellence, they pointed, at least, to substantial improvement" (Wilson 2007, 711). In other words, Cicero's optimism about the possibilities of a stable mixed regime have proven more justified than Tacitus and other doubters would have believed.

Adams expresses a similar view but specifies that the American founding extends Cicero's innovation still further. Referring to the same debate between Cicero and Tacitus over the practicality of Cicero's system of separation of powers, Adams writes in his preface:

> If Cicero and Tacitus could revisit the earth, and learn that the English nation had reduced [Cicero's] great idea to practice, and brought it nearly to perfection, by giving each division a power to defend itself by a negative; had found it the most solid and durable government, as well as the most free; had obtained, by means of it, a prosperity among civilized nations, in an enlightened age [they would be astounded].

Adams notes that the colonies of America matured under this constitution and in crafting their governments, have followed the lesson, predicting that "the institutions now made in America will never wear wholly out for

---

[91] Whether Wilson was unaware of the versions of such a scheme presented by Aristotle and Polybius or if he believed that their versions lacked something essential that Cicero's possessed, I do not know.

thousands of years" (*Defence* preface). In short, for Adams and Wilson, the experiment of mixed government in England and still more in America have proved Tacitus's skepticism wrong and have made Cicero's "visionary" dream a reality. In explicit terms, then, Adams and Wilson see the American experiment as a *realization of the Ciceronian principles of government*. America is, for them, Cicero's dream brought to life.

This dream of mixed government was the primary bulwark of liberty for Adams. According to him, Americans have a "habitual, radical Sense of Liberty," which consists both of freedom for the individual against unjust governmental coercion and the freedom of the community to make its own decisions undominated by an outside power. The proper mixture of powers in a constitution ensures that no group achieves that domination, averting threats to the liberties of the citizens. Those liberties are "not the grants of princes or parliaments but original rights, conditions of original contracts."[92] In other words, Adams, like Locke and Cicero, conceives of the same relationship between the "republican" liberty of the community and the liberal freedom of citizens. The former is necessary to secure the latter. But the former is bound and limited by the moral limitations of the law of nature not to violate the rights of individuals. Wilson again connects the lesson to Rome, saying that "while they enjoyed the blessing of liberty" under republican government, the Romans were secure in their "rights to property" and "the rights of persons" but that those were gradually lost once the domination of a single individual was achieved (Wilson 2007, 758).[93]

This American agreement with Locke and Cicero about the relationship between the rights of individuals and free government might help us to understand why Wood might see the Constitution as a liberal coup against the republican ethos of the Revolution. There is a necessarily chronological

---

[92] Quoted in Thompson 1998, 54–55.

[93] As I said, I have chosen to focus on Wilson and Adams because they seem (roughly) representative of the views that ultimately prevail among the founders of both "moments" and because at the same time, they were more attentive than most to the relationship those views had to their historical antecedents and underlying philosophical bases. Nevertheless, to illustrate how representative their ideas were, compare the foregoing to this short summary of Madison's theoretical principles by Marvin Meyers: "God created men equal, free, and independent; obliged them by natural law to preserve themselves; and endowed them with reason and passions to realize their preservation. With reason, they should recognize the equal rights of others to life, liberty, and the pursuit of happiness. . . . Thus the convention that establishes government and subjects citizens and magistrates alike to law. Thus the constitution that defines the boundaries of legitimate power and reserves all else— belief especially—to individual choice. Thus the republican form of commonwealth that perpetuates the principle of consent in the regular workings of government" (in Madison 1973, xxiv). This linking of individual liberty to republican self-government was common among the founding generation.

priority built into the two concepts, which Wood misses. If the Americans believed (and they did) that the British government had become corrupt and was threatening their freedom through its illegal (i.e., contrary to natural law) taxation and regulation of American lives and property, the first thing necessary was to establish a new political regime, justified according to the Lockean right of revolution. The conflict sparked by such a revolution required the patriotic willingness to sacrifice for the common good, calling forth the republican rhetoric of virtue that so occupies Wood. But once the first task of establishing a new regime was complete, the next task would naturally be to order it better to protect the liberty of individuals that had been the entire purpose of the rebellion in the first place.[94] To then establish a constitution that featured rights centrally would not be a betrayal but a fulfillment of the republican aspirations of the Revolution.

Writing the *Res Publica*

But the idea of a constitution also posed a special problem for Americans, even if—as Adams and Wilson (not to mention Hamilton and others) believed—Americans would be wise to follow the models of Rome and England in establishing a mixed government. What Cicero said of Rome, Edmund Burke would say of England: that its admirable constitution and distribution of powers emerged over the course of a long historical development. The Americans, however, needed new government right away.

Their teachers from Cicero to Locke assured them that they were right to resist tyranny and entitled to establish a new, just government. But it is not immediately clear how to realize that principle in practice under conditions of oppression. Locke attributed the right of resistance to tyranny to the people, who could withdraw their consent, abolish their current government, and establish a new one (II 211–243). The Declaration of Independence affirms this logic. But how are the people to establish a new government? Moreover, even if they do, how do they ensure that the new balance of powers erected to protect liberty persists, instead of degenerating into domination and tyranny again?

---

[94] Adams's famous claim that "I must study Politicks and War that my sons may have liberty to study Mathematicks and Philosophy" (letter to Abigail Adams 1780) echoes this progressive sentiment about the lexical priorities of first establishing good government—for the sake of freedom for individuals to order their own lives.

The fact that Americans could not simply sit back and wait for their regime to emerge out of a historical process necessitated some rethinking of what a constitution is. Bailyn illustrates how the prevailing understanding of a constitution in the anglophone world prior to the Revolution implied a vague, all-encompassing notion of the laws, customs, morals, and powers that made up a discrete political community. In that speech of James Otis that Adams looked to as the start of the independence movement, Otis suggested that an act of Parliament could violate the "constitution" and that any such act would be "void."[95] There began to emerge a sense that a "constitution" expressed certain first-order moral rules for a political community that somehow bound or limited the formal legislating and executive elements of government.[96] When the Americans finally declared their independence, their need for some new organizing principle for government expressed itself in the call for new "constitutions."

Thompson relates how leading men of these colonies eagerly sought Adams's advice on how to do this, his reputation for knowledge of ancient and modern political thought making him the nearest thing to an expert. So inundated was Adams with such requests that he ultimately wrote and published *Thoughts on Government* to provide a general response to these pressing concerns. Thompson describes the situation:

> Their [the other founders'] ignorance was understandable. There were simply no examples in modern history of nations or states framing constitutions *de novo*. But Adams had reflected on the subject for some time. . . . He began immediately to look "into the Ancient and modern Confederacies for Examples." The first and most important question for Adams was: "How can the People Institute Governments?" (Thompson 1998, 40)

Following Locke and Cicero, Adams believed that such new governments would have to depend on an initial act of consent. But for the people to formally consent, something concrete to consent to needed to be presented to them. Thus, Adams proposed that "Conventions of Representatives chosen by the People" be called to frame the new governments. As Thompson puts it,

[95] As quoted in Bailyn 1992, 176.
[96] See Straumann 2016 for an argument that this idea long predates this period and traces back to Cicero himself.

"John Adams was the first American to advocate having constitutions drafted and ratified by special conventions representing the consent of the people."[97]

Adams's solution resolves a less theoretical but profoundly important practical puzzle left over from Cicero and even Locke. Cicero and Locke both agree that consent of the people is essential for legitimate government. They also agree that the consent cannot be given to any political arrangement but only to one that reflects the demands of natural law. But neither Locke nor Cicero (nor Adams and most of the American founders) believed that the details of the natural law were clear and readily apparent to the mass of average people. How, then, could consent to a good regime be obtained prior to the existence of consent (and thus any legitimate authority). Adams's solution—later copied by other framers of state constitutions and ultimately the 1789 Constitution—was that wise statesmen could draw up such constitutions and present them to the people for ratification.[98] Although Cicero offers no such solution himself, the idea that wise statesmen would guide the people in this momentous choice but also need their consent is wholly consonant with the core of his republican thought. We may even see in it a modern echo of Cicero's idea in *Pro Sestio* that wise and eloquent practitioners of rhetoric were necessary to establish commonwealths in the first place, persuading people to leave the state of nature and join society. This is a far more top-down and less democratic vision of the founding of society than envisioned by Locke, but it more closely resembles how the American founders solved the problem: frame constitutions, then persuade the people to ratify them.

Adams reinforces the idea that such new governments would be solidly grounded on the consent of the truly sovereign people. Once the plans for the new governments were drafted—with an aim to mix powers so that the natural rights of the people could be protected—they must be presented to the people for a vote, so that "the People may make Acceptance of it by their own Act" (Adams 1851, 3:16). By the time of the 1787 convention, Hamilton could testify that Adams's principles of constitution making had become generally accepted and would soon be put to a national test of world-historical significance:

---

[97] Thompson 1998, 40.

[98] Of course, these constitutions were not created de novo. As Lutz has illustrated, colonial governments and charters also provided a wealth of resources for new constitution makers (Lutz 1988).

It has been frequently remarked that it seems to have been reserved to the people of this country, by their conduct and example, to decide the important question, whether societies of men are really capable or not of establishing good government from reflection and choice, or whether they are forever destined to depend for their political constitutions on accident and force. (*Fed.* 1)

Both Bailyn and Wood rightly see this theoretical development as one of the greatest practical/theoretical contributions of the American founding to modern political thinking: "it not only enabled the constitution to rest on an authority different from the legislature's, but it actually seemed to have legitimized revolution."[99] Wilson—referring as usual to Cicero's authority—summarized the new American view of a constitution:

I mean that supreme law, made or ratified by those in whom the sovereign power of the state resides, which prescribes the manner, according to which . . . the government should be instituted and administered. From this constitution the government derives its power: by this constitution the power of government must be directed and controlled. (Wilson 2007, 712)

Cicero's code of primary laws outlined in *De legibus* does in many ways resemble this "new" understanding of a constitution.

As discussed, Adams would (largely by himself) craft the state constitution for Massachusetts (he would insist on calling it not a state but a "commonwealth"), with its unitary executive, bicameral legislature, independent judiciary, and declaration of rights. When Wilson, Madison, Hamilton, and others would later draft the US Constitution, they followed almost precisely the procedures laid down by Adams for the creation of the first state governments, keeping as well most of its salient features. Richard Ryerson has illustrated how Adams consciously developed what he hoped would be a "republican orthodoxy" for Americans of all the states and that this project was at least partially successful in shaping the development of the new constitutions.[100]

Other scholars have explored at length the debates, bargaining, and controversies that attended the drafting and ratification of the Constitution and

---

[99] Wood [1969] 1998, 342. See also Bailyn 1992, 175–182.
[100] Ryerson 2016, 158.

the Bill of Rights. But there is little dispute that behind them both stood the following set of ideas that supporters and opponents alike largely agreed with: that there is a moral law prior to political life to which it ought to conform (natural law); that from this moral law, human beings derive rights to their lives, liberty, and property; that legitimate governments rest on consent and ought to be constrained by this moral law to protect the freedom of their citizens; and that the best way to achieve such limitation on state power is the checks and balances of mixed government. This higher law need not be entirely codified in written law, but it must inform all legitimate written law.[101]

All of these are likewise central elements to the Ciceronian tradition, revived and extended by Locke. To this tradition, the Americans themselves contributed theoretical innovations in constitutionalism, reflecting the practical demands of the endeavor: that constitutions ought to be written, that they ought to express (or at least reflect) those highest moral commitments of the political community, that they should be drafted by representatives of the people chosen for that purpose, and that they must finally be submitted back to the people for approval.

Adams was not the only eighteenth-century figure to wish Cicero could see his political philosophy brought into reality. Montesquieu, Madison's "oracle" (*Fed.* 47), expressed his wish that Cicero had "come in an age more enlightened" (Montesquieu 2002, 734). When Adams and Wilson suggest that the American regime is a vindication of Cicero's dream, they, in a sense, suggest that Montesquieu's prayer has been answered. In the "Age of Enlightenment," the American founders established a government that realized the aspirations of a tradition of liberty that began with Cicero's declaration of the foundations of a just *res publica*.

---

[101] This is especially reflected in the Ninth Amendment's reference to unenumerated rights retained by the people. See Grey 1978; George 2000; Berns 1982; Hamburger 1993.

7

Epilogue

The End of the Ciceronian Tradition?

What difference does it make, that those who will be born after you
should speak of you? . . . What others say about you is their business,
and they will say it anyway. . . . No one's reputation has ever lasted
forever; it fades with the death of men and is extinguished by the for-
getfulness of posterity.

—*Rep.* 6.23–25

No man who composed an epic poem about his own consulship could plausibly be considered uninterested in glory. Indeed, few of Cicero's writings are
free from references to his own achievements and reputation. Yet Cicero's
most profound thoughts on glory reflect a deep ambivalence toward it.
Although the very best statesmen are likely to be motivated in part by a desire
for eternal fame, Cicero insists that such hopes are doomed to disappoint-
ment. In the last book of *De re publica*, Scipio reports a dream in which he is
shown the heavens and the workings of the cosmos. Amid all these wonders,
he still cannot help turning his head back to glance at the tiny dot on the
surface of the earth that constitutes Rome's dominion. His grandfather and
guide chides him, pointing out how small Rome's empire truly is, telling him
that his fame will never reach the far regions of the globe, much less touch the
rest of the vast universe. Even among the people over whom Rome's empire
spreads, Scipio's name will eventually fade into oblivion (*Rep.* 6.20–23). In
writing this, Cicero signals his awareness that he would share Scipio's fate—
his fame, too, would eventually fail.

Perhaps Cicero himself would have accepted this languishment. Just as his
passionate patriotic attachment to Rome is moderated by his belief that our
true home is the universal cosmopolis of gods and men, so, too, is his passion
for glory moderated by his recognition that "true glory" (*verum decus*) can

Natural Law Republicanism. Michael C. Hawley, Oxford University Press. © Oxford University Press 2022.
DOI: 10.1093/oso/9780197582336.003.0007

be found only in that same heavenly commonwealth (*Rep.* 6.25). Admission to that realm requires no praise but only that one be *worthy* of praise (*Rep.* 6.29).[1] Nothing is worthier of praise than contributing to the preservation and protection of "those communities and groups of people bound together by justice, called states" (*Rep.* 6.13). During his life, Cicero sought most of all to contribute to that goal directly, by political action and service to his particular *res publica*. Yet when forced out of politics, he acknowledged that philosophical writing *about* republics could be the next-greatest service one could render: "even those who did not govern commonwealths, nevertheless did them a certain significant service by studying and writing so much about them" (*Rep.* 3.12). It may be that at the end of his life, Cicero recognized that his writings constituted a far more lasting service to the cause of republican government generally than his actions (however heroic) in defense of the Roman one. From the standpoint of history, at least, that is undoubtedly the case.

Cicero's fame recovered more quickly and lasted far longer than anyone would likely have expected who saw his head and hands on the Rostra in 43 BCE. Not his deeds as a republican statesman but his philosophical contributions secured his lasting posthumous renown. Yet even Cicero, it seems, could not escape the oblivion Scipio is warned about. The period leading up to the American founding corresponded roughly to the high-water mark of Cicero's historical influence. This is undoubtedly true when we compare him with other classical sources. Google's Ngram Viewer reveals that references to Cicero reach a peak around the middle to the end of the eighteenth century, at times more than double the references to Plato and Aristotle combined. But in the nineteenth century, those references go into an extended decline, becoming decisively overshadowed by the two Greek philosophers (see figure 7.1). To this day, Cicero lags well behind Plato and Aristotle as a classical source.[2] Part of the reason for his demotion lies in the rise of German classical scholarship, which largely took the Greeks to be the truly profound classical thinkers. For them, Cicero and the Romans were at best pale imitators. Cicero's style—pompous, bombastic, and often full of his own praises—does little to seduce the modern ear. His work is less systematic

---

[1] Cf. Hawley 2019, 710.

[2] This does not even take into account the fact that Cicero during the seventeenth and eighteenth centuries was often referred to as "Tully"—likely, his superiority over Plato and Aristotle during this period was even greater, once we take this into account.

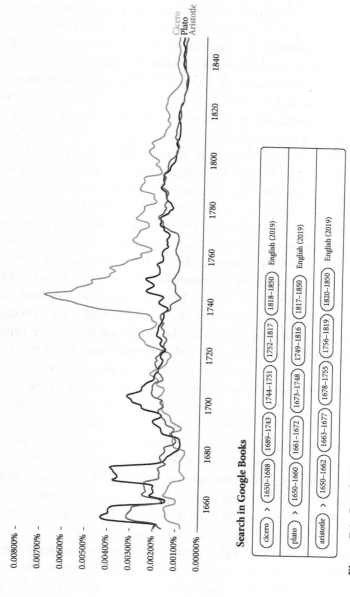

Figure 7.1 Google Ngram Viewer: Cicero, Plato, Aristotle (accessed February 2020).

than Aristotle's and less mysterious and beguiling than Plato's—making him perhaps a less obvious subject to intrigue scholars of political theory.

The most general claim of this book is that we ought not yet consign Cicero to obscurity. Curricula in political theory especially tend to skip over Cicero as they leap from Plato and Aristotle to Augustine, Aquinas, or Machiavelli. So it is hardly surprising that we would miss the staggeringly influential role he has played in the development of the ideas and institutions we now take for granted. Accounts of quarrels between "the ancients and the moderns" or "republicanism and liberalism" ring false because we tend to assimilate Cicero into the families of Greek idealism or republican virtue theory when, in fact, he stood independent of both. Cicero understood the value both of utopian thinking and of moral virtue. Yet his political theory rested on neither the one nor the other. In this book, I have sought to contribute to the burgeoning recovery of Cicero both as a deep thinker in his own right and as an immensely important historical influence. On both counts, there remains far more work to be done. But I hope to have contributed to that work, already begun by such scholars as Jed Atkins, Walter Nicgorski, Benjamin Straumann, Joy Connolly, Tim Stuart-Buttle, Daniel Kapust, and others.

In this work, I have sought to grapple with one significant (yet still fractional) element of that great story. I have attempted to show how Cicero inaugurated a tradition of thinking about politics that seeks to reconcile two apparently conflicting ideas: that the people are the rightful supreme sovereigns and owners of their political community and that there is some universal morally binding law that trumps any positive law the people or their agents might want to make. For Cicero, liberty is the product of this uneasy combination. In the rest of this epilogue, I want merely to illustrate how much is lost if we lose sight of the tension that animates this particular Ciceronian tradition. I will not here argue that we ought to accept its specific conclusions about natural law, rights, and popular sovereignty. But I do suggest that our political thinking is impoverished if we assume that the questions raised by this Ciceronian tradition do not require answers. Should the sovereignty of the people be limited? If so, according to what standard? Is liberty really opposed to limitation, or is it constituted by it?

To see how this project might enhance our own self-understanding, it is important to see that Lockean-Ciceronian natural law is not only present for us implicitly in documents such as the Declaration of Independence and the Constitution, but it is also explicitly part of the justification for considerable portions of the American legal regime. Many early yet still binding precedents of the US Supreme Court appeal to this natural law. For instance, in *Ogden* v. *Saunder* (1827), the Court sought to resolve whether the obligation to fulfill a contract derives from positive law alone. The Court determined that it did not:

> The constitution meant to preserve the inviolability of contracts, as secured by those eternal principles of equity and justice which run throughout every civilized code, which form a part of the law of nature and nations, and by which human society, in all countries and all ages, has been regulated and upheld. It is said that the obligation of contracts is derived from the municipal law alone. . . . This is what we deny. It springs from a higher source: from those great principles of universal law, which are binding on societies of men as well as on individuals. The writers on natural law are full of this subject.

One could hardly imagine a more faithful Ciceronian interpretation of the way in which natural law limits the scope of positive law, however democratically enacted. In *Watson* v. *Tarpley* (1855), the Court even appeals to Cicero's construal of natural law explicitly. The idea that there is a universal moral law that justifies and thus informs our constitutional arrangements is thus present today for us in the continuing applicability of these rulings.

But there is an even deeper sense in which our self-understanding is impoverished if we fail to grasp the significance of this blending of popular sovereign and natural law. Muddy thinking about these questions makes it easier to pull apart the ideas of rights and democratic self-government. Despite our awareness of the possibility of "illiberal democracy,"[3] most of us tend to assume democracy and individual rights belong together. Yet it is the Ciceronian tradition that did much of the work to forge that link, on the basis of a particular construal of rights and self-government grounded in natural law. Stripped of that grounding, both rights and self-government appear once more as potential rivals for priority. Rights may seem to be simply the dispensation of democratic will and thus insecure and discardable on the same grounds. Especially with the rise of populism on the right and the left, rights that thwart expressions of democracy may grow ever harder to defend rhetorically.

[3] Zakaria 1997.

Alternatively, rights can become a different sort of problem when they appear as a kind of metaphysical absolute: "rights as trumps,"[4] claims that a person or group can make that automatically supersede any democratic choice. Today rights have indeed become by far the most ubiquitous way of articulating limits to the sovereignty of the people. But there is a strong incentive to frame one's general policy preferences (or even pure self-interest) as rights claims—if such a move is successful, not only does one achieve one's political objective, but one also takes that objective out of the jurisdiction of present or future democratic decision-making. We therefore face a "proliferation of rights" with no end in sight.[5] Every day brings new alleged rights into the political discourse, with advocates hoping that their claims can join the pantheon of rights, thus shrinking further the legitimate scope of democratic judgment and, with it, the sovereignty of the people.

Locke and Cicero would undoubtedly agree that rights limit what a self-governing people may choose to do in the name of general utility. But our theories of rights and popular sovereignty were originally derived from a common source in the Lockean-Ciceronian natural law. Once that link is severed, we lose the original framework for discriminating between legitimate rights claims and spurious ones. Without a new framework, we run the risk of a discursive impasse of the sort described by Alasdair MacIntyre. According to MacIntyre, modern life confronts the problem that when "claims invoking rights are matched against claims appealing to utility . . . there is no rational way of deciding which type of claim is to be given priority or how one is to be weighed against the other."[6]

It is not unusual for people to take both horns of the dilemma—to denounce checks on the people's will yet also to want to carve out preferred exceptions to that will in the name of specific rights. This may be because the framework worked out by the Ciceronian-Lockean tradition still operates implicitly at the back of our mind—but without its philosophical underpinning in natural law. In part, the success of the later part of the Ciceronian tradition may have inadvertently made it easier to ignore its natural law premises—a lack of tension makes for a lack of attention. Locke and the American founders begin from Ciceronian premises but achieve a far more philosophically stable solution than Cicero did. Following the ratification debates, there is a noticeable decline in philosophical and public discourse

---

[4] Dworkin 2009, 335.
[5] Wellman 2018.
[6] MacIntyre 2007, 70.

over the relationship of rights and popular sovereignty, perhaps because the issue seemed satisfactorily settled.

For Locke and the founders, the people's sovereignty is not a rival source of authority to universal moral law; the former is *nested* within the latter. Popular sovereignty is legitimated by natural law; it is not a free-floating moral claim, based on some intuition of the people's justness, but rather a logical deduction from natural rights, supported by a coherent framework of universal moral equality, human sociality, natural freedom, and human dignity. From this perspective, a populism that denies natural law in the name of the people's right to rule saws the branch it sits on. After all, what moral right do the people have to rule in the first place, without natural law? The same Lockean reasoning yields clear guidelines on what sorts of rights are legitimate limitations to the people's authority. The natural law reveals that human beings are different but morally equal bearers of dignity, naturally free and naturally social. As a result, citizens have rights to equality under the law, to protection of their persons and property from arbitrary harm or interference, to participation in that very process of self-governing, and so on. But they do not have rights beyond this—at least, no rights that can be asserted *over* popular sovereignty.[7]

With the decline of natural law reasoning in the nineteenth century and beyond, not only does one see the rising possibility of conflict between rights and popular sovereignty, but it becomes far easier to challenge the wholesale legitimacy of either or both. For instance, MacIntyre himself takes just such a skeptical attitude toward the concept of rights that human beings possess merely by virtue of their humanity: "there are no such rights, and belief in them is one with belief in witches and in unicorns."[8] Without some grounding in universal moral law, democratic self-government in turn rests on dubious calculations of efficacy, for example, the very contestable "wisdom of the crowd" thesis.[9] Or it may rely on the brute logic of Polemarchus in the opening lines of the *Republic*: "do you see how many of us there are? . . . Well, then, either prove stronger than these men, or stay here" (*Republic* 327c). But

---

[7] That is to say, they may enjoy a large number of rights that go beyond this but downstream from democratic choice, in other words, as conventional or civil or legal rights.

[8] MacIntyre 2007, 69. In part, MacIntyre's position is born of a rejection of a non-teleological natural law of the sort that the Ciceronian-Lockean tradition espouses. For MacIntyre, this Stoic position infects much of Western moral philosophy and crowds out the possibility of virtue (MacIntyre 2007, 169–171).

[9] There is considerable debate over whether crowds are indeed wise, or whether we should instead defer to experts. See, among others, Waldron 1995; Schwartzberg 2016; Bell 2016.

such lines of reasoning fail the moment some other force *does* prove stronger or more effective at governing.

None of this is to say that it is impossible to defend a coherent theory of democratic legitimacy or universal human rights without appealing to the Ciceronian-Lockean tradition. There are myriad different philosophical and scholarly traditions that do one or the other (more rarely both). I wish to call attention, however, to the fact that the *particular* reconciliation of those two principles that we often intuitively take for granted, which the Declaration of Independence could pronounce as "self-evident," depends on a natural law theory that we have largely abandoned.

It seems uncontroversial to say that if the grounds for an opinion are abandoned, the opinion is no longer reasonable to hold. Now we might decide that the attacks on the very idea of innate human rights or democratic self-government are justified. In that case, there is nothing to lament in the decay of the natural law reasoning undergirding the Declaration. We need only continue the deconstructive work already begun on notions of rights and democratic legitimacy. But if we would like to retain our loyalty to the basic arrangement of democratic authority and individual rights that we have inherited, we have a few options.

First, we might seek out new paradigms by which to unite and justify our received arrangement of rights and democratic legitimacy. Much modern democratic theory attempts to do something like this. However, it balks at the idea of natural law—a term that appears in virtually no modern democratic theory.[10] Yet if it truly aims to stake a claim to universal moral rightness (a key feature of that framework we have inherited, with its "self-evident" truths), it may avoid the terminology but not the logic of natural law. For natural law is nothing more than the assertion of a universally binding moral obligation for human beings. For this reason, we may see all modern moral realism and deontological moral theory to be the modern heirs of natural law theory.[11] Indeed, one could be forgiven for thinking it was Kant—and not Cicero in *De finibus*—who said, "we understand moral worth to be of such a nature that, stripped of all utility, without any rewards or fruits, it can still be praised justly in and of itself" (*Fin.* 2.45). The basic logic of Cicero's natural law remains very much with us, even if we discard the term.

---

[10] As far as I know, no major contemporary democratic theory rests on an explicit doctrine of natural law.

[11] Nussbaum has illustrated how deeply influenced Kant was by Stoic philosophy, much of which he accessed through Cicero (Nussbaum 1997).

So perhaps we might choose to return openly to natural law thinking, as John Finnis has done. Finnis argues that natural law has been unjustifiably rejected and that a legal and moral order can still be erected and preserved on the grounds of natural law. However, Finnis (like MacIntyre) rejects what he considers to be the Stoic natural law teaching, along with its "post-Renaissance formulations," in favor of a teleological one directed toward human "flourishing."[12] In other words, Finnis seeks a return to the original teleological natural law tradition of Aristotle that carries on through Aquinas. However, Finnis's treatment, while it might secure a very stable and coherent list of rights, leaves little room for robust popular sovereignty.[13] Moreover, unless we are prepared to relitigate the early modern debates that discredited teleological reasoning and come to a different conclusion about inherent naturally given ends, this solution will not avail us much.

Alternatively, we might attempt to resuscitate the Ciceronian-Lockean natural law doctrine itself. Precisely because its premises are latent within a still-common political attitude, it might seem best simply to return to it. Yet we have seen that this natural law doctrine depends quite heavily—if subtly—on the role of a divinity providing the sanction for those "Laws of Nature and of Nature's God." Such a premise is no less contestable than Finnis's archaic teleology and no more likely to gain common acceptance.

There may be ways of excising the controversial theological premises of the doctrine to make it palatable to a secular age; again, much contemporary moral realist philosophy does something along these lines. But part of the function of this book has been to show that Locke's success within the tradition depends to a significant degree on his offering the Christian God as the guarantor of the Ciceronian natural law.[14] This is what enables natural law to have the binding status of true *law* and enabled Locke to speak of "natural rights" where Cicero had only spoken of the rights of citizens. Is it possible to get the good out of this natural law without appealing to its compromised (from a modern point of view) natural theology?

---

[12] Finnis 2011, 374–376, 416. Although both MacIntyre and Finnis refer to the natural law doctrine they oppose as "Stoic," it is clear—especially in Finnis's case—that Cicero is the primary source for it. See Finnis 2011, 374–375.

[13] Finnis 2011, 248–250. Here Finnis seems indifferent to modes of government and dismisses the idea that ultimate authority is located in the people as a whole. Finnis's position seems close to that of Grotius and Pufendorf and is unsatisfying for some of the same reasons.

[14] As noted in chapter 5, this is not a novel view. Dunn goes furthest along these lines when he argues that Locke's theological views render him irrelevant to the modern world (Dunn 1982).

To that, I have no firm answers. But it is clear that such a project would be monumental. I will end by pointing out how Cicero himself may offer some resources that we moderns could still profit from. Consider, for instance, this idea of natural rights. Locke's solution rendered rights as a kind of "property" held by each individual in usufruct from God. But for Cicero, rights were not *primarily* a kind of property; they were instead the structures of relationships, of *just* relationships. To make a rights claim for Cicero was not so much to assert something that one *owns* but rather to appeal to a common link between oneself and another—an appeal to duty that arises out of our shared dignity as rational creatures. Perhaps we have lost something in abandoning that way of thinking about rights. Rights as a form of relationship could conceivably stretch to include democratic rights of self-government as well as rights to life, speech, and property. The justness of these relationships might be found in the nature of human beings, in their fundamental equality to one another, their inherent dignity, and so on. This would make such rights fixed and universal, without appealing to any disputed notion of the divine.

Now, just because such a framework *could* be imagined does not by any stretch imply that it would be easy to establish and defend philosophically. One would have to provide an account of justice that informs the idea of "just relationship," and even Cicero did not manage to do this without an appeal to the divine. But his appeals were far more muted than Locke's and perhaps could be minimized further still.

There is no way to adjudicate among these options here. The purpose of this book has been to advance our understanding of how we got to where we are, not where we ought to go. But it is hard to attempt the latter without doing the former. The Ciceronian tradition examined in this book is responsible in large part for determining the contours of the otherwise unintuitive liberal union of popular sovereignty, transcendent moral law, and personal liberty. To the extent that such a union ought to be defended, attacked, or reformed, it is first necessary to grasp the ground on which the arrangement was formed.

References

Aarsleff, Hans. 1969. "The State of Nature and the Nature of Man in Locke." In *John Locke: Problems and Perspectives*, John W. Yolton, editor. Cambridge: Cambridge University Press: 99–136.

Adams, John. 1805. "Letter to Benjamin Rush." In *The Adams Papers Collection of the National Archives*. https://founders.archives.gov/documents/Adams/99-02-02-5110.

Adams, John. 1851. *The Works of John Adams, Second President of the United States: With a Life of the Author, Notes and Illustrations*. 10 vols. Edited by Charles Francis Adams. Boston: Little, Brown.

Adams, John. 1979. *The Adams Papers, Vol. 4: February–August 1776*. Edited by Robert J. Taylor. Cambridge, MA: Harvard University Press.

Alonso, Fernando H. Llano. 2012. "Cicero and Natural Law." *Archiv für Rechts- und Sozialphilosophie* 98 (2): 157–168.

Altman, William H. F., ed. 2015. *Brill's Companion to the Reception of Cicero*. Leiden: Brill.

Arato, Andrew. 2017. *The Adventures of the Constituent Power*. Cambridge: Cambridge University Press.

Arena, Valentina. 2012. *Libertas and the Practice of Politics in the Late Roman Republic*. Cambridge: Cambridge University Press.

Arena, Valentina. 2016. "Popular Sovereignty in the Late Roman Republic." In *Popular Sovereignty in Historical Perspective*, Quentin Skinner and Richard Bourke, editors. Cambridge: Cambridge University Press: 73–95.

Arendt, Hannah. 2006. *On Revolution*. New York: Penguin.

Aristotle. 1984. *Aristotle: The Politics*. Translated by Carnes Lord. Chicago: University of Chicago Press.

Aristotle. 2014. *Aristotle: Nicomachean Ethics*. 2nd ed. Translated by Roger Crisp. New York: Cambridge University Press.

Ashcraft, Richard. 1986. *Revolutionary Politics and Locke's Two Treatises of Government*. Princeton, NJ: Princeton University Press.

Asmis, Elizabeth. 2008. "Cicero on Natural Law and the Laws of the State." *Classical Antiquity* 27 (1): 1–33.

Atkins, Jed W. 2013. *Cicero on Politics and the Limits of Reason: The Republic and Laws*. Cambridge: Cambridge University Press.

Atkins, Jed W. 2014. "A Revolutionary Doctrine? Cicero's Natural Right Teaching in Mably and Burke." *Classical Receptions Journal* 6 (2): 177–197.

Bailyn, Bernard. 1992. *The Ideological Origins of the American Revolution*. Cambridge, MA: Harvard University Press.

Balot, Ryan, and Stephen Trochimchuk. 2012. "The Many and the Few: On Machiavelli's 'Democratic Moment.'" *Review of Politics* 74 (4): 559–588.

Barlow, J. Jackson. 1999. "The Fox and the Lion: Machiavelli Replies to Cicero." *History of Political Thought* 20 (4): 627–645.

Barlow, J. Jackson. 2012. "Cicero on Property and the State." In *Cicero's Practical Philosophy*, Walter Nicgorski, editor. Notre Dame, IN: University of Notre Dame Press: 212–241.

Baron, Hans. 1938. *Cicero and the Roman Civic Spirit in the Middle Ages and the Early Renaissance*. Manchester, UK: Manchester University Press.

Bell, Daniel A. 2016. *The China Model: Political Meritocracy and the Limits of Democracy*. Princeton, NJ: Princeton University Press.

Benner, Erica. 2013. *Machiavelli's Prince: A New Reading*. Oxford: Oxford University Press.

Berlin, Isaiah. 2000. *The Proper Study of Mankind: An Anthology of Essays*. Edited by Henry Hardy and Roger Hausheer. New York: Macmillan.

Berns, Walter. 1982. "Judicial Review and the Rights and Laws of Nature." *Supreme Court Review*: 49–83.

Binney, Matthew W. 2010. "Milton, Locke, and the Early Modern Framework of Cosmopolitan Right." *Modern Language Review* 105 (1): 31–52.

Bodin, Jean, and Richard Knolle. 1962. *The Six Books of Commonwealth*. Cambridge: Cambridge University Press.

Buckle, Stephen. 1991. *Natural Law and the Theory of Property: Grotius to Hume*. Oxford: Oxford University Press.

Burchell, David. 1998. "Civic Personae: MacIntyre, Cicero and Moral Personality." *History of Political Thought* 19 (1): 101–118.

Burnet, Gilbert. 1689. *An Enquiry into the Measures of Submission to the Supream Authority*. London: n.p.

Carlyle, A. J. 1963. *Political Liberty: A History of the Conception in the Middle Ages and Modern Times*. Reprint ed. London: Frank Cass.

Cartledge, Paul, and Matt Edge. 2009. "'Rights,' Individuals, and Communities in Ancient Greece." In *A Companion to Greek and Roman Political Thought*, Ryan K. Balot, editor. Malden, MA: Wiley-Blackwell: 149–163.

Caspar, Timothy W. 2011. *Recovering the Ancient View of Founding: A Commentary on Cicero's De Legibus*. Lanham, MD: Lexington.

Cicero, Marcus Tullius. 1928. *Cicero: The Verrine Orations I: Against Caecilius; Against Verres, Part I; Part II, Books 1–2*. Translated by L. H. G. Greenwood. Cambridge, MA: Harvard University Press.

Cicero, Marcus Tullius. 1939. *Brutus; Orator*. Translated by G. L. Hendrickson. Cambridge, MA: Harvard University Press.

Cicero, Marcul Tullius. 1949. *Brutus and Orator*. Translated by H. M. Hubbell. Oxford: Clarendon.

Cicero, Marcus Tullius. 1960. *Selected Works*. Translated with commentary by Michael Grant. Harmondsworth, UK: Penguin.

Cicero, Marcus Tullius. 1961. *The Speeches: Pro archia poeta; Post reditum in senatu; Post reditum ad quirites; De domo sua; De haruspicum responsis; Pro planico*, Vol. 11. Cambridge, MA: Harvard University Press.

Cicero, Marcus Tullius. 1966. *The Speeches Pro Sestio and in Vatinium*. Portsmouth, NH: Heinemann.

Cicero, Marcus Tullius. 1994. *De officiis*. Edited by Walter Miler. Cambridge, MA: Harvard University Press.

Cicero, Marcus Tullius. 1998. *De finibus bonorum et malorum: Libri Quinque*. Oxford: Clarendon.

Cicero, Marcus Tullius. 1999. *Cicero: On the Commonwealth and On the Laws*. Translated by James E. G. Zetzel. Cambridge: Cambridge University Press.

Cicero, Marcus Tullius. 2010. *Cicero, XVa, Orations: Philippics 1–6.* Edited by John T. Ramsey and Gesine Manuwald. Translated by D. R. Shackleton Bailey. Cambridge, MA: Harvard University Press.

Clarke, Michelle. 2014. "Doing Violence to the Roman Idea of Liberty? Freedom as Bodily Integrity in Roman Political Thought." *History of Political Thought* 35 (2): 211–233.

Cohen, Lester H. 1978. "The American Revolution and Natural Law Theory." *Journal of the History of Ideas* 39 (3): 491–502.

Cohler, Anne M. 1988. *Montesquieu's Comparative Politics and the Spirit of American Constitutionalism.* Lawrence: University Press of Kansas.

Colbourn, H. Trevor. 1965. *The Lamp of Experience: Whig History and the Intellectual Origins of the American Revolution.* Chapel Hill: University of North Carolina Press.

Cole, Thomas J. B. 2019. "Ciceronian Thought at the Constitutional Convention." *Global Intellectual History*: 1–19. https://www.tandfonline.com/doi/full/10.1080/23801883.2019.1637271.

Colish, Marcia L. 1978. "Cicero's De Officiis and Machiavelli's Prince." *Sixteenth Century Journal* 9 (4): 81–93.

Colish, Marcia L. 1990. *The Stoic Tradition from Antiquity to the Early Middle Ages: Stoicism in Classical Latin Literature*, Vol. 1. Leiden: Brill.

Connolly, Joy. 2014. *The Life of Roman Republicanism.* Princeton, NJ: Princeton University Press.

Constant, Benjamin. 1988. "The Liberty of the Ancients Compared with That of the Moderns." In *Benjamin Constant: Political Writings.* Cambridge: Cambridge University Press: 308–328.

Curran, Eleanor. 2013. "An Immodest Proposal: Hobbes Rather Than Locke Provides a Forerunner for Modern Rights Theory." *Law and Philosophy* 32 (4): 515–538.

De Grazia, Sebastian. 1989. *Machiavelli in Hell.* Princeton, NJ: Princeton University Press.

Deneen, Patrick J. 2019. *Why Liberalism Failed.* New Haven: Yale University Press.

Donahue, Charles, Jr. 2001. "Ius in the Subjective Sense in Roman Law: Reflections on Villey and Tierney." In *A Ennio Cortese*, Domenico Maffei et al., editors. Rome: Il Cigno: 506–535.

Douglass, Robin. 2012. "Montesquieu and Modern Republicanism." *Political Studies* 60 (3): 703–719.

Duff, Alexander S. 2011. "Republicanism and the Problem of Ambition: The Critique of Cicero in Machiavelli's Discourses." *Journal of Politics* 73 (4): 980–992.

Dunn, John. 1982. *The Political Thought of John Locke: An Historical Account of the Argument of the "Two Treatises of Government."* Cambridge: Cambridge University Press.

Dunning, William. A. 1896. "Jean Bodin on Sovereignty." *Political Science Quarterly* 11 (1): 82–104.

Dworetz, Steven M. 1990. *The Unvarnished Doctrine: Locke, Liberalism, and the American Revolution.* Durham, NC: Duke University Press.

Dworkin, Ronald. 2009. "Rights as Trumps." In *Arguing about Law*, Aileen Kavanagh and John Oberdick, editors. London: Routledge: 335–344.

Edge, Matt. 2009. "Athens and the Spectrum of Liberty." *History of Political Thought* 30 (1): 1–45.

Farrand, Max. 1911. *The Records of the Federal Convention of 1787.* New Haven: Yale University Press.

Finley, M. I. 1983. *Politics in the Ancient World.* Cambridge: Cambridge University Press.

Finnis, John. 2011. *Natural Law and Natural Rights*. Oxford: Oxford University Press.

Fott, David S. 2008. "How Machiavellian Is Cicero?" In *The Arts of Rule: Essays in Honor of Harvey Mansfield*, Harvey Claflin Mansfield, Sharon R. Krause, and Mary Ann McGrail, editors. Lanham, MD: Lexington: 149–166.

Fox, Matthew. 2013. "Cicero during the Enlightenment." In *The Cambridge Companion to Cicero*, Catherine Steel, editor. Cambridge: Cambridge University Press: 318–336.

Fox, Matthew. 2016. "Cicero and Historicism: Controversies in Cicero's Reception in the Eighteenth Century." In *Afterlife of Cicero*, G. Manuwald, editor. London: Institute of Classical Studies: 144–161.

Garnsey, Peter. 2007. *Thinking about Property: From Antiquity to the Age of Revolution*. Cambridge: Cambridge University Press.

Garsten, Bryan. 2009. *Saving Persuasion: A Defense of Rhetoric and Judgment*. Cambridge, MA: Harvard University Press.

Gawlick, Günter. 1936. "Cicero and the Enlightenment." *Studies on Voltaire and the Eighteenth Century* 25: 657–682.

George, Robert P. 2000. "Natural Law, the Constitution, and the Theory and Practice of Judicial Review Colloquium: Natural Law Colloquium." *Fordham Law Review* 69 (6): 2269–2284.

Gill, Christopher. 1988. "Personhood and Personality: The Four-Personae Theory in Cicero, De Officiis I." *Oxford Studies in Ancient Philosophy* 6: 169–199.

Gilmore, Nathaniel K. 2020. "Montesquieu's Considerations on the State of Europe." *Journal of the History of Ideas* 81 (3): 359–379.

Grant, Ruth W. 1987. *John Locke's Liberalism*. Chicago: University of Chicago Press.

Grey, Thomas C. 1978. "Origins of the Unwritten Constitution: Fundamental Law in American Revolutionary Thought." *Stanford Law Review* 30 (5): 843–893. https://doi.org/10.2307/1228166.

Grotius, Hugo. 2005. *The Rights of War and Peace*. Edited and with an introduction by Richard Tuck, from the edition by Jean Barbeyrac. Indianapolis: Liberty Fund.

Grotius, Hugo. 2013. *The Illustrious Hugo Grotius of the Law of Warre and Peace: With Annotations, III. Parts, and Memorials of the Author's Life and Death*. Translated by Clement Baksdale. Introduction by William Elliott Butler. Clark, NJ: Lawbook Exchange.

Haakonssen, Knud. 1985. "Hugo Grotius and the History of Political Thought." *Political Theory* 13 (2): 239–265.

Hahm, David E. 2009. "The Mixed Constitution in Greek Thought." In *A Companion to Greek and Roman Political Thought*, Ryan K. Balot, editor. Malden, MA: Wiley-Blackwell: 178–198.

Hamburger, Philip A. 1993. "Natural Rights, Natural Law, and American Constitutions." *Yale Law Journal* 102 (4): 907.

Hamilton, Alexander, James Madison, John Jay, and Robert A. Ferguson. 2006. *The Federalist*. New York: Barnes & Noble.

Hammer, Dean. 2014. *Roman Political Thought: From Cicero to Augustine*. Cambridge: Cambridge University Press.

Hammersley, Rachel. 2013. "Rethinking the Political Thought of James Harrington: Royalism, Republicanism and Democracy." *History of European Ideas* 39 (3): 354–370.

Hamowy, Ronald. 1979. "Jefferson and the Scottish Enlightenment: A Critique of Garry Wills's *Inventing America: Jefferson's Declaration of Independence*." *William and Mary Quarterly* 36 (4): 503–523.

Hamowy, Ronald. 1990. "Cato's Letters, John Locke, and the Republican Paradigm." *History of Political Thought* 11 (2): 273.

Harrington, James. 1977. *The Political Works of James Harrington.* Edited by J. G. A. Pocock. Cambridge: Cambridge University Press.

Harrison, John R., and Peter Laslett. 1971. *The Library of John Locke.* 2nd ed. Oxford: Clarendon.

Hartz, Louis. 1991. *The Liberal Tradition in America: The Classic on the Causes and Effects of Liberal Thought in the U.S.* New York: Houghton Mifflin Harcourt.

Hawley, Michael. 2018. "Cicero on the Problem of Unjust Origins." *Polity* 50 (1): 101–128.

Hawley, Michael. 2019. "Cicero's Duties and Adam Smith's Sentiments: How Smith Adapts Cicero's Account of Self-Interest, Virtue, and Justice." *History of European Ideas* 45 (5): 705–720.

Hawley, Michael. 2020a. "Individuality and Hierarchy in Cicero's *De Officiis*." *European Journal of Political Theory* 19 (1): 87–105.

Hawley, Michael. 2020b. "'The Protectorate of the World': The Problem of Just Hegemony in Roman Thought." *Polis* 37 (1): 44–71.

Hawley, Michael. 2021a. "Beyond Persuasion: Rhetoric as a Tool of Political Motivation." *Journal of Politics* 83 (3): 934–946.

Hawley, Michael. 2021b. "Review of Cary J. Nederman, *The Bonds of Humanity: Cicero's Legacies in European Social and Political Thought, ca. 1100–ca. 1550.*" *Review of Politics* 83 (1): 136–139.

Hawley, Michael. 2021c. "Locke's Ciceronian Liberalism." *Perspectives on Political Science* 50 (2): 72–86.

Hobbes, Thomas. 1682. "An Answer to Arch-Bishop Bramhall's Book, Called the Catching of the Leviathan." In *Tracts of Mr. Thomas Hobbs of Malmsbury.* London: W. Crooke: n.p.

Hobbes, Tholmas. 1972. *Man and Citizen (De Homine and De Cive).* Indianapolis: Hackett.

Hobbes, Thomas. 1994. *Human Nature, or, The Fundamental Elements of Polity; De Corpore Politico, or, The Elements of Law.* Edited by G. A. J. Rogers. Bristol, UK: Thoemmes.

Hobbes, Thomas. 2012. *Leviathan.* Edited by Noel Malcolm. Oxford: Clarendon.

Hochstrasser, Tim J. 2000. *Natural Law Theories in the Early Enlightenment.* Cambridge: Cambridge University Press.

Hulliung, Mark. 1983. *Citizen Machiavelli.* Princeton, NJ: Princeton University Press.

Hume, David. 2011. *The Letters of David Hume*, Vol. 1. Edited by J. Y. T. Greig. Oxford: Oxford University Press.

Jacob, Margaret. 2010. "Was the Eighteenth-Century Republican Essentially Anticapitalist?" *Republics of Letters* 2 (1): 11–20.

Jefferson, Thomas. 1984. "Letter to Henry Lee, May 8, 1825." In *Writings*, Merrill D. Peterson, editor. New York: Library of America.

Jefferson, Thomas. 1989. *Jefferson's Literary Commonplace Book.* Edited by D. L. Wilson. Princeton, NJ: Princeton University Press.

Kahn, Victoria. 1994. *Machiavellian Rhetoric: From the Counter-Reformation to Milton.* Princeton, NJ: Princeton University Press.

Kapust, Daniel J., and Gary Remer. 2021. *The Ciceronian Tradition in Political Theory.* Madison: University of Wisconsin Press.

Kendeffy, Gábor. 2015. "Lactantius as Christian Cicero, Cicero as Shadow-Like Instructor." In *Brill's Companion to the Reception of Cicero*, William H. F. Altman, editor. Leiden: Brill: 56–92.

King, Preston. 2013. *The Ideology of Order: A Comparative Analysis of Jean Bodin and Thomas Hobbes*. London: Routledge.

Kramnick, Isaac. 1990. *Republicanism and Bourgeois Radicalism: Political Ideology in Late Eighteenth-Century England and America*. Ithaca, NY: Cornell University Press.

Laks, André. 2007. "Freedom, Liberality, and Liberty in Plato's *Laws*." *Social Philosophy and Policy* 24 (2): 130–152.

Laslett, Peter. 1988. "Introduction." In *Two Treatises of Government*. Cambridge: Cambridge University Press: 3–127.

Lee, Daniel. 2011. "Popular Liberty, Princely Government, and the Roman Law in Hugo Grotius's *De Jure Belli Ac Pacis*." *Journal of the History of Ideas* 72 (3): 371–392.

Lee, Daniel. 2016. *Popular Sovereignty in Early Modern Constitutional Thought*. Oxford: Oxford University Press.

Lévy, Carlos. 2012. "Philosophical Life versus Political Life: An Impossible Choice for Cicero?" In *Cicero's Practical Philosophy*, Walter Nicgorski, editor. Notre Dame, IN: University of Notre Dame Press: 58–78.

Levy, Jacob T. 2006. "Beyond Publius: Montesquieu, Liberal Republicanism and the Small-Republic Thesis." *History of Political Thought* 27 (1): 50–90.

Lim, Elvin T. 2014. *The Lovers' Quarrel: The Two Foundings and American Political Development*. Oxford: Oxford University Press.

Lindsay, Thomas K. 1992. "Liberty, Equality, Power: Aristotle's Critique of the Democratic 'Presupposition.'" *American Journal of Political Science* 36 (3): 743–761.

Lloyd, Howell. 1991. "Sovereignty: Bodin, Hobbes, Rousseau." *Revue Internationale de Philosophie* 45 (179): 353–379.

Locke, John. 1954. *Essays on the Law of Nature: The Latin Text with a Translation, Introduction and Notes, Together with Transcripts of Locke's Shorthand in His Journal for 1676*. Edited by W. von Leyden. Oxford: Clarendon Press.

Locke, John. 1988. *Locke: Two Treatises of Government*. Edited by Peter Laslett. Cambridge: Cambridge University Press.

Locke, John. 1989. *Some Thoughts Concerning Education*. Edited by John W. Yolton, and Jean S. Yolton Oxford: Oxford University Press.

Locke, John. 1990. *Questions Concerning the Law of Nature.*, Edited and translated by Robert Horwitz, Jenny Strauss Clay, and Diskin Clay. Ithaca, NY: Cornell University Press.

Locke, John. 1979. *An Essay Concerning Human Understanding*. Edited by Peter H. Nidditch. Oxford: Oxford University Press.

Long, Roderick T. 1996. "Aristotle's Conception of Freedom." *Review of Metaphysics* 49 (4): 775–802.

Loughlin, Martin. 2014. "The Concept of Constituent Power." *European Journal of Political Theory* 13 (2): 218–237.

Loughlin, Martin, and Neil Walker, eds. 2007. *The Paradox of Constitutionalism: Constituent Power and Constitutional Form*. Oxford: Oxford University Press.

Lutz, Donald S. 1988. *The Origins of American Constitutionalism*. Baton Rouge: Louisiana State University Press.

Machiavelli, Niccolò. 1988. *The Florentine Histories*. Translated by Laura F. Banfield and Harvey C. Mansfield. Chicago: University of Chicago Press.

Machiavelli, Niccolò. 1996. *Discourses on Livy*. Translated by Harvey C. Mansfield and Nathan Tarcov. Chicago: University of Chicago Press.

Machiavelli, Niccolo. 1998. *The Prince*. 2nd ed. Translated by Harvey C. Mansfield. Chicago: University of Chicago Press.

Machiavelli, Niccolò. 2003. *Art of War*. Edited and translated by Christopher Lynch. Chicago: University of Chicago Press.

MacIntyre, Alasdair. 2007. *After Virtue: A Study in Moral Theory*. 3rd ed. Notre Dame, IN: University of Notre Dame Press.

Macpherson, C. B. 2011. *The Political Theory of Possessive Individualism: Hobbes to Locke*. Oxford: Oxford University Press.

Madison, James. 1973. *The Mind of the Founder: Sources of the Political Thought of James Madison*. Edited by Marvin Meyers. Indianapolis: Bobbs-Merrill.

Malcolm, Noel. 2016. "Thomas Hobbes: Liberal Illiberal." *Journal of the British Academy* 4: 113–136.

Mansfield, Harvey C. 1998. *Machiavelli's Virtue*. Chicago: University of Chicago Press.

Márquez, Xavier. 2012. "Between Urbs and Orbis: Cicero's Conception of the Political Community." In *Cicero's Practical Philosophy*, Walter Nicgorski, editor. Notre Dame, IN: University of Notre Dame Press: 181–211.

Marsh, David. 2013. "Cicero in the Renaissance." In *The Cambridge Companion to Cicero*, Catherine Steel, editor. Cambridge: Cambridge University Press: 306–317.

Marshall, John. 1994. *John Locke: Resistance, Religion and Responsibility*. Cambridge: Cambridge University Press.

Mayville, Luke. 2016. *John Adams and the Fear of American Oligarchy*. Princeton, NJ: Princeton University Press.

McCormick, John P. 2011. *Machiavellian Democracy*. Cambridge: Cambridge University Press.

Mehta, Uday. 1999. *Liberalism and Empire: A Study in Nineteenth-Century British Liberal Thought*. Chicago: University of Chicago Press.

Miller, Fred D. 1996. "Aristotle and the Origins of Natural Rights." *Review of Metaphysics* 49 (4): 873–907.

Milton, John. 1991. *Milton: Political Writings*. Cambridge: Cambridge University Press.

Milton, John. 2014. *Areopagitica and Other Writings*. Edited by William Poole. New York: Penguin.

Mitsis, Phillip. 2003. "Locke's Offices." In *Hellenistic and Early Modern Philosophy*, Jon Miller and Brad Inwood, editors. Cambridge: Cambridge University Press: 45–61.

Montesquieu. 2002. "Discourse on Cicero." Translated by David Fott. *Political Theory* 30 (5): 733–737.

Montesquieu. 1989. *The Spirit of the Laws*. Edited by Anne M. Cohler, Basia C. Miller, and Harold S. Stone. Cambridge: Cambridge University Press.

Nacol, Emily. 2021. "Locke and Cicero on Property, Labor, and Value." In *The Ciceronian Tradition in Political Theory*, Daniel Kapust and Gary Remer, editors. Madison: University of Wisconsin Press: 140–159.

Nederman, Cary J. 1999. "Amazing Grace: Fortune, God, and Free Will in Machiavelli's Thought." *Journal of the History of Ideas* 60 (4): 617–638.

Nederman, Cary J. 2020. *The Bonds of Humanity: Cicero's Legacies in European Social and Political Thought, ca. 1100–ca. 1550*. College Station: Pennsylvania State University Press.

Nedham, Marchamont. 2011. *The Excellencie of a Free-State; or, The Right Constitution of a Commonwealth*. Indianapolis: Liberty Fund.

Nelson, Eric. 2004. *The Greek Tradition in Republican Thought*. Cambridge: Cambridge University Press.

Neumann, Kristina. 2015. "Virtuous Taxation in Cicero's *De Officiis*." *Syllecta Classica* 26 (1): 21–49.

Neville, Henry. 1691. *A True Copy of a Letter Written by N. Machiavill in Defence of Himself and His Religion*. London: R. Bentley.

Neville, Henry, and Walter Moyle. 1969. *Two English Republican Tracts*. Cambridge: Cambridge University Press.

Nicgorski, Walter. 1993. "Nationalism and Transnationalism in Cicero." *History of European Ideas* 16 (4–6): 785–791.

Nicgorski, Walter. 2013. "Cicero on Aristotle and Aristotelians." *Magyar Filozófiai Szemle* 57 (4): 34–56.

Nicgorski, Walter. 2016. *Cicero's Skepticism and His Recovery of Political Philosophy*. New York: Springer.

Nippel, Wilfried. 1980. *Mischverfassungstheorie und Verfassungsrealität in Antike und früher Neuzeit*. Stuttgart: Klett-Cotta.

Nozick, Robert. 1974. *Anarchy, State, and Utopia*. New York: Basic.

Nussbaum, Martha C. 1997. "Kant and Stoic Cosmopolitanism." *Journal of Political Philosophy* 5 (1): 1–25.

Nussbaum, Martha C. 2000. "Symposium on Cosmopolitanism Duties of Justice, Duties of Material Aid: Cicero's Problematic Legacy." *Journal of Political Philosophy* 8 (2): 176–206.

Nyquist, Mary. 2008. "Slavery, Resistance, and Nation in Milton and Locke." In *Early Modern Nationalism and Milton's England*, David Loewenstein and Paul Stevens, editors. Toronto: University of Toronto Press: 356–398.

Otis, James, and Richard Dana. 1764. *The Rights of the British Colonies Asserted and Proved*. Boston: Edes and Gill.

Pangle, Thomas L. 1988. *The Spirit of Modern Republicanism: The Moral Vision of the American Founders and the Philosophy of Locke*. Chicago: University of Chicago Press.

Pangle, Thomas L. 2020. *Montesquieu's Philosophy of Liberalism: A Commentary on the Spirit of the Laws*. Chicago: University of Chicago Press.

Pettit, Philip. 1997. *Republicanism: A Theory of Freedom and Government*. Oxford: Oxford University Press.

Pitts, Jennifer. 2006. *A Turn to Empire: The Rise of Liberal Imperialism in Britain and France*. Princeton: Princeton University Press.

Plato. 1991. *The Republic of Plato*. 2nd ed. Translated by Allan Bloom. New York: Basic.

Plato. 2017. *The Apology: A Socratic Dialogue*. Translated by Benjamin Jowett. Scotts Valley, CA: CreateSpace.

Plutarch. 1919. *Plutarch Lives, VII, Demosthenes and Cicero; Alexander and Caesar*. Translated by Bernadotte Perrin. Cambridge, MA: Harvard University Press.

Pocock, John Greville Agard. 2009. *The Machiavellian Moment: Florentine Political Thought and the Atlantic Republican Tradition*. Princeton, NJ: Princeton University Press.

Pocock, John Greville Agard. 1980. "The Myth of John Locke and the Obsession with Liberalism." In *John Locke, Papers Read at a Clark Library Seminar, 10 December, 1977*, J. G. A. Pocock and Richard Ashcraft, editors. Los Angeles: UCLA Clark Memorial Library: 3–24.

Polin, Raymond. 1969. "John Locke's Conception of Freedom." In *John Locke: Problems and Perspectives*, John W. Yolton, editor. Cambridge: Cambridge University Press: 1–18.

Powell, J. G. F. 2012. "Cicero's *De Re Publica* and the Virtues of the Statesman." In *Cicero's Practical Philosophy*, Walter Nicgorski, editor. Notre Dame, IN: University of Notre Dame Press: 14–42.

Pufendorf, Samuel von. 1991. *Pufendorf: On the Duty of Man and Citizen According to Natural Law*. Edited by James Tully. Translated by Michael Silverthorne. Cambridge: Cambridge University Press.

Pufendorf, Samuel von. 1994. *The Political Writings of Samuel Pufendorf*. Edited by Craig L. Carr. Translated by Michael J. Seidler. New York: Oxford University Press.

Raaflaub, Kurt. 2004. *The Discovery of Freedom in Ancient Greece*. Rev. ed. Chicago: University of Chicago Press.

Radasanu, Andrea. 2010. "Montesquieu on Moderation, Monarchy, and Reform." *History of Political Thought* 31 (2): 283–308.

Rahe, Paul. 2000. "Situating Machiavelli." *Ideas in Context* 57 (1): 270–308.

Rahe, Paul. 2006. *Machiavelli's Liberal Republican Legacy*. New York: Cambridge University Press.

Rahe, Paul. 2007. "In the Shadow of Lucretius: The Epicurean Foundations of Machiavelli's Political Thought." *History of Political Thought* 28 (1): 30–55.

Rahe, Paul. 2008. *Against Throne and Altar: Machiavelli and Political Theory under the English Republic*. Cambridge: Cambridge University Press.

Rahe, Paul. 2009. *Soft Despotism, Democracy's Drift: Montesquieu, Rousseau, Tocqueville, and the Modern Project*. New Haven: Yale University Press.

Rawson, Elizabeth. 1994. *Cicero: A Portrait*. Bristol: Bristol Classical Press.

Remer, Gary. 2009. "Rhetoric as a Balancing of Ends: Cicero and Machiavelli." *Philosophy & Rhetoric* 42 (1): 1–28.

Remer, Gary. 2013. "Rhetoric, Emotional Manipulation, and Political Morality: The Modern Relevance of Cicero and Aristotle." *Rhetorica* 31 (4): 402–443.

Richard, Carl J. 2015. "Cicero and the American Founders." In *Brill's Companion to the Reception of Cicero*, William H. F. Altman, editor. Leiden: Brill: 124–143.

Rose, Peter. 1995. "Cicero and the Rhetoric of Imperialism: Putting the Politics Back into Political Rhetoric." *Rhetorica* 13 (4): 359–399.

Rousseau, Jean-Jacques. 1997. *"The Social Contract" and Other Later Political Writings*. Edited by Victor Gourevitch. Cambridge: Cambridge University Press.

Rubinelli, Lucia. 2020. *Constituent Power: A History*. Cambridge: Cambridge University Press.

Ryerson, Richard Alan. 2016. *John Adams's Republic: The One, the Few, and the Many*. Baltimore: Johns Hopkins University Press.

Schmitt, Charles B. 2013. *Cicero Scepticus: A Study of the Influence of the Academica in the Renaissance*, Vol. 52. The Hague: Springer.

Schofield, Malcolm. 1990. *Saving the City: Philosopher Kings and Other Classical Paradigms*. London: Routledge.

Schofield, Malcolm. 1996. "Sharing in the Constitution." *Review of Metaphysics* 49 (4): 831–858.

Schwartzberg, Melissa. 2016. "Aristotle and the Judgment of the Many: Equality, Not Collective Quality." *Journal of Politics* 78 (3): 733–745.

Scott, John T., and Vickie B. Sullivan. 1994. "Patricide and the Plot of *The Prince*: Cesare Borgia and Machiavelli's Italy." *American Political Science Review* 88 (4): 887–900.

Sharpe, Matthew. 2015. "Cicero, Voltaire, and the Philosophes in the French Enlightenment." In *Brill's Companion to the Reception of Cicero*, William H. F. Altman, editor. Leiden: Brill: 327–356.

Shklar, Judith. 1989. "The Liberalism of Fear." In *Liberalism and the Moral Life*, Nancy L. Rosenblum, editor. Cambridge, MA: Harvard University Press: 21–38.

Shklar, Judith. 1991. "Montesquieu and the New Republicanism." In *Machiavelli and Republicanism*, Gisela Bock, Quentin Skinner, Maurizio Viroli, and Judith Shklar, editors. Cambridge: Cambridge University Press: 265–280.

Sidney, Algernon. 1805. *Discourses Concerning Government: To Which Is Added, a Short Account of the Author's Life, and a Copious Index*. Philadelphia: C. P. Wayne.

Sidney, Algernon. 1996. *Discourses Concerning Government*. Edited by Thomas G. West. Indianapolis: Liberty Fund.

Simendic, Marko. 2011. "Hobbes on Persona, Personation, and Representation: Behind the Mask of Sovereignty." PhD diss., University of York.

Simmons, A. John. 1992. *The Lockean Theory of Rights*. Princeton, NJ: Princeton University Press.

Skinner, Quentin. 1984. "The Idea of Negative Liberty: Philosophical and Historical Perspectives." In *Philosophy in History: Essays in the Historiography of Philosophy*, R. Rorty, J. Schneewind, and Q. Skinner, editors. Cambridge: Cambridge University Press: 193–221.

Skinner, Quentin. 1990. "Machiavelli's *Discorsi* and the Pre-Humanist Origins of Republican Ideas." In *Machiavelli and Republicanism*, Gisela Bock, Quentin Skinner, and Maurizio Viroli, editors. Cambridge: Cambridge University Press: 121–141.

Skinner, Quentin. 1998. *Liberty before Liberalism*. Cambridge: Cambridge University Press.

Skinner, Quentin. 2002. *Visions of Politics*, Vol. 2. Cambridge: Cambridge University Press.

Slaughter, M. S. 1921. "Cicero and His Critics." *The Classical Journal* 17 (3): 120–131.

Somos, Mark. 2019. *American States of Nature: The Origins of Independence, 1761–1775*. Oxford: Oxford University Press.

Spector, Céline. 2003. "Montesquieu: Critique of Republicanism?" *Critical Review of International Social and Political Philosophy* 6 (1): 38–53.

Spragens, Thomas A. 1973. *The Politics of Motion: The World of Thomas Hobbes*. Lexington: University Press of Kentucky.

Steel, C. E. W. 2001. *Cicero, Rhetoric, and Empire*. Oxford: Oxford University Press.

St. Leger, James. 1962. *The "Etiamsi Daremus" of Hugo Grotius: A Study in the Origins of International Law*. Rome: Pontifico Ateneo Angelicum.

Storing, Herbert, and Murray Dry, eds. 2007. *The Complete Anti-Federalist*. Chicago: University of Chicago Press.

Straumann, Benjamin. 2015. *Roman Law in the State of Nature: The Classical Foundations of Hugo Grotius' Natural Law*. Cambridge: Cambridge University Press.

Straumann, Benjamin. 2016. *Crisis and Constitutionalism: Roman Political Thought from the Fall of the Republic to the Age of Revolution*. New York: Oxford University Press.

Straumann, Benjamin. 2019. "'The Laws Are in Charge of the Magistrates': Reply to Edelstein, Sullivan and Springborg." *Global Intellectual History* 4 (3): 271–288.

Strauss, Leo. 1953. *Natural Right and History*. Chicago: University of Chicago Press.

Strauss, Leo. 1995. *Thoughts on Machiavelli*. Chicago: University of Chicago Press.

Strider, Robert Edward Lee, II. 2013. *Robert Greville, Lord Brooke*. Cambridge, MA: Harvard University Press.

Sullivan, Vickie B. 1992. "Machiavelli's Momentary 'Machiavellian Moment': A Reconsideration of Pocock's Treatment of the Discourses." *Political Theory* 20 (2): 309–318.

Sullivan, Vickie B. 2004. *Machiavelli, Hobbes, and the Formation of a Liberal Republicanism in England*. Cambridge: Cambridge University Press.

Sullivan, Vickie B. 2017. *Montesquieu and the Despotic Ideas of Europe: An Interpretation of "The Spirit of the Laws."* Chicago: University of Chicago Press.

Tarcov, Nathan. 1982. *Quentin Skinner's Method and Machiavelli's Prince*. Chicago: University of Chicago Press.

Thompson, C. Bradley. 1998. *John Adams and the Spirit of Liberty*. Lawrence: University Press of Kansas.

Thompson, C. Bradley. 2019. *America's Revolutionary Mind: A Moral History of the American Revolution and the Declaration That Defined It*. New York: Encounter.

Toland, John. 1699. *Amyntor: Or a Defense of Milton's Life*. London: J. Darby.

Tuck, Richard. 1982. *Natural Rights Theories: Their Origin and Development*. Cambridge: Cambridge University Press.

Tully, James. 1980. *A Discourse on Property: John Locke and His Adversaries*. Cambridge: Cambridge University Press.

Van Deusen, Nancy. 2013. *Cicero Refused to Die: Ciceronian Influence through the Centuries*. Leiden: Brill.

Vatter, Miguel. 2013. *Machiavelli's 'The Prince': A Reader's Guide*. London: A & C Black.

Viroli, Maurizio. 2002. *Republicanism*. Translated by Antony Shugaar. New York: Hill and Wang.

Von Fritz, Kurt. 1954. *The Theory of the Mixed Constitution in Antiquity: A Critical Analysis of Polybius' Political Ideas*. New York: Columbia University Press.

Waddicor, Mark H. 1970. *Montesquieu and the Philosophy of Natural Law*. The Hague: Martinus Nijhoff.

Walbank, Frank William. 1990. *Polybius*, Vol. 1. Berkeley: University of California Press.

Waldron, Jeremy. 1995. "The Wisdom of the Multitude: Some Reflections on Book 3, Chapter 11 of Aristotle's Politics." *Political Theory* 23 (4): 563–584.

Waldron, Jeremy. 2002. *God, Locke, and Equality: Christian Foundations of John Locke's Political Thought*. Cambridge: Cambridge University Press.

Watson, Gerard. 1971. "The Natural Law and Stoicism." In *Problems in Stoicism*, A. A. Long, editor. London: Athlone: 216–238.

Wellman, Carl. 2018. *The Proliferation of Rights: Moral Progress or Empty Rhetoric?* New York: Routledge.

Wills, Garry. 2017. *Inventing America: Jefferson's Declaration of Independence*. New York: Doubleday.

Wilson, James. 2007. *Collected Works of James Wilson*. 2 vols. Edited by Kermit L. Hall and Mark David Hall. Indianapolis: Liberty Fund.

Wirszubski, Chaim H. 1950. *Libertas as a Political Idea at Rome during the Late Republic and Early Principate*. Cambridge: Cambridge University Press.

Wood, Gordon S. 1993. *The Radicalism of the American Revolution*. New York: Vintage.

Wood, Gordon S. [1969] 1998. *The Creation of the American Republic, 1776–1787*. Chapel Hill: University of North Carolina Press.

Wood, Gordon S. 2011. *The Idea of America: Reflections on the Birth of the United States*. London: Penguin Books.

Wood, Neal. 1988. *Cicero's Social and Political Thought*. Berkley: University of California Press.

Worden, Blair. 1995. "'Wit in a Roundhead': The Dilemma of Marchamont Nedham." In *Political Culture and Cultural Politics in Early Modern England*, Susan Amussen and Mark Kishlansky, editors. Manchester, UK: Manchester University Press: 301–337.

Zakaria, Fareed. 1997. "The Rise of Illiberal Democracy." *Foreign Affairs* 76 (6): 22–43.

Zarecki, Jonathan. 2014. *Cicero's Ideal Statesman in Theory and Practice*. London: Bloomsbury.

Zetzel, James. 1996. "Natural Law and Poetic Justice: A Carneadean Debate in Cicero and Virgil." *Classical Philology* 91 (4): 297–319.

Zetzel, James. 2003. "Plato with Pillows: Cicero on the Uses of Greek Culture." In *Myth, History and Culture in Republican Rome: Studies in Honour of TP Wiseman*, Nicholas Horsfall, editor. Exeter, UK: University of Exeter Press: 119–138.

Zetzel, James. 2017. "Cicero on the Origins of Civilization and Society: The Preface to De Re Publica Book 3." *American Journal of Philology* 138 (3): 461–487.

Zuckert, Catherine. 2014. "Machiavelli and the End of Nobility in Politics." *Social Research* 81 (1): 85–106.

Zuckert, Catherine. 2017. *Machiavelli's Politics*. Chicago: University of Chicago Press.

Zuckert, Michael P. 1974. "Fools and Knaves: Reflections on Locke's Theory of Philosophical Discourse." *Review of Politics* 36 (4): 544–564.

Zuckert, Michael P. 1975. "The Recent Literature on Locke's Political Philosophy." *Political Science Reviewer* 5: 271.

Zuckert, Michael P. 1994. *Natural Rights and the New Republicanism*. Princeton, NJ: Princeton University Press.

Zuckert, Michael P. 2002. *Launching Liberalism on Lockean Political Philosophy*. Lawrence: University Press of Kansas.

Zuckert, Michael P. 2001. "Natural Law, Natural Rights, and Classical Liberalism: On Montesquieu's Critique of Hobbes." *Social Philosophy and Policy* 18 (1): 227–251.

Index

For the benefit of digital users, indexed terms that span two pages (e.g., 52–53) may, on occasion, appear on only one of those pages.

Figure are indicated by *f* following the page number